essential guide

TO

DANCE

Linda Rickett-Young

Hodder & Stoughton

ACKNOWLEDGEMENTS

To all my friends and loved ones who have tolerated my irritations/absences, supported me, cooked for me and put up with my endless delegation of duties, I would like to say a deep-felt thank you. This book is for you, and for my parents who have had a lifetime of the above-mentioned.

To all dance students, young dancers and older dancers whom I have worked with, many thanks to you also for all your inspiration:

Come and trip it as you go
On the light fantastic toe

(*John Milton,* Pastoral Ode)

Copyright holders of photographs reproduced in this book:

Catherine Ashmore, pp 118, 120; British Museum, pp 101, 115; Dee Conway, p 204; Anthony Crickmay, pp 80, 123, 208; photographs by Anthony Crickmay and Houston Rogers, Theatre Museum, V&A, pp 36, 51, 70, 95, 112, 105, 109; Zoë Dominic, p 103; James Klosty, p 110; Alexis Maryon, pp 84, 105; Chris Nash, pp 60, 76, 97, 175(b), 180; Royal Opera House, p 175(a).

Orders: please contact Bookpoint Ltd, 39 Milton Park, Abingdon, Oxon OX14 4TD. Telephone: (44) 01235 400414, Fax: (44) 01235 400454. Lines are open from 9.00–6.00, Monday to Saturday, with a 24 hour message answering service. Email address: orders@bookpoint.co.uk

British Library Cataloguing in Publication Data
A catalogue record for this title is available from
The British Library

ISBN 0 340 66361 8

First published 1996
Impression number   12 11 10 9 8 7 6 5 4
Year   2004 2003 2002 2001 2000 1999

Copyright © 1996 Linda Rickett-Young

Typeset by Fakenham Photosetting Ltd, Fakenham, Norfolk
Printed in Great Britain for Hodder & Stoughton Educational, a division of Hodder Headline Plc, 338 Euston Road, London NW1 3BH by J. W. Arrowsmith Ltd., Bristol.

CONTENTS

Acknowledgements   ii

Foreword   v

Introduction   1

1 The dancer in training   3
   Alignment   3
   Flexibility   12
   Strength and stamina   21
   Coordination   30
   General body maintenance   43
   References and resources   47

2 Recording dance: walking boldly backwards into the future   49
   The issues in question   49
   Dance notation   50
   Videodance and film   58
   References and resources   65

3 The constituent features of dance: movement and dancers   67
   The movement components   69
   The space component   79
   The time component   86
   The dynamic component   90
   The dancers   92
   References and resources   98

4 The constituent features of dance: the physical setting   100
   The performing space   100
   The set   107
   Lighting   111
   Costume   114
   Props   121
   References and resources   125

5 The constituent features of dance: the aural setting   126
   Accompaniments for dance   126
   References and resources   132

6 Form in dance   133
   Form   133
   Compositional devices   134
   Compositional structures   143
   The relationship of dance to the accompaniment   149
   Different possible relationships between music and dance   158
   Organising groups in space   164
   References and resources   171

7 Dance appreciation   172
   The significance of dances   172
   Ideas   173
   The artistic process and style   174
   Performance   178
   Evaluation   186
   References and resources   191

8 Dance today   193
   Computer technology: new realities   193
   Cross-cultural dance in society today: the 'global village'   194
   References and resources   201

9 The way ahead   202
   A brave new world – with inequalities   202
   Dance education and gender   202
   The financing of dance education   205
   Dance and disability   207
   Conclusion   209
   References and resources   209

Glossary   210

Index   216

FOREWORD

As a dancer and teacher, I have been involved in dance for many years. Having performed and taught extensively, for the past six years I have been at the head of Rambert Dance Company's Education Unit, and this has brought me into contact with students of dance the length of Britain.

I am keenly aware that there is a great need for resources for these students which will provide information, guidance and inspiration. So I was delighted to be asked to comment on *Essential Guide to Dance*, particularly those aspects dealing with the creation and appreciation of dance.

Designed to be read alongside a practical training programme, this is a comprehensive and well planned book which usefully refers to dances which are in many cases available on video. It has quite specific tasks which allow the student to experience *in their body* the point being made in the text.

The components of choreography and the devices and structures which can be employed are clearly explained, and indeed provide a handy 'checklist' of possibilities for students to refer to. The text is peppered with quotations from choreographers and performers about dance and dancing, which keep the student very much in touch with the fact that this is a performing art.

Essential Guide to Dance is a thoroughly useful resource, providing a wealth of ideas and information for students, and inspiring them in their exploration of this most fascinating of subjects.

Alison Whyte
Rambert Dance Company

INTRODUCTION

Essential Guide to Dance is for BTEC, 'A' and 'AS' Level and GNVQ Dance and Performing Arts students. This book is a practical working text *for students*. It is intended to be used as a text to be read with guidance during practical daily classes. As part of daily learning, it integrates practice with theory. To me these are inseparable, and together they come to much, much more than the sum of the parts – a bit like 'Dancing on a volcano' (Comte de Salvandy, a French nobleman, 1830, the French Revolution looming).

The blend which is the theory and practice of dance gives this book its structure. Facts, practical tasks, context and appreciation are all woven together. The sections emphasise *applied* knowledge, so rather than following the linear logic of, say, anatomy, specific parts of the body appear within a training context – for example, when addressing the issue of flexibility, the hip joint in particular is examined because the mobility of this joint is of great importance to dancers. Such practical working knowledge is helpful and supportive for any dance student.

The book is not intended to be read from cover to cover – although of course individuals may choose to do so. It would be more effective for teachers to guide the reading of it as part of a structured course. Some of the text may, for example, be used as homework or for distance learning. And it most certainly would also be well-used to animate daily practical classes.

Much of the slog of teaching syllabus work involves making the different layers of knowledge explicit for the learner. This I have tried to do, and wherever possible I have used language which is not only user-friendly but also 'syllabus-friendly'. Covering such a huge range in enough detail has made life a bit like:

> Now *here*, you see, it takes all the running *you* can do, to keep in the same place. If you want to get somewhere else, you must run at least twice as fast.
>
> (*Advice from the Red Queen to Alice, in Lewis Carroll's* Through the Looking-Glass)

Icons

Throughout this book, the tasks that are set are given suggested timings. The icons used to indicate these timings are as follows:

10 to 20 minutes:

45 minutes to 1 hour:

20 to 30 minutes:

Several hours:

chapter one
THE DANCER IN TRAINING

In your study of dance training, you may be presented with names of bones, joints, muscles and so on. These and the basic physiology of *how* the body works are important, but it is an *applied* working knowledge which is most useful and meaningful to you. For a dancer or a choreographer, an active awareness of safe practice can serve to explain both how to execute a certain movement and why a particular phrase is giving difficulty. It is with this in mind that this chapter is written. Individual parts of the body are dealt with in the context of how they may arise in class or in performance. Similarly, unsafe practice and the potential for, and how to deal with, injury are also examined.

> Don't say, 'Oh well, we did that, and I kicked my leg five inches higher than she did.' Who cares? Did you understand the movement? That is what matters.
>
> (*Hanya Holm in* The Vision of Modern Dance, *1980*)

The body of a dancer is like the piano of a musician: it is a *working tool*, and so must be finely tuned. This needs an intelligent, aware, sensitive and disciplined approach to dance training. Dance training pursues the improvement

of capabilities which the body already has naturally. As with an athlete, these capabilities need to be developed in order for their potential to be maximised. Safety and efficiency of movement need to be ensured so that injury is more likely to be avoided. A dancer, in their working life, will develop certain physical skills which respond to the demands of performance and encourage safe practice.

Dance training pursues the improvement of the following main areas of basic body fitness:

- alignment
- flexibility
- strength and stamina
- coordination
- general body maintenance.

Different technique classes vary in how much emphasis is placed on these areas. Often, because of the stop-go nature of these classes, there is not enough time for effective all-round conditioning of the body. This is a problem because these basic areas for fitness are all vital in ensuring safe practice and injury prevention.

Let us now consider each of these five main areas in turn.

Alignment

> Discipline is, or should be, a voluntary course of regulated and regular actions where effort brings about the desired results. Too often it becomes something else. I am not interested in how high a person can extend his leg or how high he jumps into the air, but rather what he looks like while he is doing these things.
>
> (*Judith Dunn, dancer*)

During movement, the body remains aligned, whether in a fall or jump or turn. In the well-aligned body, there is a feeling of freedom, easy movement, effortless carriage of the head and awareness of all parts of the body. It is a more expressive body that 'looks good' whatever it is doing, at any given moment.

Good alignment is not static, it is a dynamic position of readiness to move. There is an ever-present 'plumb line' (the straight line from the head to toes) which should be maintained during movement. Without this, movement will be inefficient and possibly unsafe, as energy is wasted pulling certain segments of the body into line. This line runs from behind the ear, through the centre of the shoulder and hip, in front of the ankle and down through the foot (see Figure 1.1). The shoulders, hips and knees should be level. Rolling in on the arches of the feet or out to the border should be avoided. Generally, a triangular distribution of weight on each foot is best (see Figure 1.2): the weight is spread evenly here between points 1, 2 and 3, under the 1st and 5th metatarsals and under the heel bone (calcaneus).

Good posture is vital for control, safety and expression: poor posture or alignment of one part ricochets throughout the rest of the body. For effective movement, each segment of the body must therefore be in proper relationship to its adjacent sections. Correct use of the muscle groups in balance with each other is the only way to allow the skeleton to do its main job which is to support the whole body. The anti-gravity muscle group is responsible for maintaining the upright posture, so that the weight-bearing points on the skeleton will be balanced and the muscles will be able to release energy for action safely and economically. Alignment thus relies on there being *reciprocal relationships* between all body parts. This means that different segments of the body give and take (are extended and contracted in muscles) in equal measure in order to maintain skeletal balance.

Figure 1.1 *To show points that the line of gravity will pass through in correct alignment*

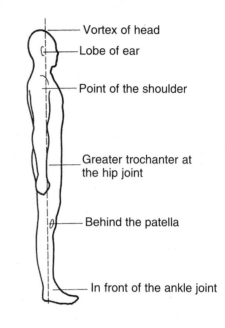

- Vortex of head
- Lobe of ear
- Point of the shoulder
- Greater trochanter at the hip joint
- Behind the patella
- In front of the ankle joint

Figure 1.2 *Correct distribution of weight on the sole of the foot*

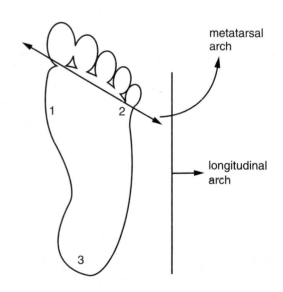

metatarsal arch

longitudinal arch

TASK 1 ⧗

1 With a partner, check each other's postural plumb line – follow Table 1.1. Write down your observations for your partner.

Table 1.1

Body area to check from front	What you may see
Feet: is the weight on the inner border (pronation) *or* on the outer *or* on the midline?	From the back, pronation appears as fatty pads on the outside of the heel. A hollow ankle shows as weight on the outside.
Knees: are they level?	Facing straight ahead *or* inward *or* both?
Hips: are they level? If not, the legs may be different lengths (check the back view for curvature of the spine).	Place forefingers on the iliac crest on the side to check they are level. At the back, place thumbs on the sacroiliac joint (where two dimples appear) to check if level.
Shoulders: are they level?	

At this point, it would be helpful to examine three specific areas of the body which are crucial for good alignment:

- the skeleton
- the spine
- the foot.

THE SKELETON

The main functions of the skeleton are:

- support;
- protection of organs, e.g. brain, heart, lungs, spinal cord;
- to allow accurate movement when muscles contract by giving rigidity;
- some bones contain red marrow which is a part of the blood-forming tissue.

Bones make up the skeleton, and the size of these depends on their function: bones bearing larger body weights are bigger and denser, whereas those bearing lesser body weights are smaller and lighter. For example:

- The *femur* of the thigh supports more weight than the *humerus* of the upper arm, and so it is larger and heavier.

- The *vertebrae* of the spine are larger near the bottom to support the increased mass from above.

In addition, the *shape* of a bone similarly depends on its function. For example:

- The *vertebrae* are like rounded building blocks stacked to form the spinal column which surrounds and protects the spinal cord.
- The *ribs* are slender and curved to protect the lungs and heart.
- Bones like those in the lower arm – i.e. the *radius* and *ulna* – are long and slender to allow the system of levers to operate efficiently.

Table 1.2   *Injuries to bones*

Injury	Symptoms/causes	Treatment
Stress fracture (including 'shin splints')	Localised cracks in bones due to repeated stress on one area of bone. Causes: Use of unsuitable (unsprung) floors. Poor alignment in any of following: *fibular* – sickle foot/inversion; *tibia bow* – weight back; *lumbar vertebrae* – weak abdominal muscles	Rest. Remedial correction of weaknesses, including specific exercise for weak musculature.
Fractures	Uncommon as a dance injury. Most common is of 5th metatarsal and of ankle, when twisted – i.e. if inverted and rotated in the fall.	Plaster cast. Immobilise for 6 weeks or many months. May be treated with strapping if a minor fracture. Dancer may not dance, but should exercise areas not in plaster to stay strong/mobile. Once out of cast: ice and ultrasound, plus exercise of inactive muscle.

The skeleton is divided into two parts:

1 the axial (head, chest, pelvis): the *skull, vertebrae, clavicle, scapula, sternum, ribs, ischium, ilium;*

2 the *appendicular* (legs and arms): the *radius, ulna, carpal bones, metacarpals, tarsals, metatarsals, phalanges, femur, tibia, fibula.*

THE SPINE

> The spine is a long limb . . . Allow the rest of the body to balance around the curving river of the spine.
>
> (*Miranda Tufnell in* Body Space Image, *1990*)

In the well-aligned dancer, the healthy spine is the power centre for moving. The way you sit, lie, stand, travel or fall is affected by the spine. Its elasticity absorbs the shock waves.

The spine has four curves (see Figure 1.3) which correspond to the four groups of vertebrae:

1 the *cervical curve*: 7 *cervical* vertebrae (neck);
2 the *thoracic curve*: 12 *thoracic* vertebrae (chest/rib area);
3 the *lumbar curve*: 5 *lumbar* vertebrae (lower back);
4 the *sacral curve*: *sacrum and coccyx* (fused at bottom).

Figure 1.3   *The curves of the spine*

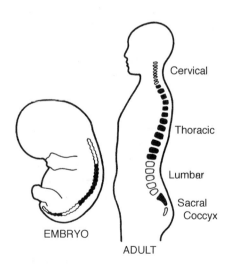

Table 1.3 *Postural problems of the spine*

Problem	Symptom(s)	Causes	Treatment
Scoliosis – lateral deviation of the spine	From the back, appears as 'S' or 'C' curve.	Numerous misalignments.	If diagnosed from childhood, dance training can help ease the condition by emphasis on symmetry of movement.
Lumbar lordosis – swayback	From side view, the normal *lumbar curve* is exaggerated.	Weak abdominal muscle/tight lumbar spine and hamstrings.	Stretch lower back, hamstrings and hip flexors/ strengthen abdominals.
Flat back	Flat lower back (opposite of lordosis), posterior tilt of pelvis/ elongated thoracic.	Weak lower back muscles/tight hamstrings	Strengthen lower back and hip flexors/stretch abdominals and hamstrings.
Kyphosis – round back	Abdominal round upper back (thoracic curve) as seen from side.	Tight chest muscles and weak upper back.	Stretch chest muscles of upper trunk and strengthen upper back.

These curves help to take some of the stress involved in weight-bearing, as do the spongy discs in between the vertebrae which act as shock absorbers. The spongy discs are essential, for example, when landing from jumps.

Postural problems/injuries of the spine

Generally speaking, if a particular form of dance training encourages bad habits and unsafe practice – for example, if movements are attempted that are beyond a dancer's ability – alignment and muscular balance will break down. Serious postural problems or injury, or both, may then result. There are also various *anatomical* defects – e.g. curvature of the spine – which require medical diagnosis and cannot be changed by exercise. In training, dancers with these defects need expert advice on how to accommodate the problem whilst maintaining correct posture. Some postural problems are listed in Table 1.3.

The neck (the *cervical curve*) is also vulnerable to strain because it is so mobile, and because the weight of the head is only held by the neck muscles, which must therefore be in good condition. In the event that the neck *extensor* muscles are weak and the *flexors* are too tight, the dancer's chin may jut up and the ear will be in front of the plumb line. This is known as *cervical lordosis/forward head.*

- Extensor muscles are those which stretch the body.
- Flexor muscles are those which curl or bend the body.

The *sacroiliac joint* (where the lumbar curve meets the sacrum) is also vulnerable. This is the point where the mobile spine meets the immobile *pelvis.* If the lower abdominal muscles are weak and combined with tight lower back muscles, then there will be weakness in this joint.

The use of the spine in different dance genres

There are interesting contrasting uses of the spine in the various genres of dance. The classical ballet genre has maintained the vertical spine as one of its characteristics from the fifteenth century. This relates back to its noble beginnings when correct deportment, how to walk, sit, stand and bow were taught and denoted status and power. The nobility would perform dances in this manner, and later this tradition was taken on by professionals to become ballet as we know it today. The style of the vertical torso gives ballet its distinctive ethereal lightness, and facilitates the execution of characteristic multiple pirouettes and soaring jumps with greater ease.

Even this defiance of natural forces was not enough, however, for the pioneers of *modern dance*, and at the start of the twentieth century individuals like Isadora Duncan emerged in rebellion. For her, the *solar plexus* was the creator of all movement, and the name of the game was freedom. Along with this went a mobile, *tilting, twisting, curving* spine. This allowed a wider range of expressivity for the choreographer, and dance has never looked the same since. Later pioneers in modern dance, like Martha Graham and Merce Cunningham, continued the exploration of the spine as an expressive limb.

THE FOOT

Another crucial part of the body for dancers' correct alignment is the foot. Isadora Duncan, with her defiant rebellious barefooted look, named dance 'the religion of the foot'. It is surprising, really, that such a small device is yet strong enough to support the whole of the rest of the body.

The many small *intrinsic muscles* in the foot are *layered* to connect the bones in the arches, metatarsals and phalanges (see Figure 1.4). These intrinsic muscles are vital because they allow the foot to point strongly with straight toes. Weak intrinsics will cause the toes to claw, because the flexor muscles will be overpowerful.

The other muscles which move the foot start below the knee and connect to the bones of the foot. The movements produced by these muscles are:

- plantar flexion – pointing downward
- dorsiflexion – top of the foot points upward
- inversion – inner border of foot lifts
- eversion – outer border of foot lifts
- adduction – turns foot inward
- abduction – turns foot outward
- supination – combines adduction and inversion
- pronation – combines abduction and eversion (looks like a flat, duck-footed walk).

Figure 1.4   *The bones of the foot*

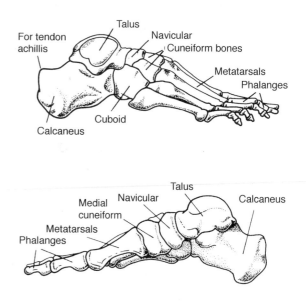

The manner in which the foot is divided into three sections – *forefoot, midfoot, hindfoot* – aids stepping and forms three arches: *inner, longitudinal* and *transverse*. We notice these sections as we walk, run or jump. When doing exercises like foot pushes and prances the 'going through the foot' is felt particularly clearly as springy and strong. Strong, flexible feet are one of a dancer's most valuable assets. These two relatively small body parts are true 'feats' of engineering!

In correct alignment, the lower leg (*tibia/fibula*) rests on the *talus* which in turn rests on the heel bone (*calcaneus*). Together, all this forms the hindfoot or *tarsus*.

The midfoot consists of the *navicular, cuboid* and three *cuneiform bones*.

The forefoot has several arches (see Figure 1.5) for normal function (support and stepping) and protection:

- the inside *medial longitudinal arch*: from heel to heads of metatarsals;
- the outside *lateral longitudinal arch*: from heel to head of the 5th metatarsal;
- the *transverse* arch is under the ball of the foot along the heads of the metatarsals;
- the *metatarsal arch*: dome-shaped, and running across the front heads of the metatarsal bones.

Postural problems/injuries of the foot
Metatarsal and toe injuries/problems

- *Fracture of the 5th metatarsal:* see the section on bone injuries on p. 6.
- *Stress fracture of metatarsals:* 'March Fracture' appears as a pain under the foot when pushing through the foot in jumps, on a rise or when stepping. Soldiers marching on hard surfaces are prone, hence the name. *Causes:* Poorly aligned body weight/barefoot work where extra pressure has been put on the metatarsal arch/increase in work. *Treatment:* rest recovery over approximately 6–8 weeks; physiotherapy which encourages the intrinsic muscles of the foot to support properly.
- *Morton's Foot. Appearance:* abnormally short and hypermobile first metatarsal which can destabilise the foot and cause pain in the metatarsal area. *Treatment:* a foot pad to correct faulty weight placement.
- *Hallux Valgus and Tailor's Bunion. Appearance:* an enlargement on metatarso-

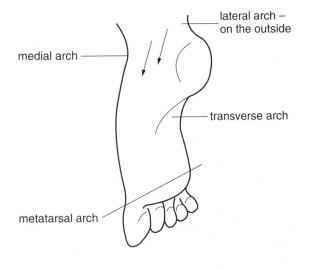

Figure 1.5   *The arches of the foot*

medial arch

lateral arch – on the outside

transverse arch

metatarsal arch

phalangeal joint of either the 1st or 5th toe. Inflammation appears on the bursa where extra mineral deposits accumulate. Pain occurs when the ankle is rolling inwards. The big toe distorts away from the midline and the little toe towards the midline. *Causes:* Hallux Valgus from foot pronation combined with walking with outwardly rotated hips. Tailor's Bunion foot supination combined with inwardly rotated hips. Incorrect weight placement results. *Treatment:* by chiropodist placing a pad. Physiotherapy may use ice/ultrasound/corrective exercise. Check weight distribution on feet. Avoid tight shoes and barefoot work.
- *Hammer toes. Appearance:* crooked toes, big toe points upward and phalanges 2 and 3 are flexed downward, and the ends are often callused. This can lead to corns. *Causes:* too narrow or short shoes. *Treatment:* keep toes in extended position in jumping and travelling. If pain becomes too great, special footwear/surgery may be necessary.

Arches injuries/problems

- *Plantar fascial strain. Appearance:* aching on the sole of the foot. *Causes:* incorrect landing from jumps. *Treatment:* ice/strapping/reduce workload/ultrasound/support pads in shoe. Can be stubborn and recurring.

- *Flat feet (pes planus). Appearance:* lowering of the medial longitudinal arch. Aching under big toe and along to heel. *Causes:* unsuitable footwear/rolling in on ankles causes longitudinal ligaments to weaken. Often related to poor turn-out and knee problems/bunion. *Treatment:* ultrasound/arch support/corrective exercises for the intrinsic muscles of the foot.

- *Rolling and sickling:* if there is a bow in the tibia bone, a misalignment in the angle of the ankle joint will result. The knee will be out of line with the ankle and foot. Rolling and sickling will occur.

TASK 2

A corrective exercise for feet to strengthen the *dorsi flexors* and to help the prevention of, or to heal, shin splints of the lower leg:

- Sit on a mat on the floor, legs straight out in front.

- Extend one foot. Place the other foot on top.

- The top foot puts downward pressure on the bottom foot. Flex the bottom foot against the pressure for 10 seconds, then pull back the foot through the whole range of flexion.

- Repeat two or three times.

The use of the foot in different dance genres

In classical ballet the foot is normally *plantar flexed* (pointed), whereas in the modern genre it is often *dorsi flexed* – this is particularly noticeable in the Martha Graham technique. Some post-modern styles prefer a more neutral, relaxed position of the non-weight-bearing foot. Obviously, these all have very different expressive qualities – the light endless line of the ballet in contrast to the harsher, broken and more natural throw-away feel of the post-modern dancer. An even length in the metatarsals and toes will assist support in *demi-pointe* (weight distributed evenly on heads of metatarsals and phalanges) and *full-pointe* (weight on phalanges only) work. The feet on the ground gives a further contrast between the genres – the floating ethereal look of the ballerina on pointe as contrasted with the earthy gravity-bound flat look of the modern dancer. Needless to say, the rigours of pointe work may cause alignment problems. Shoes must fit correctly, with, if necessary, high *vamps* (support pads) to protect high arches (*pes cavus*). Pointe work should never begin until over the age of 12 when the bones have ossified sufficiently to cope with the weight. Continual pointe work may result in a thickening of the metatarsals, and this is why the feet may seem to widen. When pointe work is stopped completely, however, the feet will return to their original size.

As well as the spine and feet, other parts and functions of the body are also crucial in maintaining correct alignment:

- the *lateral flexors* of the trunk help to hold the trunk in place, for example during multiple pirouettes.
- *Visual cues*: the eyes send information to the brain on the body's position in space.
- *Semi-circular canals in the inner ear* send information on the body's orientation in space.
- *Receptors in joints, tendons and muscles* provide continual information to the brain on the body's relative position in space.

ALIGNMENT – SUMMARY

It is clear that this fundamental skill of alignment is crucial to the prevention of injury for any dancer. Becoming aware of and correcting poor posture can improve alignment. The stretching and strengthening of appropriate muscle groups is required (see Figure 1.6) when misalignments/injuries are encountered.

Some examples of faulty alignment in training which are discussed at greater length elsewhere are:

- weight too far back;
- failing to turn out from the hips;
- twisted hips;
- feet overturning/rolling;
- misuse of muscle groups during *plié* (knees flex) and *relevé* (rise on toes either demi-pointe or full pointe).

Many dance programmes nowadays stress the importance of body awareness, as taught in the Alexander and Pilates exercise techniques which emphasise a balancing of the body. Regular attendance to good technique classes in the presence of an observant teacher will help to maintain alignment and keep the chance of injury to a minimum.

> Learning to dance is an extremely vulnerable activity ... Dancers must learn to treat themselves with respect.
>
> (*Julia Buckroyd in* Dying Swans, *New Scientist, 25 December 1993/1 January 1994*)

Figure 1.6 *The main muscles controlling alignment*

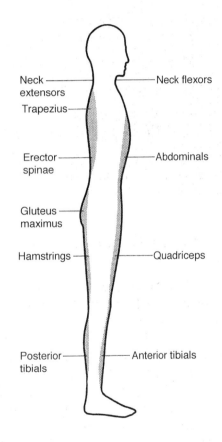

To help you check some of the information in this section, there now follows a further task.

TASK 3 ⧖

In pairs, let one read instructions and the other adjust posture. Check list for standing in parallel first position:

- Weight evenly spread over the metatarsal arch. *Check*: long toes; lift inner longitudinal arch.
- The *tibia* and *fibula* (lower leg) balance on top of the *talus*/ankle.
- The pelvis balances on the *femur* (thigh bone), so that the muscles of the lower back, abdomen and thighs are in equal contraction. *Check:* the thighs lift to support the hips; hips level; drop the tail bone (*sacrum*)/flatten the abdomen so that the pelvis is in reciprocal relationship with the *lumbar* spine; normal amount of anterior posterior curvature.
- Knees relaxed; soft patella.
- Upper back supported by *thoracic vertebrae*. *Check:* proper amount of anterior–posterior curvature; shoulder girdle rests easily on thorax. Shoulders relaxed/*scapulae* dropped.
- Weight of head even on top of cervical spine. *Check:* jaw at right angle to the floor; long neck lifted lightly from ears.
- Chest lifted, and *sternum* above balls of feet. *Do not:* lift shoulders/tighten neck/hold breath/lift chin/tuck seat under.

Now read this to your partner:

- Now hold this position and try to rise easily. [Check your partner does not: shift their weight forward or back when rising; flex at the hip or knee.]
- Move your arms and head easily without loss of balance.
- Use your bones for support – think X-ray!
- Feel control coming from the centre outwards.
- Let your arms connect to the centre of your back.

Flexibility

Increasing flexibility involves increasing muscular elasticity so that the range of mobility from a joint will increase. It does *not* involve stretching the ligaments that provide the joints with stability: the elongation of the ligaments increases the possibility of injury. The limit to flexibility is either the ligaments themselves or bony restriction. Individual structural differences like the shape of the bone will affect the range of motion/flexibility. Tight ligaments will reduce mobility, as will tight musculature.

> **MYTH: a dancer can never be too flexible:**
>
> **Natural flexibility is not necessarily a bonus for a dancer. Flexible joints which are not protected by adequate muscle strength are more susceptible to injury.**
>
> **(*Rachel Harris in* Dance Dates, *Birmingham National Dance Agency, 1994*)**

The assumption that all dancers should be able to achieve the same range of motion is thus false. Other factors which will influence flexibility are: gender; age; body temperature; training. When flexibility is increased, the range of motion in the joints increases. A more flexible body helps to avoid malalignment, muscle tears and injury generally.

THE JOINTS

Where two bones meet, there will be a *joint* which allows movement to occur. There are several types of joint which allow different degrees of mobility – from fully mobile to very restricted. In dance, we clearly need a wider range of movement in the hip/leg joint (the 'break' of the leg) than in, say, the knee which needs greater stability for its protection in actions like landing from a jump.

There are three types of joint:

- cartilaginous
- fibrous
- synovial.

Cartilaginous joints

These allow little movement but give great strength. The joints between the vertebrae where the *intervertebral cartilage* is placed is one such joint. The limitation of movement here is crucial in absorbing both the shock from, say, jumps and jarring to the skull and brain. These joints are characterised by the presence of *fibrocartilage* between the bones.

Fibrous joints

These allow little or no movement; for example, the flat bones of the skull.

Synovial joints

These are the most mobile, so in dance these are the ones that are of greatest concern – e.g. the hip joint (ball and socket – see Figure 1.7),

The main concerns surrounding flexibility are:

- *the joints – particularly the hip, knee and ankle;*
- stretching.

Figure 1.7 *The hip, showing features of a synovial joint*

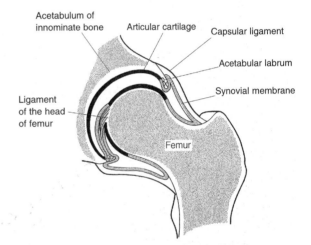

fingers, toes, knees and ankles (hinge joints) which all allow a range of free movement.

Of all the joints, the synovial ones are the most complex in structure, having the following structural characteristics:

- *Synovial fluid:* this fills the space between the ends of the bones.
- *Synovial membrane:* this surrounds the whole joint.
- *Ligaments:* these are bands of connective tissue wrapping around the outside of the joint which support and protect the joint from strain and dislocation, and connect the bones.
- *Tendons:* these are the endings of the muscles which also cross the joints and attach the muscle to the bone and help to increase the strength of the synovial joints.

As we can see, these different joints either *allow* or *restrict* movement, according to their structure. The point here is to know which movements are suitable for which joints, and to be able to move *within the body's potential*, thus avoiding injury. It is important to recognise your own limitations. Forcing or twisting a joint in directions for which it is not structured will cause injury. Therefore, it is helpful to know not only the joints' *structures* but also their correct movement range – see Figure 1.8.

Generally, joint movements include a range from the following:

- *flexing:* bending a joint;
- *extending:* straightening a joint;
- *abducting:* motion away from the centre line;
- *adducting:* motion towards the centre line;
- *rotating;* motion around the joint axis line;
- *circumducting:* a combination of the above involving motion in a circle.

Figure 1.8   *Movements possible in the joints*

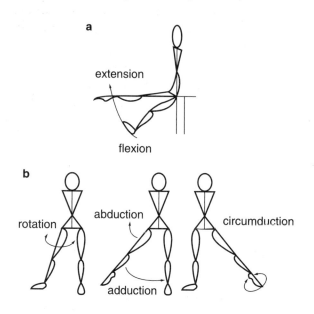

TASK 4

In groups of three or four, use sitting, standing and lying positions.

1   Experiment with bending and stretching all the joints in varying degrees – 45°, 90°, 180° – noticing which joints are more or less mobile.

- Work on circling, rotational movement in the joints.
- To music of your choice, put a phrase together to be performed in unison which contrasts rotations with bends and stretches, and uses different joints.

2   It may be fun to use chance procedures to make the phrase by writing down on separate pieces of paper the names of different joints and turning them face down. Select at random the joints, and perform the phrase in the order that you chose them.

This task can also provide an opportunity to look at *Labanotation* – see Chapter 2, pp. 50–58.

Reflecting on the task, consider now that different joints can be classified by their correct movement range, as follows:

- *nonaxial:* linear movement only;
- *uniaxial:* movement in a single plane around a fixed axis;
- *biaxial:* motion in 2 planes around 2 axes;

- *triaxial:* motion in all three planes (front to back – *frontal* plane; the *horizontal* plane divides top from bottom of body; the *sagittal* plane divides right from left) around three axes. This joint is sometimes also called a *ball and socket joint.*

Table 1.4 classifies the main joints in this way. Joints have sacs of fluid between the tendons and bones called *bursa*. These allow the smooth movement of tendon over bone. If overused, joints may become inflamed, and this is known as *bursitis*.

Table 1.4   *Classification of joints by type and movement range*

Bones	Joint	Joint type	Movement range
Scapula and humerus	Shoulder	Ball and socket, synovial, triaxial	Adduction, abduction, flexion, rotation and extension
Carpals and metacarpals	Wrist	Biaxial, synovial	Adduction, abduction, flexion, extension
Innominate bones and femur	Pelvis	Ball and socket, triaxial, synovial	Adduction, abduction, flexion, extension, rotation
Femur, tibia, fibula	Knee	Hinge, uniaxial, synovial	Flex, extend. Some rotation when *not* weight bearing
Tibia, fibula, talus	Ankle	Hinge, uniaxial, synovial	Flex, extend. Rotation when not weight bearing
Talus, calcaneus, navicular	Foot	Nonaxial	Linear only

The use of the joints in dance

As we stated earlier, certain joints are of greater importance in dance training than others. The ones most used in Western dance genres like classical ballet and modern dance are: hip, knee and ankle. There are contrasts here with non-Western styles like the South Asian *bharata natyam* where the elaborate language of hand gestures, or *mudras*, combined with articulation of the face, eyes and arms, are the mainstays of expression. The expansion into postmodern dance from the 1960s to the present day has brought with it experimentation through the mixing of genres. Choreographers like Lea Anderson combine Grahamesque floor work with Indian-influenced tiny gestures and with popular movements such as one might see on a pop-music video.

In the more conventional techniques of training, certain joints are open to overuse. It is important to look at these in more detail.

To show a dance class in the style of Martha Graham, as taught by Robert Cohan at I.M. Marsh College

The hip/pelvis

The hip/pelvis (see Figure 1.9) is the strongest joint in the body due to its heavy net of ligaments and strong musculature. The ball and socket are also deeply set to give greater stability. At the same time, the top of the head of the femur stands out from the pelvis, giving a greater range of movement in all directions. Consider this the next time you are performing *ronds de jambe en l'air*. The turn-out associated closely with classical ballet depends on the 'Y'-shaped *ilio-femoral ligament* and the angle at which the femur is set in the bowl of the *acetabulum* of the hip socket. The powerful ligament holds the femur, and if gently stretched at an early age, it can become more elastic and so increase the range of motion in the hip. This must be balanced with the strength both of the turn-out muscles and of those muscles which lift the leg:

- turn-out muscles: 6 *external rotators/ gluteals/iliopsoas/sartorius*;

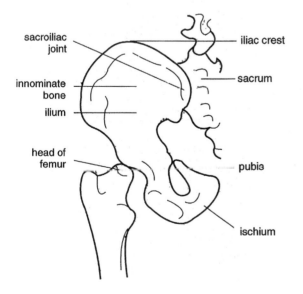

Figure 1.9 *Bones of the right side of the pelvis*

sacroiliac joint

iliac crest

innominate bone

ilium

sacrum

head of femur

pubis

ischium

Postural problems/injuries – the pelvis

Tight musculature and ligaments around the hip can affect the back and create misalignments around the body. Forcing turnout, insufficient warm-up and misalignment are all possible causes of injuries such as strains to the *rectus femoris* or *iliopsoas*. The correct tilt of the pelvis is essential in order to support the normal curve of the spine. 'Sticking the tailbone out' will increase the hollow of the back, and must be avoided.

Some dancers with too-loose ligaments may feel their hip go out of joint. Over time, this may lead to deterioration in the joint. The musculature must be strengthened in order to avoid this condition which, in time, can develop into *osteoarthrosis of the hip* where the joint narrows and the bone surface wears away – this is very painful. Many dancers trained in Graham technique in the early days forced the opening of the hips and have suffered such deterioration as a consequence.

Men who begin training later than most women usually develop less hip flexibility.

The use of the hip in different dance genres

One of the best-known characteristics of classical ballet is the turned-out position of the hips, legs and feet, which is like Indian and Eastern genres in this respect. For safety's sake, the turn-out must be controlled by the muscles of the pelvis, particularly the inside-thigh muscles and the *gluteous minimus* which links the legs to the pelvis.

Forcing turn-out at an early age by twisting the hips will over-stretch the musculature of the spine and lead to injury of the lower back, groin and knees. In the modern genre, a more 'natural' parallel hold of the hips is preferred. This originated in the work of Isadora Duncan as a rebellion against what she regarded as the artificiality of ballet. Later, Martha Graham used it with greater emphasis to give her choreography a hard-edged look in combination with flexed hands and feet.

The knee

The knee joint (see Figure 1.10) is potentially unstable, but the *cruciate ligaments* hold the femur on the tibia making it strong and robust. Also, two *semi-lunar cartilages* help to deepen the joint and circulate the synovial fluid, assisting shock absorption. These do not take weight, but if the knee is twisted whilst weight-bearing, they can be trapped between the femur and tibia and will tear.

The kneecap (*patella*) protects this joint and acts to increase the action of the big thigh muscles (*quadriceps femoris*) by serving as a point of attachment of the tendon and thereby increasing leverage for the movement of the joint. Thus, lifting the leg and extending the knee from the thigh are made possible.

Postural problems/injuries – the knee

Most knee injuries occur when bearing weight in flexion, because this is when the joint has least stability. Many such injuries result from repeated twisted misalignment which will loosen ligaments. Such often arises during pliés, when there is a failure to maintain the line of the patella directly over the midline of the feet (which extends out from the middle toe). If the knee is allowed to 'screw' because of inadequate hip flexibility, the *medial ligament* will take undue stress, and there will also be excess strain on the inside of the knee. Foot-rolling may also be a factor. The uneven pull on the patella will cause deterioration of the ligaments.

The maintenance of a straight, secure knee joint with minimal rotation during movement is the main way to protect it. After a knee injury, attention should be given to the quadriceps muscle group in order to compensate for the loss of strength due to lack of use. This muscle group wastes quickly (*atrophy*) and so needs exercise, as do the hamstrings (the pair muscle group to the quadriceps) which provide

Figure 1.10   *The knee joint (a) from the front (b) from the side*

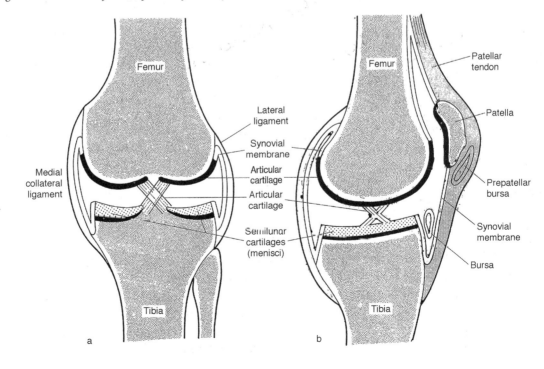

the necessary stretch as the quads contract. This give-and-take relationship of muscle pairs is called *reciprocal*.

Table 1.5 *Injuries/problems of the knee*

Injury	Symptoms	Causes	Treatment
Torn cartilage	Pain on bent leg, when weight bearing, on inside of knee. Knee locks if bent, or wasting of quads.	Incorrect pliés alignment – knee drops inward. Poor turn-out in hip.	Rest/operate if badly torn. Exercise quads/hamstrings.
Bursitis (Housemaid's Knee)	Pain on either side of patella – swelling.	Excessive bending – bursa inflame.	Rest/ice/ultrasound.
Jumper's Knee	Pain in plié and jumps, tender on patella under tibia when pressed.	Overuse during jumping.	Massage/ultrasound/ stretch/strengthen quads.

Postural defects of the knee – hyperextension

'Swayback' knees, although useful in classical ballet because they give a long, aesthetically pleasing look, are a sign of weak quadriceps. Overstretching of the hamstrings and locking of the knees should be avoided.

The ankle

The ankle joint (see Figure 1.11) lies between the *tibia*, the *fibia* and the *talus*. The ligaments on the outside and inside (*deltoid*) are the main means of support. The ankle joint is very stable, but is also the site of large stresses.

> **FASCINATING FACT: on landing from jumps, the ankle can absorb up to *8* times the body weight.**

Postural problems/injuries – the ankle

- *Sprained ankle:* the most commonly injured part of the ankle is the *anterior tibia fibular* ligament on the outside of the ankle. A sprain of a joint, indeed, is the most common injury in dance. It can happen from faulty landings causing the foot to sickle in-

Figure 1.11 *The ankle joint*

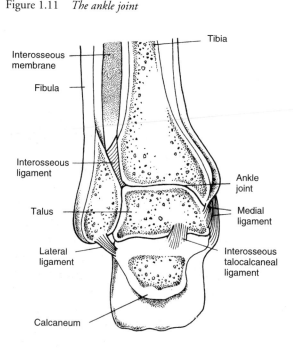

wards as it rolls over on its outside edge. The ligament is then twisted and may tear. *Treatment:* ice, rest, elevation and – if severe – a plaster or strapping. Recovery can take up to 6 weeks.

Further ankle ailments are listed in Table 1.6.

STRETCHING

Flexibility is improved by *stretching*. This action lengthens the muscle along the direction of the fibres. There should be a pleasant sensation inside the muscle. There are a number of ways to stretch correctly which may overcome the blocking effect of the *stretch reflex*. This is a protective reflex which makes the muscle contract immediately after a stretch, so that in

Table 1.6 *Injuries/problems of the lower leg*

Injury	Symptoms	Causes	Treatment
Achilles tendonitis	Aching at back of heel approx. 2 inches above top of heel bone	Overuse: hard floors/not allowing time to 'go through the heel' repeatedly/inadequate warm-up/forcing over too far on pointe.	Rest/ice/ultrasound. Tape and massage. Support pads under heels in shoes.
Achilles bursitis	Tender around heel. Pain in jumps, plié, extension of foot/swelling.	Pressure on bursa from tight shoes.	Rest/ice/ultrasound. Check ribbons not too tight, soften back of shoes or add cushion.

case of a sudden fall or twist, the muscle is prevented from overstretching to the point of injury.

- *The long sustained stretch.* During a slow action, the brain can override the stretch reflex. With conscious control, this stretch can be sustained, and *gravity* can be used to increase the extension for at least 30 seconds. Letting the muscle 'hang off the bone' and 'nudging around', combined with relaxation and constant breathing, can reach spots that other stretches do not. This relaxed type of stretching is featured greatly in post-modern anatomical release work.
- *Reciprocal inhibition.* Trying to stretch a muscle while it is in any state of *contraction* will reduce the effectiveness of the stretch and may tear the muscle fibres. For this reason, *ballistic bouncing stretches* are ineffective, and unsafe, and may cause soreness. The maximum contraction of one muscle will temporarily inhibit the stretch reflex in its opposite muscle. So, if you wanted to stretch, say, the hamstrings, a consciously held contraction of the quadriceps for 20 to 30 seconds first would then allow greater stretch in the back of the thigh. After the contraction, the hamstring stretch should then be held for a further 30 seconds to 1 minute. For this principle to work, both muscles have to be of similar mass. A bonus of the reciprocal method is the strength gained due to maximal contraction.

Both of the above reflexes are activated at a spinal level by a release of chemicals.

- *The Golgi tendon reflex.* This is another protective reflex, but one which acts as a reaction to pressure. The Golgi tendon organs are sited at the point where the tendon meets the muscle, and they are sensitive to pressure. They totally relax the muscle when the tendon is about to pull off the bone, and they block the stretch reflex for a longer time. A word of warning though to dancers who think 'Ah! I'll use this to stretch more', because the severity of the pull required to activate the Golgi reflex makes it a dangerous way to increase mobility. During intense stretching, if it is experienced, there is a feeling of warm, total release. The muscle goes to jelly, and the range of motion is increased noticeably. The safest way to reach this point is *very* slowly and carefully, and after an adequate warm-up.

Generally speaking, the following guidelines should be used to sequence an exercise programme effectively:

1 Start gently, and gradually build up to a more vigorous level. Do an all-over warm-up first.

2 After the exercise of one muscle group, take time to undo the bad effects or to notice the good effects. For example, after a maximum contraction for strength, stretch out in the opposite direction. Or vice versa.
3 Before doing a major stretch, do a maximum contraction of the opposite muscle group.
4 Pinpoint the exact muscle or group that needs stretching/strengthening.
5 Listen to your body!

FLEXIBILITY – A SUMMARY

Improving mobility in the joints is crucial if the dancer is to maintain muscular balance in the body. This of course will also help alignment, safe working methods and avoidance of injury. You should learn what proper stretching techniques feel like when you do them, and so avoid unsafe methods.

TASK 5

Check a partner's flexibility:

1 For tightness in the back: one dancer kneels down with feet flat and curls forward. Look for: flat places on the spine – these are points of tightness. Swap over.
2 For tightness in the front of the shoulder: raise an arm in abduction until it is parallel to the floor, then take the arm behind. Look for difficulty in this movement – this indicates tightness.
3 For tight hamstrings: lie on your back and raise your legs, keeping the hips on the floor. The leg should be able to reach at least 90° or more. Look out, therefore, for a leg raise of less than 90°.

If any tightness has been found, now do the appropriate corrective stretch from below:

1 For the lumbar area: kneel as before, but stretch out the arms, breathe out and hold for 30 seconds. Apply the long sustained stretch.
2 For the whole back: standing, drop from the head and curve down, lifting the abdominals; keep the legs soft and bent. Curl up again, and repeat three times.
3 For the pectorals (the front of the shoulder area): make one arm reach directly behind you. Repeat with the other arm.
4 For the hamstrings: lie on your back, bend both legs in, then softly place them on the torso. Breathe out and gently hug; hold for 20 seconds.

Any muscular tightness you may have can be lessened by stretching, but any structural limitations of bone and ligament will not be affected by stretching, and so all dancers should learn to work within their own personal range.

The next section is concerned with strength, and it is important to note that only when the muscles which control a joint are strong can a full range of mobility be achieved through gradual stretching. Weak muscles should not be stretched. Stretching and strengthening must be in balance.

Strength and stamina

STRENGTH

When combined together, increasing levels of flexibility, strength and stamina form a policy of preventative training.

Strength is the capacity to exert a muscle contraction against resistance. Contraction is the opposite muscle action to that of stretching. A strong body moves freely, efficiently and above all safely. The aim is all-round strength, not the overdevelopment of certain muscle groups.

The main concerns are:

- types of strength
- muscles

Types of strength

During exercise, there are two types of strength: *isotonic* and *isometric*.

Isotonic

This involves a dynamic resistance during which the muscle *shortens*. Exercises may be performed, in the full range of motion of a joint, in sets of 10 to 15. Repetitions slowly build to 2 or 3 sets. By adding weights, self-resistance (like another body part), pulleys or elastic bands, overloading may be increased gradually.

MYTHS:
- **Building strength = bulk.**
- **Building strength = loss of flexibility.**
- **Dancers should not use weights.**

TASK 6 ⋈

Perform the following isotonic exercise to strengthen hip abductors (*gluteus medius*). If a dancer has weak hip abductors and tight external rotators, *grand battement* and *battement tendu* will be performed with hip flexed and externally rotated, rather than in abduction.

1 Lie on your side, with legs straight and feet together.
2 Internally rotate the top leg, and abduct the hip through the full range of motion.
3 Repeat 10 times.
4 Build gradually to a maximum of 3 sets of 10. Allow 2 to 5 minutes' rest between sets.
5 When 3 sets are possible, perform the exercise standing with an ankle weight starting at 2 lb.

Isometric

This involves a static resistance during which the muscle tension increases but does not shorten.

TASK 7

Perform the following isometric exercise to strengthen the lateral trunk flexors and correct scoliosis and an uneven hip tilt.

1 Lie on your side on a mat, with legs straight and feet together.
2 Rest on one forearm, and extend the other arm to shoulder height.
3 Raise the hips sideways off the mat as far as possible, and *hold* for 10 seconds.
4 Repeat, then change to the other side.

A weight-training programme for male dancers of the Birmingham Royal Ballet was devised by Yiannis Koutedakis at the University of Wolverhampton. The dancers used free weights and machines set at high resistance for a low number of repetitions. After the programme, the dancers felt that their physical appearance had improved.

> Some choreographers initially expressed doubts about the outcome ... This meant that the project was restricted to male dancers. But the results have convinced choreographers that their sugar plum fairies are not going to turn into Ms Universe overnight, so Koutedakis is planning to extend the programme to include women.
>
> (Helen Saul in New Scientist, 25 December 1993/1 January 1994)

> ... the greatest classical dancers, such as Nureyev, Baryshnikov and Marakova ... know that their 'muscular corsets' used correctly are so strong that no matter how complicated that line, nothing can distort or tense and thus hurt their bodies.
>
> (Joan Lawson in Dancing Times)

With the above in mind, the principle of *progressive overload* to build strength can be identified. This involves increasing:

- *frequency:* increasing the number of repetitions or the speed of a movement;
- *intensity:* adding more and more resistance, as with weights;
- *duration:* increasing the length of time a movement takes.

For example, holding a leg off the floor against the pull of gravity – as is often done in dance classes – will build up strength and stamina in the quadriceps. With added progressive overload during exercise, the muscle size/strength will increase.

Muscles

> I have a big feeling about muscle – to have a muscle, to feel a muscle, to have a muscle warmed up and toned and ready to do something, it's a marvellous, sensual feeling.
>
> (Edward Villella in Dance from Magic to Art, 1982)

Muscles are the meaty part of the body. In dance, it is the *striated* or *skeletal* muscle which is of concern. This is controlled by the nervous system which sends electrochemical energy impulses which cause the muscle fibres to contract and the joints to move. Muscles are attached by tendons to the bone at each end: (a) the end of the *origin* – this stays still; (b) the *insertion* – the end which pulls and moves.

Muscles can only *pull* (i.e. contract), and movement is brought about by pulling on the bones so as to turn these bones into *levers*. The structure of each such lever has three main parts:

1 the *load* or *weight*;
2 the *fulcrum* (balance point) of the joint;
3 the muscle action producing the *effort* at the point of the muscle insertion.

There are three types of lever: *first order, second order* and *third order* – depending on the position of the fulcrum.

In Figure 1.12, F = fulcrum, E = effort and W = weight. An example of a second-order lever is shown in Figure 1.13.

Figure 1.12 *First order lever*

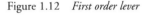
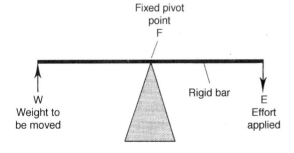

Most common levers are third-order, where the 'effort' moves a shorter distance than the 'load'. This has the advantage of allowing a large movement to be made with only a slight contraction/shortening of the muscle (see Figure 1.14), thus making it a more efficient movement.

Figure 1.13   *Second order lever in rising onto one toe*

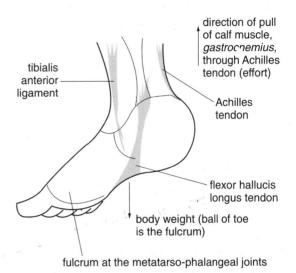

Figure 1.14   *Third order lever action of the arm*

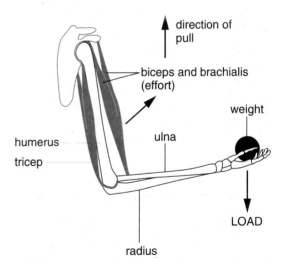

Contraction occurs when muscle fibres shorten and movement is produced. This is *concentric contraction* (as in the example of the biceps in the arm above). However, muscles also produce *eccentric contraction* – e.g. to straighten the elbow, the *biceps brachii* muscle fibres will lengthen. Here is an example of how concentric and eccentric contraction work: a plié begins with the pull of gravity, as controlled by an eccentric contraction of the quadriceps (or quads). Then, when the quads and hip extensors contract concentrically, the body is raised against gravity back to standing.

To dance without injury, a muscle needs a high level of efficiency in the *antagonistic* action of its pair muscle. This means that while a muscle is contracting, its opposite muscle must relax smoothly. Poorly trained or tired muscles do not tend to act antagonistically, and they strain easily.

Muscle pairs include:

- *biceps brachii* (front upper arm) and *triceps brachii* back upper arm);
- *rectus abdominis* (front torso) and the long muscles of the back;
- *tibialis anterior* (front lower leg) and *gastrocnemius, soleus* (back lower leg);
- thigh adductors (inside thigh) and *gluteus medius* and others (outside thigh).

Injuries – muscles and tendons

Muscles are attached to bones by the much stronger tendons. Both muscles and tendons are liable to injury. If a tendon is irritated by overuse, tendonitis may occur. Rest is then essential. The *achilles* tendon is particularly prone to tendonitis. The symptoms are tenderness and crunching, particularly when plantar-flexing the ankle. Careful stretching of the *soleus* and *gastrocnemius* (lower leg) when cooling down reduces the likelihood of tendonitis.

Muscles and tendons are usually injured by too sudden a movement, or by a recurring strain on weak muscles from poor technique or overuse. Vulnerable muscles include: the groin (*iliopsoas, rectus femoris, adductors*), the hamstring group, and the calf (*gastrocnemius*). A thorough warm-up will help to reduce muscle and tendon strains, as it will for joint sprains. If you do, however, injure yourself, the following is a good guide, and easy to remember:

Figure 1.15 *Figure showing different muscle sets*

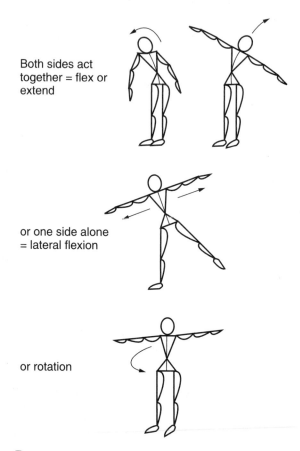

Both sides act together = flex or extend

or one side alone = lateral flexion

or rotation

R = rest

I = ice

C = compress (bandage/support)

E = elevate (raise)

Cold therapy will decrease the blood flow and bruising which damages soft tissue. It limits swelling by decreasing the muscle's need for oxygen, and thus relieves pain. Apply ice for no more than 10 to 15 minutes, and repeat if necessary every few hours until the swelling, local heat or bruising stops. After 2 days, alternate between cold and hot in order to stimulate blood flow to the injury and encourage healing. The ice should not have direct contact with the skin – a bag of frozen peas does work! (Or of course you could have rice and peas!)

Table 1.7 *Muscular functions and problems*

Location	Muscle names	Function	Problems/injuries
Feet	Intrinsic muscles intersseous lumbrical	Strengthen arches and keep toes long when foot is plantar flexed.	If toes keep curled, increases stress on Achilles tendon.
	Hallucis longus tibialis anterior	Dorsi flex foot (flexed).	
	Plantaris	Plantar flex foot (point).	
Leg Lower	Gastrocnemius	Plantar flex foot – a 'white' fast-mover muscle for travelling jumps etc.	Stretch out after use, with ankle flexed, knee straight. Reduces risk of tendonitis in Achilles tendon.
	Soleus	Maintains plantar flexion, in relevé, pointe work – red holding muscle.	After a class with lots of adagio or balances, stretch it, with ankle flexed. Knee should be flexed and legs parallel.
Knee	Quadriceps group rectus femoris, vastus lateralis, medialis	Extend the knee by increasing leverage.	In any knee injury, the quads waste/weaken during recovery.
	Hamstring group: semitendiasus, semimembranosus, biceps femoris	Strengthen alignment of knee over centre of tarsus. Flex knee and extend hip.	Pronation (knees over-rotate) injure patella.
Hip	Small rotators	Externally rotate femur and stabilise hip.	Imbalance between rotators tightens buttocks and pinches sciatic nerve.
	Iliopsoas	Medially rotate femur and flex hip.	Can appear 'duckfooted'. Cause of lumbar lordosis, lumbar back pain.
	Adductors, including pectineus, adductor brevis, longus, magnus	Laterally rotate femur (inner thighs pull together), stabilise pelvis when acting against the abductors when standing on one leg.	
	Abductors, including gluteus medius and minimus	Stabilise hip by supporting contraction on weight-bearing side.	If too weak or tense, will affect hips or knees.

Cont.

Table 1.7   *Continued*

Location	Muscle names	Function	Problems/injuries
	gluteus maximus	Extends hip. Feel it contract when lifting from being flexed at hip.	Low back pain if excess lordosis (sway-back). May 'buck' during jumping.
Torso	Sacrospinalis, quadratus lumborum, rectus abdominis obliques, transversalis	Extend spine. Flex spine.	Strong abdominals help to protect lumbar spine.

Heat sources could be in spray form, an infra-red lamp or heat packs. Only a qualified physiotherapist should apply ultrasound. An appropriate exercise routine should be followed to maintain uninjured and injured parts alike.

TASK 8

To check a partner's strength:

1 For strength in the front and back of the shoulder: one dancer lifts their arm to the side horizontally. With the partner doing the resisting, try to move the arm forwards, then, with resistance from the back, do the same backwards. Look for *unequal* forces in one or the other direction – they should be equal.
2 For the strength of the quadriceps: lie on your back, lift a leg to a flexed position and then, with partner resisting, continue to flex at the hip.
3 For the strength of the hamstrings: lie on your front and lift your leg against partner's resistance.

STAMINA

Dancing should look easy; like an optical illusion. It should seem effortless. When you do a difficult variation, the audience is aware that it is demanding, and that you have the power and strength to do it. But in the end, when you take your bow, you should look as if you were saying 'Oh it was nothing. I could do it again.'

(Helgi Tomasson in Dance from Magic to Art, *1980)*

This describes stamina. Stamina is staying power, endurance of either the muscles or the heart and breathing. As described in the quote above, it would be easy to think that stamina has to do with how you look. It is more than that, however, because it is crucial for the prevention of injury. In order to maintain quality performance over long periods, the heart and lungs need to deliver oxygen to the blood and muscles as efficiently as possible. Once fatigue sets in, mistakes in judgement or undue stresses on muscles and joints make continued dancing unsafe.

Stamina can be divided into two parts:

1 *Muscular endurance* is the ability of a muscle to continue to contract over a period of

time. It is inseparable from muscular strength and size; both these are developed by the above-mentioned principle of progressive overload. This type of conditioning needs many repetitions with light resistance, and of course this can be boring! So how many is enough? Listen to your body, and when a burning sensation is felt, the general rule is 5 more repetitions for increasing muscular endurance. Well-trained muscles are able to contract over longer periods before tiring, and so in class the dancer aims to achieve increased strength and endurance in exercises. Speed will increase if movements are practised at an increasing pace.

2 *Cardiorespiratory endurance* is the ability to continue *aerobic* activity (activity depending on free oxygen or air) over a period of time. The cardiorespiratory system includes the heart and lungs (and associated organs). It would be helpful to take a closer look at these vital systems.

The cardiovascular system

This consists of the heart, the blood and the blood vessels. Together these enable the transport of necessary nutrients and gases to and from the muscles and organs. The blood also carries heat to the skin for removal by sweating and radiation.

During exercise, changes occur in the cardiovascular system. There is:

- an improvement in the condition of the overall system;
- an increase in the size/strength of the heart muscle and the volume of the heart chambers;
- an increase in aerobic capacity;
- a lowering of the resting heart rate;
- a better venous return of waste products;
- an increase in the volume of blood;
- an increase in the red-blood-cell count (i.e. *haemoglobin* cells which carry oxygen);
- an increase in chemical buffers (potassium

and sodium) in the blood (these lower acidity and help to maintain a lower cardiovascular rate);
- an increase in *stroke volume* (i.e. the amount of blood pumped at each heart beat).

The heart

A muscular pump about the size of your fist, the heart sends fresh oxygen (O_2) through the arteries to the rest of the body. The *veins* then carry waste products and carbon dioxide (CO_2) back, to be expelled from the body.

FASCINATING FACTS: the heart

- **beats at about 70 times per minute (resting rate).**
- **pumps blood at a rate of about 5 litres per minute – i.e. about 180 million gallons in a lifetime.**

The heart rate

During exercise, the heart rate (your *pulse*) increases from its usual resting rate to a maximum rate which is related to your age. When the exercise stops, it then decreases in order to maintain circulatory balance. The deceleration here is controlled by the *vagus nerve* which stops the heart from constantly speeding up. This nerve is stimulated by increased blood pressure. In a healthy young adult, normal blood pressure is around 120/80. The higher figure refers to the blood pressure during each heart beat, and the lower figure to your blood pressure *between* beats. The more strenuous the activity and the better the person's physical condition, the more sensitive the vagus nerve is. This is thought to explain why fitter individuals have a lower resting heart rate than untrained individuals.

Other factors affecting the heart rate are:

- The *pacemaker* stimulates a steady heart rate. This rate can be speeded up by the *accelerator branch*.
- *Chemical regulation* operates when there is

an increase in the levels of CO_2 in the blood. The heart rate and blood pressure increase as *adrenalin* is released into the bloodstream.

The target heart rate

Most dance classes do not focus on cardiorespiratory conditioning. In order now to stress this type of conditioning, a medium-to-high 'target' heart rate must be maintained continuously for 15 to 20 minutes. In dance class, it is usual to cross the floor once, then rest and wait for others to do so. This means that aerobic activity is not continued over a long enough time.

The respiratory system

During exercise, both the heart and the breathing rate speed up to increase the supply of O_2 *to* and of CO_2 *away from* the muscle. When we are huffing and puffing, CO_2 is being expelled more forcefully from the *alveoli* in the lungs out of the body. This removes the CO_2 away from the muscles, making an exchange for O_2 possible in the capillaries; and in this way, exercise may continue (see Figure 1.16).

Figure 1.16   *Elements of the respiratory system and gaseous exchange*

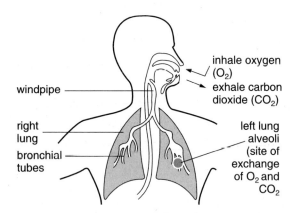

windpipe

right lung
bronchial tubes

inhale oxygen (O_2)
exhale carbon dioxide (CO_2)

left lung
alveoli (site of exchange of O_2 and CO_2)

The rate of breathing is controlled by nerve cells in the brain. These detect the levels of O_2, CO_2 and acidity in the blood and stimulate an appropriate increase or decrease in respiration.

Carbon dioxide is a relatively harmless waste gas because it is displaced easily by oxygen in the haemoglobin. However, carbon monoxide, as produced by smoking cigarettes, is extremely poisonous because it combines with haemoglobin to exclude oxygen. It therefore deprives the body of a basic requirement, and so smokers are less able to provide muscle with the necessary increased oxygen as demanded in dancing. Dancers who smoke will have less ability to maintain high-quality performance over long periods, and may be more prone to injury.

The *ribcage* protects the lungs. Attached to it are the muscles which control the expansion and contraction of the *thorax cavity*. These are: the *intercostals*; the *serratus group*; and the *diaphragm*. The lungs have no muscular power of their own.

The overall level of fitness for any sport or dance is something specific to that activity. However, the cardiorespiratory system does need a basic level of aerobic fitness, whatever the activity. An increase in the delivery of oxygen to the muscles by the heart, blood vessels and lungs is improved by slow and steady exercises, such as cycling or swimming, which gradually increase in intensity – in other words, through aerobic exercise where muscles work using oxygen.

The American College of Sports Medicine defines aerobic activity as follows:

> Aerobic activity is that requiring continuous, rhythmic use of large muscle groups at 60–90 per cent of the maximum heart rate and 50–85 per cent of maximum oxygen uptake for 20–60 minutes.

The main effects of aerobic exercise are:

● an increase in muscular endurance/stamina;

- an increase in cardiorespiratory endurance/stamina;
- a reduction of fat deposits (weight loss);
- a maintenance of bone mass.

Muscles can continue to work *without* oxygen, and this is called *anaerobic* activity. Anaerobic exercise begins when oxygen consumption by the muscle stops increasing, despite an increased performance. At this point, an oxygen debt is accumulated, and waste *lactic acid*, which the muscle produces, can only be tolerated to a certain level before exhaustion – i.e. before a point is reached where the muscle can no longer contract.

Aerobic exercise improves long-term edurance while anaerobic exercise improves short-term endurance. Dance tends to use mostly anaerobic activity – during technique class, performing repetitive movements will improve muscular endurance. However, some choreographers may also place vigorous demands on the dancers' aerobic endurance. This will result in progressive overload on the muscles and cardiorespiratory system. Preconditioning/preventative training for building up the stamina of the cardiovascular system is therefore advisable. In the event that the dance class is not providing sufficient training in this respect, the dancer should once again invest in some supplementary training. This supplementary type of work was noted earlier in this chapter in the Birmingham Royal Ballet's programme for male dancers which aimed to increase upper-body strength and power. The programme focused on developing muscle fibres quickly by encouraging anaerobic activity through the use of free weights and machines set at high resistance for a low number of repetitions. But there were also exercises for slow muscle-fibre development in the form of aerobic sports such as cycling or running.

Recovery periods are needed after anaerobic exercise so that the oxygen debt is paid back and a normal chemical balance is resumed. Often, after such exercise, the muscles may feel sore or stiff. This may be caused by mild inflammation in the muscle fibres, which often occurs after new exercises or when adapting to new techniques. This condition reduces flexibility and causes general discomfort when dancing. Warming-up before and cool-down after class is advisable in order to help avoid this.

Warm-up is a gradual physical and mental preparation for greater physical exertion which increases:

- the heart rate;
- the deep temperatures of the muscles – thereby improving their contractibility and flexibility;
- the flexibility of tendons and ligaments – so reducing the chance of injury;
- reaction speed;
- blood sugar and adrenalin levels.

The warm-up should include exercises which:

TASK 9

Prepare a suitable warm-up pattern of 15 to 20 minutes along the following lines:

- 5 to 10 minutes' easy prancing in place;
- a light easy moving of joints;
- gradual stretches;
- some 'technical' exercises, or a rehearsal of the dance about to be performed – this is important for mental readiness and the avoidance of injury;
- a gentle stretch to cool down.

raise the pulse rate; mobilise the joints; stretch the muscles (simple stretches).

Cool-down is the gradual slowing-down of the circulation in order to return to a resting heart rate. Stopping exercise too suddenly can cause the pooling of blood in previously active areas such as the lower limbs, and this can cause soreness, fainting and dizziness. Gentle stretching or breathing for about 5 minutes is advised. The wearing of warmer clothing will help to avoid pulls and aches.

During exercise, the blood supply to inactive areas – like the digestive system – will reduce so that the muscles in turn can receive *more* blood. Eating too soon before class or a performance will cause increased blood flow to the digestive system and so deprive the muscles of an essential supply.

STRENGTH AND STAMINA – A SUMMARY

A healthy, well-conditioned cardiovascular system will provide the dancer with sufficient endurance to maintain safe, expressive and efficient movement throughout technique classes, rehearsals and performances. This system, however, works only in tandem with an equally well-conditioned respiratory system.

The relationship between strength and flexibility is reciprocal. When the muscles are elastic, it takes less strength to contract – this is because there is no need to overcome excess tightness in the opposite antagonistic muscle. Likewise, muscular endurance is increased with an increase in mobility. And similarly, in reciprocal stretching, if the opposite muscle is strong, it is easier to activate the inhibition of the stretch reflex.

Strength and muscular endurance are related in a number of ways. If the muscle is strong, it can continue activity for longer. In progressive overload, which conditions for muscular endurance, the fatigue level rises, and the last few repetitions can be 'maximal'. Such overload can thus serve to build strength.

Generally speaking, prevention is better than cure when it comes to injury. Technique classes and rehearsals are not always considered adequate conditioning to build a body which is 'dancefit'. The level of conditioning in any training programme must take into account the *individual* physical system.

These most basic physical attributes – alignment, flexibility, strength and stamina – are all under the control of that most fascinating part of the body, the brain and nervous system. This is attuned to respond to the ever-changing conditions of our body and surroundings. It is the instrument which fine-tunes the high degree of coordination and skills which dance demands. It is to this control tower that we now turn our attention.

Coordination

The skills of balance, control of energy and accuracy of action are the subjects of coordination in dance training. In order to increase skill levels, the nervous system must be finely tuned. Through repeated practice, skills will improve. This may – for example, in balance – involve a decrease in the weight-bearing area.

Increasing speed will result if the pace of an exercise is gradually increased.

The nervous system consists of:

- the nerves/neurons;
- reflexes and receptors;
- the brain.

Together, these engage in a complex communication system which controls all human interaction in the internal and external environments.

There are two parts to the nervous system:

1 The *autonomic nervous system* regulates involuntary functions of digestion, hormones and the cardiorespiratory activity.
2 The *somatic nervous system* regulates both movement itself and our *perception* of movement, and so is of concern to dancers.

Both systems are controlled by the brain via *neurons*. These are individual cells capable of sending messages to and from the brain and the rest of the body. There are two types of neuron:

1 *Sensory neurons* transmit messages about tension in muscles, tendons and ligaments, and about hot, cold, pain, orientation in space and coordination to the brain.
2 *Motor neurons* pass impulses from the brain to the muscles. The two types together allow you to put your finger on your nose without having to look at it.

THE BRAIN AND NEUROLOGICAL CENTRES INVOLVED IN MOVEMENT

These centres comprise:

- the *midbrain*: the primitive control centre regulating physical reactions like sweating and cardiorespiratory activity;
- the *cerebral cortex*: the centre of fine motor control, involving decision-making for initiating and arresting motion. When new movement combinations are being learnt, the new information may cause a feeling of awkwardness, but gradually, in dance, most movement becomes reflex as training develops;

- the *cerebellum*: this transmits information to the midbrain and cerebral cortex regarding the status of the body. It is crucial in maintaining upright posture and balance. When you miss the last step on the stairs, it is because the cerebellum has been misinformed by the eyes and so sends the wrong messages; and in turn, the wrong amount of muscle contraction required for ascent or descent is then executed.

RECEPTORS AND REFLEXES

In order for the centres in the brain to function, receptors must send information from muscles, tendons and joints about tension, coordination and spatial orientation. The brain then reacts by sending messages via motor neurons so that appropriate adjustments are made. Earlier in this chapter in the section on flexibility, the spinal reflexes affecting stretching were mentioned. These are muscular reflexes which are designed to protect the joints and muscles. There are three other such reflexes as shown in Table 1.8.

There are also reflexes relating to the senses of

sight, touch and hearing: receptors in the eyes, skin and ears react to stimuli from the outside and send messages to the cerebellum, and appropriate adjustments are made on command from the brain. These reflexes are known as the *righting reflexes* (see Table 1.9) because they are primarily concerned with maintaining balance and orientation, and they comprise the *aural, skin and visual righting reflexes.*

Table 1.8 *Muscular reflexes*

Name of reflex	Action	Applications
Flexor reflex	All flexor muscles are activated when one is powerfully activated.	Increases intensity of abdominal contraction by accompanying it with flexors for hands, feet, knees – as seen in the Martha Graham style. When learning new skills, sometimes powerful flexions are accompanied by unwanted tightness in neck, shoulders etc.
Extensor reflex	Activates all extensor muscles when one is powerfully activated.	Explains 'bucking' when beginners start to jump. The powerful contraction of the extensor muscles of the feet, ankles, knees and hips causes an overflow of neural activity to the extensors of the spine, and the head and shoulders are thrown backwards.
Crossed extensor reflex	Activates the active contracting muscle of the diagonally opposite limb, and facilitates the antagonistic muscles of the parallel limb.	For balance, when the right hip flexes, the left hip extends; and when the right shoulder extends, the left shoulder flexes. This is active in all balance and travelling. In Graham-technique spiral exercises. In opposition – e.g. skips. Often, beginners flop about. The wise teacher may not mention arm position, but allows the body to 'take over', thus allowing the natural reflex to establish itself as the norm without the conscious control of the cerebral cortex.

Table 1.9 *Righting reflexes*

Name of reflex	Action
Aural righting reflex	Organs of balance in inner ear. Three semi-circular canals are filled with fluid and have hairy linings. As the fluid moves, the cilia (hairs) interpret messages to adjust balance. When infected, say, during a cold, there is a distortion in the feedback sent to the nervous system, and a loss of balance may result.
Skin righting reflex	Receptors called *exteroceptors* are sensitive to pressure, and send messages on where the body weight is placed. Whether lying or standing on feet or hands, the receptors in the skin are active. They can be of help to dancers on stage under blinding lights who may not be able to rely on visual righting sensations. These reflexes can be improved by practising movements with eyes closed.
Visual righting reflex	We depend on these mainly to maintain balance. Try standing on one leg with eyes closed. Activation of visual reflex is attempting to keep both eyes on the horizontal. This is not so appropriate during tilting, and so then the other reflexes may be of more use.

THE PSYCHOLOGY OF DANCE TRAINING

As seen in the explanations above, there is a definite connection between mind and body: the mind can affect the way the body feels and reacts. In dance, where the focus is such a personal one as your own body, there is a need to avoid unhelpful, harmful practice when learning new coordinations. The concerns involved here are:

- tension and stress
- kinesthetic sense
- the use of imagery/feedback.

One look at a beginner's dance class will tell you how much of an increase in the overall tension level there is in order to achieve a desired movement. As we know, the cerebral cortex activity and other muscular reflexes are the reasons for this. It is incredible that the students can move at all when trying to use such high levels of tension to perform relatively easy tasks. In addition, localised tension in fingers, face, shoulders etc. interferes. Known as 'Beginner's Paralysis', this does lessen as the dancer's general skill level and coordination increase. The ability to inhibit undesired movement in one part of the body is necessary in order to focus on a new skill. The paralysis may return with each new difficult skill, but gradually tension is lowered. In this trial and error process, the dancer may try different muscular combinations, and may encounter blockage in motor learning and coordination.

> You cannot help facing movement blocks that will stand in your way. No one can remove these blocks except you yourself, and only when you are able to remove them will you eventually discover yourself. This is the only way to improve . . .
>
> (*Hanya Holm in* The Vision of Modern Dance, *1980*)

Movement blocks to coordination vary, and are due to any of the following:

- specific weakness in the musculature – e.g. an inelastic antagonistic muscle;
- variations in potential according to body type (*somatype* – see Figure 1.17): *mesomorphs*, *ectomorphs* and *endomorphs* have preferences for different types of movement. The mesomorph prefers faster turns and jumps, whereas ectomorphs prefer a slower pace. All have different areas of weakness. Mesomorphs need to stretch their heavier muscles, whereas ectomorphs work to improve strength and stamina. Endomorphs work to improve their endurance and may need to control their weight.
  Similarly, males, with narrower hips and a more direct connection between the femur and the pelvis than females, tend to be able to run faster but have less of an outward hip rotation. And other individual anatomical differences include different lengths of torso and legs: those who have long legs and a short torso easily allow their limbs to reach out around them, whereas the long-torso and short-legged dancer would be more mobile in the torso and have a greater range of tilt, curve and bend;
- stylistic blocks: unfamiliar patterns between techniques – say, between the Martha Graham style and the classical ballet/Merce Cunningham technique.

The emphasis should be, whenever possible, on relaxing and allowing natural reflexes to guide the way. Once the conscious use of the cerebral cortex cuts in, the intuitive powers of the dancer have less of an influence, and stress and tension start to mount.

How you treat your body can influence your thoughts and feelings. Regular exercise makes one feel good, builds body awareness and should build confidence and an overall sense of health and well-being.

Figure 1.17 *Somatypes*

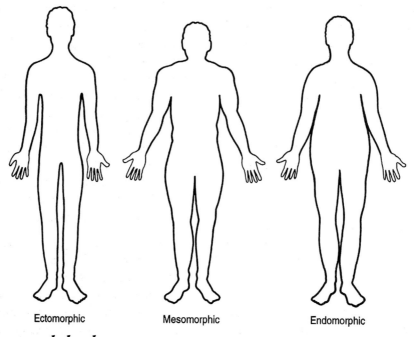

Ectomorphic   Mesomorphic   Endomorphic

Tension, stress and the dancer

Body type may be a contributing factor to the high tension levels common in dance. There are so many *ectomorphs* engaged in the art, and evidence suggests that this body type may experience more anxieties. Constant demands to have utmost physical control results in high muscular tension, sometimes in specific parts of the body. This can cause muscular imbalance, pain and a subsequent *spread* of the tension. The specific demands of dance can increase levels of neuromuscular tension for dancers, making this a major cause of injury in dance training. An overanxious dancer may have high levels of neuromuscular tension, and this may have any of the following effects:

- There is more injury than usual (the accident-prone dancer).
- The dancer starts to imagine injury and then feels actual pain.
- A dancer pretends to be injured in order to avoid a stress situation.
- There is a loss of flexibility.

- There is a loss of smooth coordinated movement.
- There is an increase in the heart rate and blood pressure.

A relaxed dancer will have better coordination, circulation and respiration. Tight muscles can constrict blood vessels and so impede blood flow, cutting down the exchange of O_2 and CO_2. Any long-term effect of anxiety which impedes performance – like pretending to be injured – needs firm handling.

Pre-performance nerves, butterflies, breathlessness, nausea, dry mouth and a need to sit on the lavatory, are all normal nervous responses associated with an increased release of adrenalin into the blood. Once the dancer is on stage, however, the fear vanishes and the show goes on.

Sometimes, after a long intense period of training or rehearsal or a tour, dancers become stale. All the hours of repetition and practice are suddenly gone, and fatigue and depression follow.

A dancer may be injury-prone at this time. Symptoms such as a loss of appetite, weight loss, depression, tiredness and digestion problems are common. A change of routine or environment or a few words of support may be simple but effective anecdotes to aid the recharging of the emotional batteries.

80% of learning difficulties are related to stress. Remove the stress and you remove the difficulties.

(*David Whiteside, Gordon Stokes, President, 3 in 1 Concepts, Burbank, California 1987*)

Often, a dancer will be *unaware* of neuromuscular tension until pain is actually felt: it will have been gradually building up, allowing the nervous system to tolerate its presence. Until the tension is released, the dancer will not even be aware of its presence: it has been successfully hidden for so long because it would otherwise have interfered with progress in training.

There are certain areas of high tension which are most difficult to release:

- An habitual posture is a learned habit often adopted in order to over-achieve in a specific skill (leg higher/more turn-out etc.).
- The tension has become part of the *expected* feedback during dancing, and changing it can cause real feelings of disorientation and disturbance.
- Emotional or physical pain from the past is often cloaked in neuromuscular tension, and so reducing it can cause fear, often related to a loss of control. This may manifest itself as nausea, weeping or exhaustion, and needs careful handling. The need for relaxation techniques such as yoga, 'release' and the Feldankrais and Alexander techniques is now widely recognised.

Let us take an example of neuromuscular tension in the shoulder joint. Raising the arms and 'keeping the shoulders down' is a learned coordination. Naturally, the *scapulae* (shoulder blades) will rise. In training, this involves constant contraction of the antagonistic muscles, and so the tension level may build. It is the *latissimus dorsi* which holds down the scapula. Careful stretching and relaxation will lessen the tension.

Figure 1.18   *(a) shoulder girdle (b) shoulder joint*

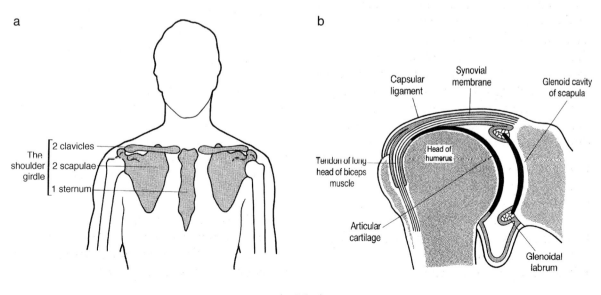

To show lifting: Nina Sorokina and Mikhail Lavrosky of the Bolshoy Ballet

The shoulder joint (see Figure 1.18) is an area of great mobility, and special conditioning is needed before such skills as lifting are taught. There is perhaps more concern here for male dancers, although much post-modern work makes this a potential danger area for females too.

A general strengthening of the following muscle groups should proceed by progressive overload to a point where more weight is being lifted than will be lifted in performance:

- the flexors/abductors of the shoulder: *deltoid, trapezius, serratus anterior, rhomboid major* and *minor, latissimus dorsi, pectoralis major;*
- the torso generally;
- the upward rotators of the scapula: *subscapularis, teres minor, infraspinatus;*
- the extensors of the knee and hip.

Six basic principles for safe lifting in dance

1 Maintain proper alignment.
2 Apply force close to the centre of gravity of the person to be lifted.
3 Apply force as close to the vertical as possible.
4 The lifter should lower their own centre of gravity with a plié in order to harness the powerful force from the knee and hip.
5 The lifted dancer should be kept as directly above the lifter's centre as possible.
6 Use the muscles of the leg, but the torso/back must also be strong and stable during the lift.

When lifting a partner above head height, abduction and flexion of the shoulders is important. There should be no backwards tilt in the lumbar spine. If the elbows or wrists are *swayback* (hypermobile), there may be an increased vulnerability to injury. In order to avoid injury, greater strength is needed. Restriction of the dorsi-flexion of the wrists may also cause lifting problems.

Problems/injuries of the shoulder joint

The constant contraction increases tension deep in the muscle, and as a result the scapula will be pulled forward and eventually the muscles will go into spasm. This is known as *pectoralis minor syndrome*, and it may be painful to rotate the neck. There may also be numbness in the fingers and arm (on the *ulna* side). When the muscle is very tight, the nerve is pressed, in a way similar to *sciatica* in the hip. The source of the problem is mainly in the front in the *pectoralis minor*. Deep-pressure massage can relieve the pain, though it would seem that it takes considerable time for the posterior muscles – i.e. the *trapezius* and *deltoid* – to get the message that they can finally relax. *Pectoralis minor syndrome* is common in dancers because of the demands to keep the shoulders down. However, non-dancers such as typists, swimmers, flautists and string players are also susceptible.

Clearly, there are some complex coordinations and timings to be learnt in order to acquire correct lifting techniques. Learning any coordinations in dance has traditionally been taught by verbal instruction, 'monkey-see-monkey-do', and touching the dancer. This approach has been tried and tested over centuries of dancing. Relatively recently, however, a new school of thought has introduced alternative approaches which put more emphasis on the *inner self*. This holistic approach involves seeing life as a whole, with mind and body together; and it is an altogether more *internal* approach, starting from the inside out.

The kinesthetic sense, sensory feedback and imagery

The mind can work in a negative way in training, as we have read. It is only common sense, therefore, to assume that it can also be put to *positive* use – namely, by allowing our minds to use pictures and images that affect every cell in our bodies through sensory feedback. In the traditional list of the five senses – touch, taste, sight, hearing and smell – the forgotten *sixth* one is the *kinesthetic sense*. This involves the perception of *motion* and of *position*, and it depends on the proprioceptors and sensory organs involved in the righting reflexes. These send information to the central nervous system regarding muscle contraction, relaxation, joint position and speed of motion. Accurate kinesthetic perception requires the integration of this information with the perception of spatial coordinates, and it operates in the skills of balance, accuracy and the control of energy.

When the kinesthetic sense is operational, it can act as a link between mind and body in order to improve coordination. The receptors and brain centres can link up and use *imagery* to cause changes in, and to deepen the dancer's understanding of, movement. The post-modern dancer Remy Charlip called such release work 'bone meditations'.

> Take an image, let it hang in the mind, let the sensation of the thought dissolve through the body. Let the movement inside of the body ... move the outside.
>
> *(Miranda Tufnell in* Body Space Image, *1990)*

In these exercises, there is no visible movement. Often, the body is in a position of 'constructive rest' (Lulu Sweigard, 1989). This involves lying on the back and allowing the pull of gravity to relax the muscles and joints. The knees are bent and the feet are flat on the floor. The arms are either folded across the front of the torso or resting at the sides.

● *Kinesthetic imagery* involves using feelings that accompany body movement, so that when a movement is performed correctly, it has a certain feel. For example, when doing foot 'pushes', use the image that the floor is covered with sharp pins to improve the use of the intrinsic muscles of the foot and the articulation of the arches and metatarsals. This exercise increases strength and mobility in the feet.

- *Visual imagery* involves a mind picture, maybe of a rainbow, which the fingertips may draw in the space above your head as you do large side-to-side triplets. It must relate to a *desired* shaping or placement of body parts, and be an image which you can hold in your mind's eye. Visual imagery can also be helpful for relaxation exercises. Set a scene in your mind which will be clear to you — say, a deserted beautiful beach where a warm soft breeze blows and the waves lap gently at the shore.

- *Anatomical imagery* can help with alignment; and as with all images, returning to the same picture or feelings each time a certain movement is executed should trigger the same muscle response, thereby improving accuracy and safe practice. Anatomical imagery is based on a sound understanding of body structure — of the size and shape of bones, joints and muscles.

TASK 10 ⧖

In pairs, play some quiet soft music in a warm quiet space. One person reads out the task slowly and quietly for the other who is lying in the constructive rest position:

'In a relaxed state, surround the head with a cushion of air, and let the jaw hang softly. Allow the brain to rest lightly in the bones of the skull. The brain is a control tower of information, sending and receiving, quietly humming, pouring, sifting. The brain sends messages that flow out into the spinal cord, down the spine and out to all over the body, networking to the six senses. Relax and listen to the world around you. Let the sounds and sights be felt and reflected through your body.
[Allow time here for the dancer to absorb these thoughts.]
'Open the body through the senses. Allow the body to move out amongst these sensations. Send these feelings back to the fluid-filled corridors of the mind where over 10 billion cells await the arrival of the information. Repeat this feeling of to-ing and fro-ing from brain, to body and outside a few more times.'

- *Pictoral imagery:*

TASK 11 ⧖

Standing, let the shoulder girdle rest on a rounded ribcage. See the shoulder girdle like a ring circling, opening. See the scapulae like a pair of rafts floating on the ocean of the back. The arms hang from the scapulae. Imagine the scapulae as a pair of ears opening … listening out to the tips of the shoulders … down in the lift to the basement of the spine.
(Based on an image in Body Space Image, *Tufnell, 1990)*

- *Body image.* These days, the stereotyped image of the dancer's sylph-like body is gradually being eroded away. Yet, *anorexia nervosa* and related illnesses are still common. Dancers who have a negative body image, or who block out parts of their body that displease them, may be on the road to injury, failure and illness. A complete, clear and accurate body image is required for dance work. Too often these days we are bombarded with media-approved images of men and women. Whilst we know anyone can dance well, and whilst our teacher may encourage all the politically correct attitudes, there are still always the magazines, television programmes etc. contradicting what we want to believe.
- *Mental rehearsal:* this is an imagery technique that uses the body image to improve motor skills. You review the performance of an action in the mind. The aim is to see yourself executing the desired move effortlessly and accurately. Many believe that this technique releases impulses over the neuron pathways and taps into natural movement. New coordinations result as appropriate muscles are triggered. Research has found that this technique produces action potential in the muscles.

- *Motor memory* is separate from the kinesthetic sense. It is stored in the cerebral cortex and *assisted* by the kinesthetic sense. Motor memory is developed by repeating movements in class or in rehearsal. As with any repetitive activity, the ability to pick up a movement quickly improves, and a larger and larger storehouse of movements to draw from is developed.

The mind is a muscle.

(From the dance of the same name by Yvonne Rainer, 1966)

The movement becomes second nature as it is memorised. The more experience you have in memorising movements, the easier memorising *new* movements becomes, because the greater the range of movements you have already memorised, the *smaller* the amount of new information that needs to be remembered with a new movement. So, just like the training of a muscle, the more you use the memory, the fitter it becomes. Indeed, the physical senses of experienced dancers are so well-tuned to their minds that they can later reproduce a movement learnt *by observation only.* This is one reason why repetition of movement in class is so important.

PHYSICAL SKILLS IN DANCE TRAINING

The concept of coordination in dance training is a complex one. It takes into consideration the many aspects of the nervous system in the psychology of dancers, as well as psychological strategies which can improve the quality of training. What are the actual skills which a dancer may improve by adopting such strategies? A general heading of 'coordination' covers a number of individual skills. These are listed below, and along with each is a task which adopts the use of psychological strategies as mentioned earlier. The skills are:

- control of energy
- balance
- accuracy.

Control of energy

An important part of control of energy is the use of the force of gravity. In classical ballet, the lifted centre is the accepted norm. Learning to lift the weight up from the centre of the body, away from the pull of gravity, gives a look and feel of lightness, and also enables you to move, stop and change direction easily.

(Do not hold the breath here.) Movements such as plié, falls, turns and jumps are all performed more safely and effectively with a lifted centre. In a fall, the centre keeps lifting as the body drops. This prevents too hard a landing and enables recovery for the next move (similarly for a jump).

TASK 12

Sitting, breathe in and lift the torso, stretch long into the lower back, and at the same time lift under your ribs and up through the sternum. Counterbalance this by pulling down the scapulae and pulling up through the back of the neck. Breathe evenly and start to move off the spot, letting the limbs move freely whilst maintaining the first sensations of lifting through the torso. Feel easy and relaxed. Let the torso adjust easily as the energy flows out into the legs and arms.

A swing requires the dancer to drop with gravity on the downward phase. Too *much* tension/resistance will prevent the arc of the swing from giving in to gravity.

TASK 13

Standing, swing one arm back and forth. Notice how energy is required to lift your arm, but that gravity takes over on the downward phase. Try swinging other parts of the body – the leg, neck, hips, upper body from the waist. Too much resistance, as you will see, will block the natural swing.

Balance

This has to do with:

- alignment and stability;
- directing energies through the body.

Balance is developed as a dance skill through training. Stability is decreased by lessening the base on the floor – thus, balancing on, say, one foot makes it more difficult to keep the centre of gravity over the base. Energies are directed out from the centre through the extremities of all the limbs, and whenever one body part reaches away from the centre, an opposing part has to be stretched in the opposite direction in order to maintain balance. For example, on a rise (*relevé*), balancing is easier if you think about pressing down smoothly into the floor whilst sending energy up through the centre. What about in an *arabesque*? Copy Figure 1.19 and fill in the direction of five energy arrows;

Figure 1.19 *Fill in the correct lines of energy during an arabesque balance*

see Figure 1.20 on page 42 for a correct drawing.

Being *centred* is crucial to achieving good balance. Unlike alignment, centring is both a physical and a psychological concept: it refers to the *physical* centre of gravity and, psychologically, to the satisfying *feeling* of being whole and grounded. Physically, the centre of gravity is in the pelvis slightly below the navel (lower for women than for men).

In ballet, the placement of the centre is fairly stable in order to enable multiple pirouettes and so on, but in modern genre the centre shifts more frenetically as the body tilts, curves, bends and extends continuously.

TASK 14

Walk around the room slowly, moving from your centre rather than from your feet. Feel your energy move out of your centre, keeping it over your feet with each step – the body acting as a whole, not in separate parts. Walk backwards and sideways, keeping the centre with you.

Accuracy

The dancer must be able to move not only well but also accurately. This comes about with the ability to reproduce movement that has been seen in a demonstration. Beginners need to see movement in terms of placement, shape and direction. As dancers become more experienced in coordination, they are able to see more of a whole picture and yet be sensitive to detailed positioning at the same time.

Dancers also need to develop sensitivity to changes in dynamics and spatial orientation, so that these may also be performed accurately each time. For dance, the fullest movement potential of each individual dancer should be developed, and whatever the genre, this entails controlling movements more efficiently, harmoniously and expressively. This makes them more pleasing to watch for the audience, safer for the dancer and, for the choreographer, presumably more capable of expressing the intentions of the dance. What is crucial to expression should also be so to injury prevention and safe practice in dance training.

The use of breath with the movement can help accuracy. It also adds vitality and reduces tension in the body. And it further assists with the control of active muscles and with the relaxation of those not required. The overall effect is to give movement an effortless look and a greater expressive quality – in phrasing, rhythm, balance, jumping and stretching. *Restricted* breathing will limit both the movement of the thorax and stamina.

Here are a few things to try which show how breathing can either enhance or restrict movement.

TASK 15

1 Lie with arms above head, but half-bent, and legs relaxed. Check with your hand to see how much arch there is in your thoracic/lumbar spine. Breathe in through the nose, stretching your arms away from your feet. Breathe out forcefully, making a hissing sound, allowing arms, legs and back to relax. Imagine your lungs to be two balloons emptying and filling. Repeat 3 times. Check to see if the spine arch has lessened – i.e. relaxed.

2 Stand with your weight on both feet, arms abducted to your sides. Lift one leg directly in front of your body to a comfortable height and breathe into it at the same time. Release the breath beyond the toes.

3 Improvise and compose a short original phrase of movement. Practice it until it is memorised. Repeat it, trying out different patterns of breath until you find one which is most suitable for the movement.

4 From standing, collapse down and exhale. Rebound up, and inhale. Repeat a few times. Now reverse the breathing pattern, and choose which of the two worked the best for you. (Note: in general, dancers inhale when a movement suspends and exhale when giving in to gravity.)

Well-timed breathing will assist in accuracy. It also reduces stress and tension which are a major cause of injury in dancers. Relaxation techniques can play a crucial part in safe practice, and it is ultimately each dancer's responsibility to ensure adequate rest and relaxation for themselves. This may be a regular daily routine attached to a class or rehearsal schedule, or participation in a yoga or meditation or some other relaxation-based technique. A lack of it can produce staleness and proneness to injury (real or imagined).

TASK 16 ⧗

Work in pairs. Lie down flat, and close your eyes. Allow your partner to take one arm; do not resist or assist as it is lifted a little by the hand. Allow it to be moved up, down and sideways and rotated, giving the full weight to your partner. Where resistance is met, this is a likely point where you hold neuromuscular tension.

Repeat with the other arm and legs, and as you work, note where points of tension are discovered in your body.

Figure 1.20   *Correct lines of energy during an arabesque balance*

COORDINATION – A SUMMARY

In training, the dancer is clearly engaged in a complicated day-to-day workload, not least of which is to improve the many complex coordinations of the nervous system as demanded by any dance style or genre. Be it ballet, modern, post-modern, African or South Asian, all ask a great deal in terms of coordination. Control of energy, balance and accuracy are all essential when performing any dance actions.

General body maintenance

To be fit for dance, all the aspects mentioned in this chapter are essential. What is required is a balance of exercise, training in skills, rest and relaxation, and finally an adequate diet.

DIET

> You are what you eat.
>
> *(Brian and Roberta Morgan in* Brain Food, *1987)*

So what are *you* then? A can of diet coke? That means you're sweet but go flat too quickly. A chocolate bar? Fatty and satisfying but prone to constant cravings. A fresh mackerel? A cool alert customer. Recent research has proven that eating oily fish regularly provides the right chemicals to improve transmission between brain cells. So the old wives' tale that fish is brain food is true! Therefore, if you wish to improve your coordination in dance training, then cut out the junk food and settle for the fish.

Dancers are notorious for food abuse, and possibly even more so for pretending that it is not happening. Mention the word 'diet' to a dancer, and the response will be cloaked in terms of *eating less*. 'Diet' should instead, however, be a term which implies eating a sensible range of foods adequately. Enough calories, vitamins and minerals etc. must be consumed to keep you healthy now and in later years.

Basic considerations are:

- what to eat
- when to eat
- how to eat
- eating disorders.

> We need to reeducate dancers and get them to establish good nutritional habits. They should be eating carbohydrate and eating every three hours. We want the dancers to be slim, but with healthy, strong muscle tone so that they can resist injury.
>
> *(Tony Geeves in* New Scientist, *25 December/1 January 1994)*

Appearances can be deceptive. You may look thin, but snack-based high-fat diets produce underdeveloped muscles which leave space for a substantial layer of fat on a seemingly slim body.

What to eat

An ordinary person with a quiet lifestyle needs 1,500 calories daily just to maintain normal body functioning and minimum activity. It is only reasonable, therefore, to assume that dancers need more in the region of *2,000* calories daily. About two-thirds of calorie intake is needed just to maintain the normal functioning of muscles, organs and body temperature.

The rest of the day's activities – eating, walking, dressing, working, playing – need about 800 calories. The equation is easy – whatever calories we use up day-to-day come from food. If you consume more calories than you use, you put on weight. If you consume fewer calories than you need, you lose weight.

The following are essential components of a healthy diet:

- *proteins* – for building up the body;
- *carbohydrates* – to provide energy;
- *fats* – for energy and flavour;
- *vitamins* – small but essential;
- *minerals* – for bones and blood;
- *water* – for basic physiological functions.

Table 1.10 *Essential components for a healthy diet*

Nutrient	Sources	Needed for	Amount per day	Lack of: the effects
Proteins	Lean meat, fish dairy, bread, cereals, beans	Muscle and tissue development and repair. Normal metabolism	40 g per day = 400 g bread or 200 g meat	Loss of muscle. Illness – e.g. flu – causes loss of protein
Carbohydrates (sugars, starch, cellulose)	Sugar, potatoes, wheat, rice, cereals	Energy	50–60% of food intake	Fatigue – weakness, headaches, irritability, poor coordination, nervousness
Fats	Dairy, meat, eggs oily fish, cooking oils/fats	Improving the taste and feeling full. High energy source = high calories! Carry vitamins A, D, E & K		Too much is more the issue: heart disease, high level of cholesterol in blood
Vitamins	Most foods, particularly vegetables	Proper body functioning	Small daily amounts; e.g. 30 g vitamin C, 1 g vitamin B12	Vitamin D: rickets, bones soften. Vitamin C: scurvy. Too much: vitamin A: harms eyes; Vitamin D: upsets metabolism
Minerals	Most foods	Producing enzymes and hormones which control a number of functions in: blood, bones, teeth	Some, like calcium (in dairy products), are needed in large amounts. Others, like zinc, sodium, potassium, in smaller amounts	Lack of iron (18 g): anaemia. Lack of iodine: low metabolic rate, energy loss, weight gain. Lack of calcium (1200 mg daily): long-term brittle bones
Water	Water! Tea and coffee are diuretics and increase fluid loss. So does alcohol	Physiological processes, e.g. flush waste from kidneys maintain blood volume, sweating	Drink plenty daily	Dehydration, muscle fatigue, cramp, injury, exhaustion

The reduction of specific fatty areas, like under the upper arm, can be brought about by certain strengthening exercises for targeted spots. For example, lots of abdominal curls will remove fat from the abdomen; and similarly with strengthening exercises for the hips, thighs and upper arms.

Starvation diets are dangerous, and not likely to succeed. They cause dehydration and long-term damage to basic body tissues and functioning if followed regularly. Similarly, the spot reduction of weight in specific sites such as the thighs is not helped by wearing plastic trousers. These do not reduce fat, and in fact promote a loss of fluid and so can cause dehydration and heat stroke; they are only useful for keeping warm. The best way to lose weight is a calorie-controlled diet in combination with aerobic exercise. Burning off fat from all over the body by breaking it down for use as energy is the result of aerobic exercise.

Losing weight should be a carefully monitored affair. Height and weight tables are not the best way to gauge whether you are over- or underweight. The use of skin-fold callipers to measure fat on, say, the triceps are recommended and the fat here should not exceed 8–10 mm in women and 6–8 mm in men. Losing weight is a long-term process: it takes months.

Remember, the calories required for energy will vary with the individual metabolic rate. Thus, anxious ectomorphs may well burn food off more quickly than laid-back endomorphs. *Muscle* tissue burns off calories more quickly than other forms of tissue because it has a higher metabolic rate. It is also heavier than *fat* tissue. There is a possible cause of confusion here. Through exercise, muscle tissue builds up, and therefore weight increases. Weight loss is thus not an indication of fitness. Although muscle weighs heavier, it also burns off more calories, so weight loss is easier! With regular exercise, dancers who burn calories slowly can become high calorie burners (there is a general

increase in the metabolic rate as muscle increases), and fat stores are reduced more rapidly. More muscle and less fat results in an improvement of body shape and general fitness, but not necessarily weight control.

There is nothing nutritionally wrong with being vegetarian; in fact, nutritionists favour such diets. However, the recommendation is to eat foods from all food groups. Eating more carbohydrates or protein than fats will ensure fewer calories and more energy.

When to eat

An important consideration here is that when the body is digesting food, the blood flow moves away from muscles to the digestive system. Obviously, this would not, therefore, be a good time to be exercising. Pre-performance eating needs careful scheduling. A small meal at least 2 hours before the show gives enough time for digestion. Foods like pasta or a sandwich, containing complex carbohydrates, are best because they will allow a steady release of energy throughout the performance. Concentrated sweet fluids are to be avoided because their absorption is too slow to enhance energy levels. These fluids may produce a peak of glucose in the blood (the body will release a burst of insulin to deal with this) and then a fall and a trough (see Figure 1.21) below the normal level which will make the dancer feel fatigued. And obviously, a tired dancer is one prone to

Figure 1.21 *Changes in blood sugar level after drinking sweet liquids*

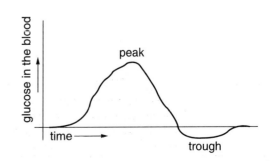

injury. The daily rush and demands on a dancer can cause a tendency to skip meals. Several small meals daily – 'grazing' – is an effective eating regime to accommodate such schedules.

TASK 17

Make a large (A3-size) poster which gives advice to dancers on what to eat. Use drawings, magazine cuttings, food labels etc. Make it bright and informative. Research the calorific values of food to include on the poster.

How to eat

Weight loss and weight gain are often concerns for dancers, and this reflects the preoccupation with abnormal thinness that permeates today's society. Gymnasts, models, some athletes and more and more men are targets of this 'look'. The eating disorders which arise from these unreasonable demands will be discussed below.

TASK 18

Keep a food diary over 2 weeks of all the foods, and their weights, that you eat. From this you can work out the total calories taken in and divide this figure by 14 to obtain your daily intake. Compare your food diary with an *activity* diary for the same period. You can then work out the daily expenditure of calories per 24 hours. Then you will know the average number of calories you will need daily to maintain your present weight. If weight loss is desirable, decrease your daily intake by 500 calories – which comes to a weight loss, per week, of 2 lbs or 900 g. If weight *gain* is required, *add* 500 calories daily to give 2 lbs or 900 g weight gain per week.

Eating disorders

Ballet dancers have a notoriously high incidence of anorexia and bulimia – eating disorders in which dieting becomes an obsession.

(Tony Geeves, New Scientist, *25 December 1993/1 January 1994)*

Anorexia nervosa is self-starvation and *bulimia* is a related disorder involving binges of eating and then vomiting, the abuse of laxatives or diuretics, or fasting. Both of these disorders will disrupt menstruation and give a long-term risk of *osteoporosis* (thinning of the bones). The first conference about osteoporosis was held in 1993. Many findings were brought to light. Here are some of them:

- Poor nutrition may be a contributory cause to hormonal imbalance; and when hormonal imbalance is combined with intensive exercise, the menstrual cycle may be upset. Any dancer weighing less than 47 kg (7 st 6 lbs) is at risk. (This information was supplied by Dr Ashley Grossman, Professor of Neuroendocrinology (nerves, glands and hormones) St Bartholomew's Hospital.)
- In adolescence, 50% of the bone mass is acquired. Loss of bone density correlated with missed periods over a five-year span. Adequate nutrition is essential if stress fractures are to be avoided. (This information was supplied by Dr Victor Grossman, GP to Birmingham Royal Ballet.)

As always, prevention is better than cure.

Taking extra calcium and avoiding smoking, drinking and drugs are advised. Oestrogen therapy for younger dancers can help alleviate loss of period and fragile bones later in life.

In the next decade it is not inconceivable that a dancer who becomes crippled with arthritis or suffers an osteoporotic fracture will sue her company or school for knowingly exposing her to undue risk, in the same way as sufferers from repetitive stress injuries do now. Will it take the threat of litigation to make the companies' artistic directors, choreographers and teachers take this problem seriously?

(Fiona Dick in Dance Theatre Journal, *vol. 11, no. 2, 1994)*

In extreme cases, both disorders can be fatal. If you think that you have such problems, or that a friend does, then it is important for you or your friend to talk about it and seek help. Some symptoms are: obsessive preoccupation with weight, guilt about eating, unrealistically high expectations of oneself.

Diet – a summary

The food you eat should be organised to give you:

● maximum energy;
● minimum body fat;
● enough variety to ensure efficient body functions and so avoid injury.

This chapter should have given you enough information in text, pictures and practical assignments to increase your understanding of what your body needs and how it functions. *You* have the main responsibility for its maintenance. Be good to it, and it should last you a lifetime of dancing and living.

References and resources

You can never have too many bags and shoes.

(From the television series Absolutely Fabulous*)*

BOOKS AND ARTICLES

Arnheim, D. D., *Dance Injuries: Their Prevention and Care*, London: Dance Books, 1992

Blakey, P., *The Muscle Book*, Stafford: UK Bibliotek, 1992

Dance UK (ed.), *The Dancer's Charter for Health and Welfare*, London: Dance UK, 1992

Dancing Times, *Study Supplement 5 'A' Level Anatomy* (A. McCormack) *Dancing Times*, LXXX 953, February 1990

Dick, F., 'Fit but fragile', *Dance Theatre Journal*, vol. 11, no. 2, 1994 (article about osteoporosis)

Doyle, W., *Teach Yourself Healthy Eating*, London: Hodder & Stoughton, 1994

Foley, M., *Dance Spaces*, Arts Council of England, London, 1994

Geeves, T., *The Difference Between Being Warm and Warming Up*, Dance UK Information Sheet No. 3, Dance UK, 1991

Gelabert, R., *Anatomy for the Dancer – as Told*

to *William Como (Vols 1 & 2)*, New York: Danad Publishing, 1964

Howse, J. and Hancock, S., *Dance Technique and Injury Prevention*, A. & C. Black, 1988

Ryan, A. J. and Stephens, R. S. (eds), *The Healthy Dancer*, Dance Books, 1987

Sweigard, L., *Human movement potential: its ideokinetic facilitation*, New York: Dodd, Mead & Co, 1974

Tufnell, M. and Crickmay, A. *Body, Space Image*, Dance Books, 1990

Vincent, L., *Dancer's Book of Health*, New Jersey: Princeton Book Co., 1988

Vincent, L., *Competing With the Sylph*, New York: Andre and Mckeel Inc., 1979

VIDEO

Ballet Floor Barre by Nicole Vasse, New York: Dance Videos, 45 mins, £15.99, 1995. Includes warm-up, work on turn-out and pelvic control, flexibility and cool-down.

MUSIC

For rest and relaxation: *The Way of the Dolphin*, NWC 200, Medwyn Goodall.

USEFUL INFORMATION

Most of the books and videos named in this book are available from Dance Books Limited, 15 Cecil Court, London WC2N 4EZ.

The Dance UK Medical Register Helpline gives advice from a medical practitioner used to dealing with dancers' specific problems. Ring: 0181 741 1932/0181 788 6905.

The general number for Dance UK is: 0171 741 4040.

chapter two
RECORDING DANCE: WALKING BOLDLY BACKWARDS INTO THE FUTURE

The issues in question

Ballets are the most transitory of things – once a step has been danced it is dead.

(*In* Making a Ballet, *by C. Crisp and M. Clarke, 1974*)

This chapter will question the truth of this statement, and offer alternative options which may allow us to *record* dances so that they may be a part of the future:

The future is made of the same stuff as the present.

(*Simone Weil, philosopher*)

The two main ways of recording dance which will be compared in this chapter are:

- notation
- film and video.

Videotape is a fairly accurate way of making a record of a dance which can be used for study or for a choreographer's/dancer's own development.

For all of its obvious limitations, the technology is here to stay and it does perform some vital functions; dancing moves forever into history on a practical note, important decisions are being made today on the basis of viewing videotapes.

(*Daniel Nagrin in* Dance Theatre Journal, *1988, vol 6, 1, pp. 33–36*)

Many dancers are using video to tape their rehearsals and improvisations as a way of finding new material for choreography. This medium can also be used for making archives to monitor their own growth and development. A simple camera set-up may be adequate for these purposes, but is it able to deal with the complexities of teaching *large-group* choreography to new dancers? This may be made more difficult if the original dancers are not present at a reconstruction, or if the original dancers remember it differently – which happens a great deal, as dancers' long-term motor memories are notoriously awful! Is video adequate to record complete and accurate versions? Do the problems described in the previous section present so many obstacles that it is too time-consuming and expensive? What if a video recording of a particular performance contained mistakes, and this then becomes the archive? What if the camera could not cover the whole stage area? Questions and problems arise if video is the only record. What, then, are the alternative options?

Certainly, it is worrying to think of how much of our dance heritage has been lost forever. In comparison to music, visual art and literature, we have little record of the past. These days, most large dance companies employ *choreologists*. Their job is to take notes during rehearsals when new dances are being choreographed. They give advice to the choreographer about what was done in previous rehearsals, how much music is left in a section, and so on. Choreologists also are responsible for reconstructing old repertoires. This means that a dance can be reconstructed and performed centuries after it was created, just like a Mozart symphony. Many dancers, however, are revived without scores, and one has to wonder how accurately they are remembered.

An example of how this works may be helpful here. The innovative and far-sighted Mats Ek mad-house version of *Giselle* may never have come about if the original classic has not been kept for posterity throughout the centuries. Similarly, the brilliant Mark Morris 1992 version of *The Nutcracker*, entitled *The Hard Nut*, has been a source of such great enjoyment, and a real flagship for the dance world.

... a black-and-white Sixties comic strip, where instead of Sugar Plums and Christmas pies round the fire, we get bubblegum kids and an apple-pie Mom, and the fire is an image on the TV set.

(Ismene Brown, in a review of The Hard Nut in The Guardian, *August 1995)*

Bringing the classics into the present and giving them a new lease of life which complements the more traditional reconstructions is lifeblood to dance.

So let us now first look more closely at *dance notation* as a means for revival, reconstruction and study.

Dance notation

A HISTORY

In the fifteenth century, dance steps were recorded on paper. In 1588, the *Orchesographie* by Thoinot Arbeau was published. This recorded well-known steps using abbreviations – e.g. s = single, d = double, R = reverencia – written next to the music score. The steps and dance terms themselves were explained in detail in the form of a lesson to a pupil.

A system called *Feuillet notation* was devised by Pierre Beauchamps and published in his *Choregraphie* in 1700. This was adopted by French ballet master Raoul Feuillet at the time. In Kellom Tomlinson's English dance manual *The Art of Dancing*, published in London in 1735, an engraving shows a couple dancing the minuet. The steps are drawn in Feuillet notation at their feet, rather like a floor pattern for each dancer. It can still be read today, although it only gives information about footwork.

Later, in 1852, there was an attempt to show *whole* body movement, rhythm and timing when Arthur Saint Leon published *Steno-choregraphie*. Here, stick figures were drawn under the music score. A modified version of this by Albert Zorn in 1887 was used quite widely in the USA and Europe.

The classics of *Giselle* and *Sleeping Beauty* survived in Russia partly as a result of the notation of Vladimir Stepanov. He was a teacher and dancer with the Imperial Maryinsky Theatre in St Petersburg. In 1892, he published *Alphabet des Mouvements du Corps Humain*. This was used mainly in ballet, and tried to show whole body movements in *anatomical* terms. The continuity of training and performance in Russia also contributed to the survival of the above works. One wonders what their fate would have been without the notation. The

The Minuet: the conclusion, or presenting both arms. An illustration from The Art of Dancing, *Kellon Tomlinson, 1775*

works were staged by Nicholas Sergueyev and the UK's Royal Ballet in the 1930s using the Stepanov notation which he brought with him from Russia. In this way, the classics had not only been preserved (an important enough achievement in itself) but had also been communicated across international borders.

In ballet, the use of words to describe movement is very helpful. But the dance of today can be very complex in its use of gesture, space and lifting, so an adequately sophisticated system of notation is required to deliver precision. Within the last 75 years, two systems have been developed. *Benesh Notation* and *Labanotation* are both used extensively today. The two systems look very different, but their aims are the same.

Rudolf Benesh (1916–1975) was a mathematician who was married to a ballet dancer. They were concerned about the loss of dances, and after 8 years' work they launched a system in 1955.

Benesh uses a musical stave (see Figure 2.1). It is read across the page from left to right, and each of the five lines represents a different area of the body. Benesh also uses the same Italian terms as found in music to show dynamic qualities – like *adagio*, for example. The timing of the movements corresponds to the bars of music. Symbols show both where body parts are placed and the direction of movement. There are also signs to show actions like jumps and turns. The movement is traced by the pathways that the body parts make as they change position.

After Benesh had been taken up by the Royal Ballet, other ballet companies also used it to record their repertoires.

Rudolf Laban (1879–1958) (yes, it is odd that *both* are named after famous reindeer!) was one of the pioneers of modern dance. German-born, he moved to the UK in 1938 to escape Nazi Germany. Laban's influence in the world of dance teaching, mainly within the world of

Figure 2.1   *To show Benesh notation*

The movement reads from right to left along the stave. *Limb and body movements are drawn in the stave.* '+' is a bend sign

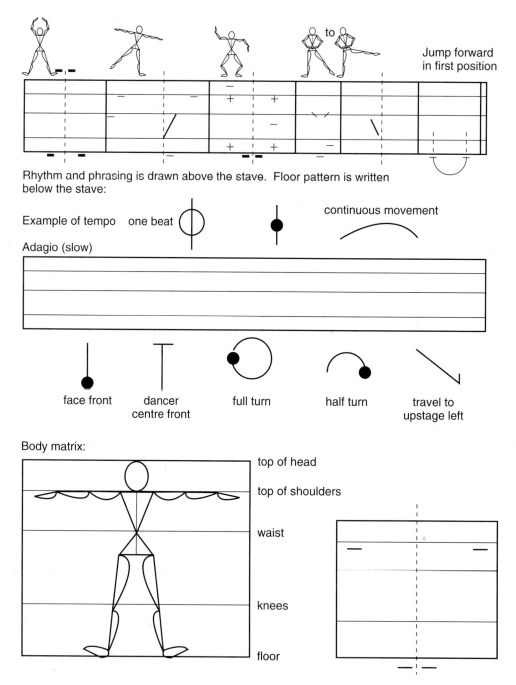

Jump forward
in first position

Rhythm and phrasing is drawn above the stave. Floor pattern is written below the stave:

Example of tempo   one beat   continuous movement

Adagio (slow)

face front   dancer   full turn   half turn   travel to
              centre front   upstage left

Body matrix:

top of head

top of shoulders

waist

knees

floor

Figure 2.2 *Labanotation signs to show extension and flexion of limbs*

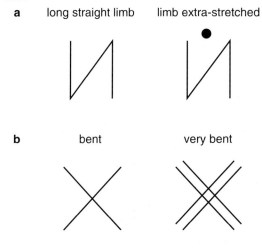

a long straight limb   limb extra-stretched

b bent   very bent

Figure 2.3 *Notation for (a) leg extension (b) arm extension*

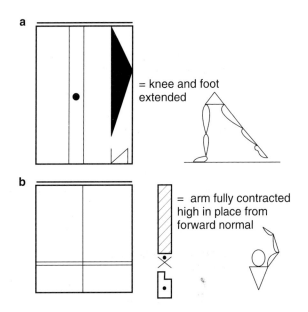

a

= knee and foot extended

b

= arm fully contracted high in place from forward normal

women's physical education, is regarded as a crucial influence in the building of dance education in the UK today.

Laban's work centred on the analysis of human movement. He choreographed *movement choirs* from 1910 onwards, firstly in Germany and later in his own dance company. He was also ballet master of the State Theatre of Berlin during the 1920s. But his main work was in the analysis of dance and the training of dancers, which he worked on with his pupil and collaborator Kurt Jooss.

The analysis which he produced was called *eukinetics* and *choreutics*. This divided movement into two categories, 'outgoing' and 'incoming', and carefully broke movement down in terms of *dynamics* and *direction*. Laban also devised a complicated movement scale within an *icosahedron*, which is a 20-faced geometric form. This was used as a systematic base for dance training. His pupils Kurt Jooss and Mary Wigman in turn made huge contributions to the development of modern dance in Europe. Wigman also influenced modern dance in the USA through her pupil Hanya Holm.

Labanotation (see Figures 2.2, 2.3 and 2.4) is read from the bottom to the top of the page, in a three-line stave. The advantage of this strat-

Figure 2.4 *Other Labanotation signs*

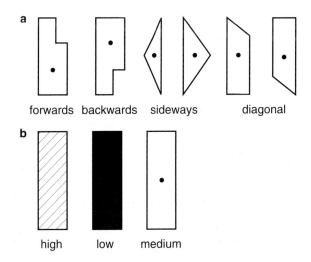

a forwards backwards sideways   diagonal

b high   low   medium

egy is that it gives the body movement continuity and shows the dancer's actual right and left as it is read. Symbols on the right of the column are for the right side of the body, and those on the left are for the left side. Basic symbols indicate the directions, levels, timings and duration of a movement. Bar lines indicate the music timings. The notation also allows for the recording of dynamics and quality changes. Labanotation is useful in many ways: for dance, in sport and in physiotherapy.

Today, libraries of dance scores are available. This addresses another issue which is controversial in the dance of today and of the future, namely copyright. A choreographer can protect the rights of an original work by making an accurate written score. In terms of the future, these libraries can form an invaluable source both of study, for dance students and researchers, and of revivals for public viewing. This makes dance history more accessible for all, and in valuing this history we strengthen the value of present-day works also.

New computer technologies are also involved in the future of dance notation. There is an Apple Macintosh software package for Benesh called MacBenesh and Labanotation programmes called Caliban, Labanwriter and Lifeforms.

TASK 1 ▽

Choreograph a simple 4-bar phrase in 4/4 meter. Include a turn, a jump and some steps in different directions. Indicate that it is repeated on the other side of the body. Notate it in either Labanotation or Benesh.
Exchange scores with another student, and read each other's. Compare how accurately the phrase is reproduced. (Suggested music: the 'Gavotte' from Parampara's *Moving in Time*.)

NOTATION FOR RECORDING AND RECONSTRUCTION

Obviously, in dance, studying a notation score can give insight into the composition, structure and style of a dance. By noticing the variations and developments of motifs through an observation of the way in which they are repeated on a score, you can gain an understanding of how a choreography is structured. If the signs for toe and heel feature numerously in a score, the style may be quite folky. Or if there appears to be a great deal of stamping, a dance may be within South Asian or African genres. Or again, the Martha Graham style or modern dance genres may show through if there is lots of floorwork – i.e. where the knees, hips and torso make contact with the floor.

TASK 2 ▽

Read the Labanotation in Figure 2.5, and suggest in what genres the styles of walking shown here are most likely to be. (Answers at the end of this section.)

As already mentioned, choreologists are responsible for the process of reconstructing and reviving past works. Where possible, it is best to use also a video record. Notating dances from rehearsals is a time-consuming business. As Monica Parker wrote in a Sadler's Wells Ballet programme: 'It is common for one minute of choreography to take two hours of rehearsal – and a further six hours for the full notation of that minute to be made.' This is

Figure 2.5 *Notation for Task 2*

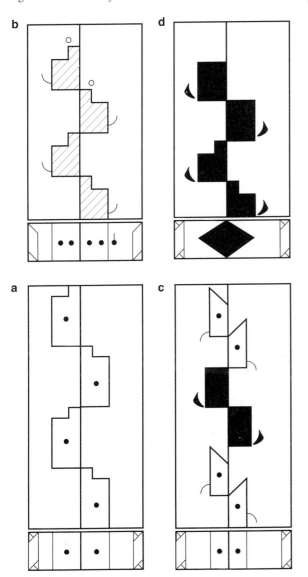

certainly slower than making a video record! However, in other instances, reconstructing from a videotape alone may actually prove to be slower and less accurate, if the following example is anything to go by. In 1973, notator Anne Whitley notated Tippett's *The Ice Break*. Over 100 performers, multi-level staging, dry ice and other theatrical effects had to be recorded. The work was revived two years later, and she used the score to teach from. It was staged in four days! This would seem to be

accurate, fast and cost-effective. In such cases, notation plays a vital part in conserving our dance heritage.

Revivals and stagings of past ballets or modern dances, seen through the eyes of another era, may sometimes look dated, but they may still nonetheless have value as a 'dance antique'. However, as already mentioned, classic ballets are often reworked in a modern style, and this approach may also even be considered for those modern works which are already now a part of our dance past. As with new interpretations of Shakespeare, such reworkings can remain accurate to the basic form but convey new emotions and fresh dynamic colour, and this may bring to the surface new ideas which lay hidden in the original dance. Or, they may have different and possibly more up-to-date costumes, sets or lighting arrangements. A museum of dance reconstructions faithfully copying the originals is one possibility, but this alone may only have 'cobweb potential'. Reviving dances to live again in *new* times with *new* relevance for *new* audiences should also, therefore, be a possibility.

Some of choreographer Doris Humphrey's work from the 1930s only exists today because it was notated and filmed. It has been suggested by the Doris Humphrey Foundation that such reconstructions should be faithful to the original.

> ... the history of modern dance needs these living illustrations, particularly while the first 'generation' dancers can still provide them.
>
> (Lesley Main, director of the UK Doris Humphrey Foundation, in Dance Theatre Journal, 1995, vol 12, 2)

Three works of Doris Humphrey, *Shakers* (1930), *Water Study* (1928) and *Air for the G String* (1928), were reconstructed with students from The Place (the London Contemporary Dance School) by one of the dancers from the original cast, Ernestine Stodelle. The reconstruction promised much, using not only the score as the base but also memories of the original performance. However, as observed by dance critic Sarah Rubidge (*Dance Theatre Journal*, 1995, vol 12, 1), the final performance of *Shakers* was not entirely successful owing to the failure on the part of the students to commit the level of energy which the work required. The new dancers were from another era, and did not seem to have the particular physical or mental outlook that was required for dances from the early twentieth century.

There is no doubt that live performances of authentic reconstructions contribute an immediacy of energy and a view of history that film and notation may not be capable of providing. But this is not the only option. An alternative view was also expressed in the same article by Sarah Rubidge, namely that experienced professional directors should be allowed responsibility to use the *scores* as a starting point for giving life to the work. The professional dance director is the equivalent of the conductor of an orchestra, and as such there will always be some that are better than others at pitching the new version sensitively to the original.

The suggestion that less experienced or able dancers should not be allowed access to these scores is, I find, questionable. The value of scores to dance students (and let's face it, that's what we *all* are in the end) is that they offer an insight into the past of a kind not otherwise available. The physical experience of a score or film is the most important thing a student can have. All the books in the world cannot recreate the intimate learning experience that a physical reconstruction can offer. Of course, we are not saying that these reconstructions *must* be performed, but only that they ought, at least, to be *experienced*. Such reconstruction will be vulnerable to inaccuracies, and the student should be aware of this.

Recently, I took part in a class by Dee Wernham who has been taught the Isadora Duncan technique by one of Duncan's original pupils. It was an odd experience, and I feel that I had been whisked back nearly a century. There was something about this authentic reconstruction that had the pioneering spirit of the origins of modern dance. Once described as 'pithy' by Jane Dudley (an original student of Martha Graham), the Duncan style had a surprising strength, integrity and natural weighty feel that I had not expected. No doubt, like all things over time, inaccurate reproductions produce watered-down versions. But an authentic reproduction is quite a different matter. The original energy and style was of course noticed in Frederick Ashton's (1976) *Brahms Waltzes in the Manner of Isadora Duncan*.

So where does this leave us? Well, it would seem that the dance world needs to respect and cherish its heritage. Whether this should be done by notation, film or live reconstructions is debatable – from now on, maybe it should always be all three. What *is* certain is that the heritage of dance can only serve to *enrich* the future of dance, and to help all to value the art of dance.

OTHER USES FOR DANCE NOTATION

Information provided by movement notation can be used for many different purposes.

Labanotation has been used to record the movements of workers in factories in order to find ways of increasing productivity. Once the relevant movements were notated, the analysis showed up which were productive and which were non-productive. In this way, machinery could be repositioned to make use of the most efficient order of movements.

Notation is also used in psychiatry, medicine and therapy. Benesh notation has been used in the treatment of cerebral palsy. When the patients' movements have been recorded over time, the results can be analysed to see how the patients are responding to different types of treatment. Labanotation has been applied to sufferers of schizophrenia, and again this has involved the observation, recording and analysing of body posture – for study by psychiatrists.

In scientific research, movement notation has been used to record motion in a weightless state, and it has contributed to the computerisation of instructions for movements for robots. There has also been some use in anthropological research: a study of the dances of different cultures in the Pacific Islands and South Africa has used notation to make comparisons between the roles of the male and the female in the community.

DANCE NOTATION – CONCLUSIONS

Being able to access our dance past is vital. For young choreographers, studying past originals in a systematic way brings them into line with students of other arts. The research and study of tradition is not academic and inhibiting as the dance world sometimes seems to think. It is a way of moving on and improving on the past, and this can only be done if we have an *accurate knowledge* of the past – it is not possible to develop on from nothing. Video, being such a relatively recent form of recording, is limited in terms of how far back into the past it can go. It also fails to give the kind of detail, depth and accuracy that a notation score can offer.

Important choreography like that for *Giselle* may have been lost forever if it had not been notated in Russia. We cannot afford to ignore our past; nor to neglect putting on record the present, as this will be the *past* for students of the future! So, for all dance students who feel that notation is the drudgery of your dance life, try to adjust and look at it in a new light. It is part of your own future, and may even be contributing to the future survival and growth of dance generally.

ANSWERS TO TASK 2

Figure 2.5:

(a) modern genre, because parallel and medium/natural level.
(b) classical ballet genre, because turned-out and high level on toes.
(c) folk dance, because uses heels and stamps.
(d) African or South Asian, because uses low level and stamps.

Videodance and film

There has been a rapid rise in interest in television commissions for dance. In recent years, there have been various dance series, including Channel 4's *Tights Camera Action!* (1993 and 1994), as hosted by Lea Anderson, and BBC2's *Dance for Camera* (1995), and there are more in the pipeline. So why this growing interest in dance on screen rather than live at the theatre? The answer is connected to the availability of new technology and the breaking-down of barriers to 'what dance can be and do'. This is not a huge step away from creating *virtual realities*. Certainly, with the massive range of special effects now available, dancers on film can perform superhuman feats beyond their wildest dreams. For example, in the 3-minute 1994 video *Waiting*, directed and choreographed by Lea Anderson, with The Cholmondeleys dance group, the dancers are seen to be flying and floating around in a state of suspended animation as they simply wait around. Similarly, in *Mothers and Daughters* (1994), choreographed by Victoria Marks and directed by Margaret Williams, the dancers spin at unbelievable speed in a close embrace.

DANCE ON FILM – A SHORT HISTORY

To understand why this new art form within dance is developing so quickly, it would be worth looking at where and when it all started.

The first dance films to become widely seen were the Hollywood musicals like those of Fred Astaire and Gene Kelly of the 1930s. Some ballet and ballroom dances were also broadcast on television at the same time. In the late 1940s, ballet became popularised through such feature films as *The Red Shoes* (choreography Leonide Massine, 1946) and later in the 1950s several blockbuster musicals, like *Seven Brides for Seven Brothers*, were released. The combined effect of these films inspired many to take up dancing.

In the USA in the late 1960s, the concern shifted towards making dance films. For example, Merce Cunningham, who is often regarded as the pioneer of dance on video, collaborated with composer John Cage and CBS-TV on a version of *Field Dances*. Cameras panned everywhere, and there were out-of-focus shots, unexpected interruptions with fragments of interviews, and shots of Cage at the piano. Sometimes there was no sound or picture at all! Cunningham's usual strategy of *random composition* was clearly in place! As a result of this collaboration, Cunningham decided to research further into how the two art forms of dance and video may work together, and this led to a later collaboration between Cunningham and Charles Atlas in the early 1970s. This produced some innovative ideas. They experimented with making a new form of dance especially for the screen, called *videodance*. Here, the camera was located in amongst the dancers, moving with the action rather than relying on a zoomlens close-up. This gave a greater feel for the *energy* involved in dance, a factor which is usually washed out in film/video productions. The camera strapped to the body of the operator – called a Steadicam – was found to give a smoother look. Cunningham and Atlas went on to make many more videodances, including *Walkaround Time* (1969–73) and *Locale* (1978–80).

Atlas went on in the early 1980s to work with other post-modern dance artists such as Karole Armitage and Douglas Dunn. He developed a very distinctive style which had the following characteristics:

- quick-moving, hand-held cameras to give a look of spontaneity;
- abrupt editing which looks almost amateur and experimental;
- documentaries that have a slight fictional, surreal feel.

These techniques, combined with very careful planing, created intense visual interest for the viewer. The film-biography on dancer Michael Clark, *Hail, The New Puritan* (1986), shows these characteristics very clearly. It portrays Clark's life in punk London combined with several dances. The opening section featuring many of his friends – including the late fashion designer Leigh Bowery – is full of surreal images. As the introductory titles then start to roll, Clark is filmed waking up (in Chisenhale Dance Studio, London, but you would be forgiven for thinking it was his flat), and you realise the opening was all his dream! It is full of humour and startlingly clear observations.

> I wanted a psychological element, not so much a mystery but to do with personalities. ... It's a sort of blurring of forms ... Fiction and reality.
>
> *(Charles Atlas in* Dance Theatre Journal, *1986)*

More and more television coverage in art-magazine-type programmes like *The South Bank Show* and *Arena* gave dance more exposure. These usually involved straightforward films of stage works. This type of dance film is generally regarded as limited in scope nowadays.

In the UK in the 1970s, the producers Bob Lockyer and Colin Nears led the field. Lockyer collaborated with the London Contemporary Dance Theatre, concentrating mainly on the works of choreographer Robert Cohan. From then on, dance-on-film series became more regular.

One such early series of *Dance on 4* (Channel 4, 1983) showed a range of genres and styles, including: a documentary of *Backstage at the Kirov* with excerpts from *Swan Lake*; *Plainsong* and *Carnival* by Siobhan Davies with Second Stride; Robert North's *Troy Games* for the London Contemporary Dance Theatre; and Twyla Tharp's *Dance Scrapbook*. There was a wide range of use of camera and approaches to the filming of dance across the whole series. The Twyla Tharp film was an autobiographical study of her experimental work with dance and film, and it had a raw, exciting energy. This work contrasted with a more conventional use of film in the stage performance of *Troy Games*, where the camera angles and some of the timings employed shut out some of the humour of the original. When cameras were used more freely, moving amongst the dancers, there were varying levels of success. In *Swan Lake*, there was an increase in the physical impact for the viewer, as the camera almost became one of the *corps de ballet*. However, in *Plainsong*, the same technique produced rather a mismatch. Here, the cameras seemed to intrude on the calm quality and clear structure of the choreography.

In 1986, television directors Terry Braun and Peter Mumford formed an independent production company called Dancelines. This aimed to research the different possibilities involved in making dance for television. Their first project, itself called *Dancelines* involved a collaboration with Siobhan Davies, Ian Spink and a group of dancers/choreographers including Paul Clayden, Lucy Burge and Matthew Hawkins. The idea was to involve the *whole* team in the use of camera, editing and choreography. Dancers used the cameras, and camera operators joined in with the dancers' daily class. In this way, a close exchange of skills and understandings occurred. Everyone was on a very steep learning curve, and very valuable communication channels between the different art forms opened up. The final programme documented the whole process.

The *Dance on 4* series was repeated in 1988.

All the featured work was made for film or television. *Dancelines 2* featured in this series, and it carried on, in a more sophisticated way, from where the earlier research had left off.

As a part of this series also, Richard Alston collaborated very closely with Peter Mumford on an adaptation of the stage work *Strong Language*. This was no simple adaptation. It is still very recognisable as *Strong Language*, but it shows off certain features of the original dance which were less emphasised in the live performance. For example, the music and overall form of the piece was reorganised to suit a 25-minute programme instead, and there was substantial re-choreographing: one whole section of the original was missed out. Furthermore, the use of sudden changes in images, angles and perspectives resulted in more highlights than the original dance had. In place of the original contrapuntal structure, a new concern with close-ups involved the audience more with each individual dancer, and the former could now relate to the whole piece by building relationships with individual dancers rather than with the broad compositional structure of the piece. This approach was far more suited to small-screen viewing than to a live stage work. It was a radical piece of dance filming.

Dance on 4 (mentioned above) also included *Newark* by Trisha Brown (USA), which cleverly used the edges of the screen as wings for entrances and exits, as well as taking advantage of the way the small screen can emphasise the depth of a shot. The cameras were static, but they were used to enhance the sculptured look of figures in the foreground juxtaposed with figures who seemed to be far away in the background. In fact, the background figure was only a few feet away. This clever technique of perspective was used to enhance the central idea behind the piece, which was, in Brown's words, to honour the way men move. The women's movement in the dance is similar but more continuous. One female dancer, who is particularly strong, works in a dynamic

The Featherstonehaughs in Immaculate Conception. *To show the use of photographic effects similar to the use of video, to distort and create unusual images*

that is somewhere between the two genders. A few choreographic changes to the original stage work were required in the adaptation to videodance, but the adaptation was nonetheless generally accepted as a successful one.

From the 1980s into the 1990s, there have been many more series of specially commissioned works, as well as showings of earlier works. A comprehensive view was given in the above-mentioned Channel 4 *Tights Camera Action* Series 1 and 2 in 1993 and 1994. Many superb and experimental works from Europe, the USA, Canada and the UK were shown. The point was clearly being made that dance made for film had matured into a new genre. It enabled choreography to reach new heights of possibilities in terms of increasing movement vocabulary from the real to the superhuman. There were wonderful tricks, effects and fun to be had. Lea Anderson was involved in three works: *Flesh and Blood* and *Perfect Moment* (both adaptations of stage works, in Series 1) and *Waiting* (commissioned for the series and directed by Anderson herself).

In 1995, a series broadcast on BBC2 called *Summer Dance* showed a wide mix of work: a full-length ballet of Kenneth Macmillan's *Mayerling;* a documentary on Martha Graham; a videodance by Merce Cunningham called *Beach Birds* (director Eliot Caplan); *Outside In*, a post-modern work by Candoco choreographed by Victoria Marks and directed by Margaret Williams; *White Bird Featherless* by Siobhan Davies; *Rooster, Ghost Dances* and *Moonshine* by Christopher Bruce; and a full helping of Balanchine as the grand finale to the series. All in all, a mixed bag of genres and intentions showing the whole spectrum of dance, from stage works on film to videodance in the twentieth century.

PROBLEMS OF FILMING DANCE

The future of dance on film is a complex one, needing a close regard for the *aim* behind the filming of any particular dance. Depending on *why* a dance is being filmed, various problems will appear. These problems arise from a certain amount of incompatibility between how the human eye works and how the eye of the *camera* – as controlled by the film director – works.

Problem: long shots versus alternative options

Long shots from one or several static cameras serve to show the broad structure of a work but do not allow the viewer a clear image of the movements involved because the figures appear so small. The human eye, when watching dance at the theatre, will choose *what* to watch and *when* – from a broad overall scan, including exits and entrances, to a focus on a particular piece of detail or a particular soloist. Some stage works do not adapt to filming easily.

If we consider Mats Ek's Freudian interpretation of *Giselle* as an example of fine choreography which is difficult to film, we see the point. This director used cameras in a *conventional* format when transferring the stage work onto screen. The basic problem here is that if the usual number of cameras is employed, the field of view is insufficient to include large casts in one shot. And because the director is trying to be faithful to the choreographer, the result is a no-win situation. As an audience watch the dance on the stage, both their eyes and the choreography itself work mainly *side-to-side*. Television, by contrast, works mainly *foreground to background,* and so the two are not easily compatible. Long shots from static cameras is thus not an answer. Figure 2.6 shows the problem. (For a fuller explanation of this, see Bob Lockyer's article 'Dance and video: random thoughts', in *Dance Theatre Journal,* Vol. 4, Autumn 1983.)

Figure 2.6 *Showing problems of filming dance caused by camera angles/field of vision*

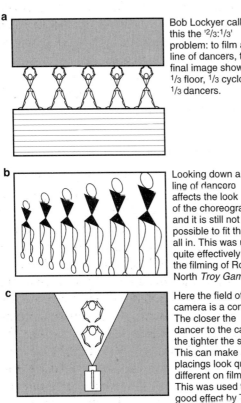

Bob Lockyer called this the '2/3:1/3' problem: to film a line of dancers, the final image shows 1/3 floor, 1/3 cyclorama, 1/3 dancers.

Looking down a line of dancers affects the look of the choreography, and it is still not possible to fit them all in. This was used quite effectively in the filming of Robert North *Troy Games*.

Here the field of a camera is a cone. The closer the dancer to the camera, the tighter the shot. This can make stage placings look quite different on film. This was used to good effect by Trisha Brown in *Newark* and by Cunningham in *Points In Space*

Bob Lockyer went some way to solving this problem in attempting to stay true to the original stage work of Robert Cohan's *Forest* (filmed for television in 1983). At the start of the dance, the company enter in canon (see Chapter 6, pp. 139-140) from stage right. Lockyer adapted this for the small screen by playing with the time element of the film. He *superimposed* one dancer doing the calling motif over the next and the next. This gave a filmed look which was close to the original canon that the audience would have seen in the original stage work.

In his early research, Merce Cunningham discovered an important strategy in regard to this problem:

> The triangular floor (as seen by the camera's eye) has led Merce's exploiting depth as a way of choreographing. One of his achievements is that he has made dancing look very spacious in a very small area so that you don't necessarily feel that the camera is confining the dancers.
>
> *(Charles Atlas in* Dance Theatre Journal, *1983)*

In *Points in Space* (1987) for BBC2, Cunningham collaborated with director Eliot Caplin to create a videodance plus a documentary of the process of its making. The footage shows Cunningham watching rehearsals in New York through a camera viewfinder in preparation for the later filming which took place in London. There is a clear concern with making exits fit into the small screen scale, and some clever uses of foreground and background. It also shows the cameras moving amongst the dancers – Caplin calls this 'cameras dancing'. Interestingly, the final dance was later reworked for the stage – a complete turn-around from the usual convention of filming a stage work.

The problem of adapting stage works and long shots was also encountered by the Mumford–Alston collaboration on *Strong Language*. The form and structure of Alston's choreography did not work on film because it relied on the eye seeing *broad* shots of how movements played off one against the other. The restructuring of the choreography for television opted for closeups in order to build the interest of the viewer in relation to individual dancers and the small subtleties of their movement. Braun and Alston also used *split screen* so that a number of different images from the dance could be seen at once. This helped to fit the dance into the small screen without losing a sense of the original whole – even if this whole was now seen in a different way.

A possible solution

Long shots have their uses if a major-scale production, say of a classical ballet, is to be filmed for audiences who may not otherwise see it. However, they are limited in scope. In order for dance to have an impact on the small screen, *alternative ideas* for how best to put across the original kinetic feel and energy need to be generated.

The use of long shots versus alternative options relate closely to the next problem which we will examine, in that the performance of any dance is reliant on the eye of the viewer, and there may – as already mentioned – be problems of incompatibility between that eye and the eye of the camera or director.

Problem: the camera's eye versus the spectator's eye

> 'You're the choreographer' Glen Tetley said to me a few years ago ... 'You select the images the viewer sees.'
>
> (Bob Lockyer in Dance Theatre Journal, 1983)

There is a key question to be asked here: should the director use the camera simply to present the dance to us, *or* should there be a creative freedom in the use of the camera which generates something entirely new? The first assumes that the camera is a mere substitute for the *audience's* eyes. The other is more about film using the dance as the subject matter to be *worked on* – just as a choreographer would choose certain *ideas* to work on. The choices of camera focus and angle and of editing styles are like choreography but in a different medium. There may be an approach which lies somewhere between the two.

The reality of being true to a stage work is not, however, quite so straightforward as it may first appear. At a basic level, each member of an audience will see and perceive a performance in their own individual way. So what hope is there of filming a 'perfect' view?

Furthermore, the camera can never see the same as the human eye. The *director's* view will always be the one finally seen, and this can never reproduce the whole of the live performance with all its dynamics and visual freedoms. Filming diminishes the three dimensions of space – as well as the raw energy, which is scaled down enormously.

Possible solutions

One solution preferred by some is to move the camera itself rather than to zoom in and out from static cameras. This solution is more suited to catching the energy and kinetic feel of dance, and it is often seen in work by Merce Cunningham in collaboration with directors like Charles Atlas and Eliot Caplin. It may not act as the perfect human eye, but it perhaps behaves more like one than do any alternative approaches. It still reduces the choices that the eyes of an audience in a theatre may have in what to watch – or what *not* to watch – but when combined with appropriate choices of effects, editing and cutting, it can give an enjoyable and fresh view of dance. For example, in the videodance *Outside In* (1994) featuring Candoco (with Margaret Williams as director and Victoria Marks as choreographer), the choice of changing locations, which works so well on film, is used to add interest for the viewer. The locations switch from green countryside to dark warehouse space. This is very much selecting what the audience sees, but it's a fair deal because it adds to the creative and imaginative impact of the final film. It also uses overhead shots in order to give greater insight into the differing qualities and ways of moving of the different performers. In this way, the director becomes almost like an additional choreographer, directing the viewer's eye in a very specific, organised way.

In adapting stage works to film, there may be

more success to be found in looking for imaginative solutions which will *enhance* the original qualities rather than water them down. This may require subtle or drastic changes to the choreography in order for it to be better seen in a small-scale format. The art form of videodance is about creating new possibilities in how dance uses time, space and energy. It requires a different approach to the filming of dance, and could not operate in the way that a straightforward stage performance does. On the other hand, there may be some scope for imaginative adaptations of videodance to the theatre.

TASK 3

Using a dance which you have choreographed, think about how you might treat it in order to make a videodance. Remember, this is only a paper exercise, so let your imagination run away with you! Consider the possibilities of distorting a movement to enhance its inherent qualities and structures. What special effects and use of cameras would you choose? Which parts might be better shot in close-up, or in a long panning shot? Would you consider using any of the following: blurred shots; speeding up or slowing down; reversing the action; pauses; chopping up and rearranging movements into a different order from that in which they appeared in the original piece; overhead shots; upside-down shots; harsh cuts; moving cameras; the superimposing of one image over another; changing the accompaniment completely?

Problem: working with dancers

Dancers in rehearsal normally have to repeat many movements over and over again in order to improve the quality of execution, and so that the choreographer has a better idea of whether the dance is working or not. This repetitious and potentially injurious process is worsened by the addition of the demands of the camera operators and the film director, since there may be long gaps between shots when the dancers' muscles can cool down very quickly.

Solutions

There are various solutions to this problem, most of which require adequate preparation by the director in collaboration with the choreographer and the film team. In describing his approach to filming stage works, Bob Lockyer explains how he initially tries to remember his reactions on seeing the dance for the first time, before learning the dance and then, finally, writing it down. Clearly this is a time-consuming process, but a necessary one if dancers are to be spared endless repetitions and long waiting times. After such detailed preparations, Lockyer gives copies of the action plan to the camera operators and the vision mixer. Detailed lists of shots are made and given to the crew, so that after the dancers have done their usual warm-up, it's straight into the action. In this way, hopefully, excessive repetition may be avoided.

Problem: expense

The above detailed preparation can also help to keep down costs on what is already an expensive process. In *Dance Theatre Journal*, 1983, Bob Lockyer stated: 'Sadly, I can't seem to find, inside or outside the BBC, the money to make videodance.' Gladly, this situation seems to have improved, but budgets and funding remain a problem; and for a student, it must seem a problem of impossible proportions. Everyone seems to own some sort of camcorder these days, but producing a videodance is not always that simple. For the best results, more than one camera is needed – ideally, three at different angles and levels, and each of them with their own monitor so that shots can be seen clearly. On a low budget and with a single camera, there would have to be a great deal of imagination and skill in the treatment of the dance and its filming to make up for the lack of equipment.

The cutting and editing process is where much of the creativity and artistry of the art form lies, and access to editing suites may not be so easy to obtain. Collaborating with students on media courses may be helpful here. Perhaps, making a joint assignment for a team of dancers, film crew and musicians might be exciting.

TASK 4

This is a lengthy task which will require scheduling over a whole term, as well as a close liaison between your teacher and people in other departments, if it is to be worth pursuing. The aim is to produce a 4-to-5-minute-long videodance. It is important to discuss things together as a whole team – dancers, film crew and musicians – right from the start. Considerations about sound accompaniment, costumes and other physical settings should be looked at as early as possible in the project.

As a team, draw up a schedule to include rehearsal times, the shooting of the film, and the editing and final showing of the video. Using two or three outdoor locations (remember, you may need written permission for this) and a unifying theme, create small pieces of choreography for filming. As you work, allow the film crew to watch and to consider how they might video and edit the work in order to enhance the chosen theme. During the editing process, continue wherever possible to work as a team.

VIDEODANCE – FINAL WORDS

Videodance is an exciting new art form with many possibilities. Try to watch out for new series and commissions on television. The eye of the choreographer and that of the camera/director may be very similar in the final credits.

References and resources

BOOKS AND ARTICLES

Atlas, C., 'Filming Cunningham dance', *Dance Theatre Journal*, vol. 1, no. 1, 1983

Burnside, F., 'Television's summer of dance', *Dance Theatre Journal*, vol. 12, no. 2, 1995

Dancing Times, *Study Supplement 3 Reconstruction and Revival, Dancing Times*, LXXX 951, December 1989

de Marigny, C. and Rubidge, S. (conceived

and devised), the 'Dance and television' issue, *Dance Theatre Journal*, vol. 6, no. 1, 1988

Hutchinson Guest A. UK Available from the Language of Dance Centre (see address below):
— *Your Move*, London: Gordon & Breach, 1995
— *Dancer's Glancer – a Quick Guide to Labanotation*, London: Gordon & Breach, 1992
— *A History of the Development of the Laban Notation System*, Cervera Press, 1995
— *Labanotation*, New York, 1977

Kane, A. 'Notation moves on', London: Dance Books, *Dance Theatre Journal*, vol. 4, no. 4, 1986

Kipling Brown, A. and Parker, M., *Dance Notation for Beginners*, London: Dance Books, 1983 (a good guide to both Laban and Benesh Notation)

Lockyer, B. 'Dance on video – random thoughts', *Dance Theatre Journal*, vol. 1, no. 4, 1983

Partsch-Bergsohn, I. 'Laban: magic and science', *Dance Theatre Journal*, vol. 4, no. 3, 1986

Rubidge, S., 'Reconstruction and its problems', *Dance Theatre Journal*, vol. 12, no. 1, 1995

MUSIC

For Task 1: *Moving In Time*, by Parampara, is available from: Mandy de Winter, 3 Brandywell Road, Broseley, Shropshire TF12 5ST. This tape has many useful tracks. Tel.: 01952 883 242. Parampara also give workshops in Circle Dance. Recommended for Task 1.

SOFTWARE

Labanwriter, for use with Apple Macintosh computers, is available from The Labanotation Institute – see address below.

USEFUL ADDRESSES

For information on courses and publications:

The Labanotation Institute
University of Surrey
Guildford
Surrey GU2 5XH
Tel.: 01483 509 351

The Language of Dance Centre
17 Holland Park
London W11 3TD
Tel.: 0171 229 3780

The Institute of Choreology
4 Margravine Gardens
Barons Court
London W6 8RH

The Benesh Institute
12 Lisson Grove
London NW1 6TS
Tel.: 0171 258 3041

chapter three

THE CONSTITUENT FEATURES OF DANCE: MOVEMENT AND DANCERS

With every new ballet that I produce I seek to empty myself of some plastic obsession and every ballet I do is, for me, the solving of a balletic problem.

(Sir Frederick Ashton in Dance from Magic to Art, *1976)*

Composing dances may be said to be a process of *problem-solving*. Dance training prepares the body for the physical demands of dance and improves coordination skills. The next step may be making your own dances. Using the physical intellect imaginatively to compose dance involves learning about the components that make up a dance. The process of making dances, as outlined in Figure 3.1, is the focus of this chapter.

As choreographer, you must be able to make clear for your dancers exactly what movements you require. This will help you to collaborate with the dancers and bring out their best in

Figure 3.1   *Process of composing a dance*

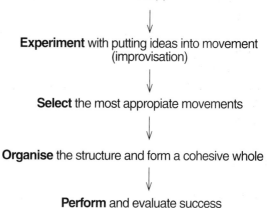

performance. Therefore, you need to be able to observe and analyse in order to find the most appropriate and successful movements. You also need a sound knowledge of the rules – even if only to go on to *break* them successfully.

TASK 1

(This is a good task to do if you happen to be injured or ill.) Watch a class of dancers perform a taught phrase. Choose three of the dancers, and make notes on:

- individual differences in how they perform the phrase;
- individual differences in how *successful* they are in performing the phrase.

In addition, evaluate *why* some are more successful than others, and suggest how those that are less successful can improve their performance.

Figure 3.2 is a mind map showing the various constituent features that all dances, of any genre, possess:

- the movement components;
- the dancers;

- the physical setting;
- the accompaniment (the aural setting).

The last two features will be discussed in Chapters 4 and 5. Let us now analyse the first two in detail.

Figure 3.2   *Mind map of constituent features of a dance*

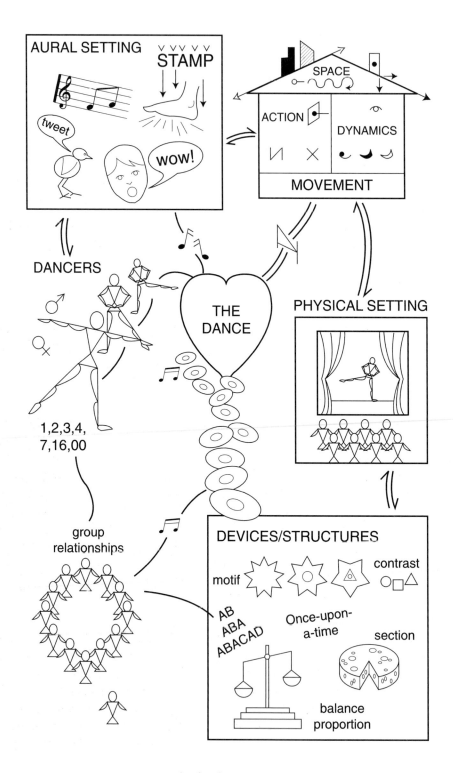

The movement components

The basic movement components are:

- actions
- space
- time
- dynamics.

THE SIX DANCE ACTIONS

There are three basic anatomical actions that the body is capable of performing: flexion, extension and rotation (see Chapter 1). The dancer in training will use these three basic actions in endless combinations to produce the six dance actions. These are:

- travelling (locomotion);
- elevation;
- turning;
- gesture (isolation);
- stillness;
- falling.

Travelling (locomotion)

Walking is a fundamental human activity, one which takes us from A to B.

> Every time you step you fall only to catch yourself from falling ...
>
> *(Laurie Anderson from the album* Big Science*)*

The natural human walk involves heel down first. The endless other possibilities – rolling, knee walks, sliding, crawling etc. – are where choreography begins.

TASK 2

- Walk slowly, feeling the moment of loss of balance as your centre shifts forward.
- Gradually accelerate to a fast walk – feel the natural walking action of heel down first (*dorsi flexion*).
- Change to a stylised dance walk: toe down first (*plantar flexion*).
- Carefully explore and experiment with different walks: on heels; on toes/balls of feet (*metatarsal arch*); on the outside of the foot; on the inside of the foot.
- Walk on different levels.
- Walk in different directions.

Walking involves an even rhythm. The ankle must extend to push off the back foot and shift the body weight forward. The centre needs to pull up to maintain a smooth, even quality. The eyes should focus on eye level, not downwards, and the arms should work naturally in opposition to the legs.

A *parallel walk* is more common in modern dance, while walking with *turn-out* from the hips is more usual in classical ballet – although the famous classical dancer and choreographer Vaslav Nijinsky caused a sensation by breaking this rule when he used a parallel walk in *L'Après-midi d'un Faune* (1912). Nijinsky wanted to give a look of classical Greek 2-dimensionality, and so he used parallel legs with arms also unnaturally parallel to the leg action. At its première, the audience at the Paris Opera rioted!

Running is a fast walk using a greater extension of feet and legs, and the emphasis here is upward and forward. Running also involves an even rhythm.

Runs, triplets and prances are all variations of walking. Triplets are in a 3/4 waltz time signature, with the accent on the first downward step. Prances are runs which emphasise the upward knee lift sharply with a sudden extension of the foot. Both prances and triplets are often used in the Martha Graham style of technique training.

TASK 3 ⧗

Select three from the following: walking; runs; triplets; prances; skips.

- Combine them to make a phrase which can be repeated on alternate sides continuously. Keep it simple – i.e. no arms, turns.
- Practice the phrase until you have it very clear and accurate.
- Repeat it 4 times.
- Notate it to show the repetitions.

Ronald Emblen in the clog dance from La Fille Mal Gardee, choreographed by Frederick Ashton

When a number of steps are patterned together, they become recognisable dances. Frederick Ashton's use of folk steps in *La Fille Mal Gardée* (*The Unchaperoned Daughter*, 1960) includes clog dance, maypole dancing and a morris dance. The start of his *Facade* (1931) is a Highland fling, and later a polka is danced by a woman in her bloomers. There is also a Charleston danced by two flappers, four waltzing girls and a mock-passionate Tango. The choreographer Christopher Bruce, appointed artistic director of the Rambert Dance Company in 1994, has often used folk-influenced steps – for example in *Sergeant Early's Dream* (1984), where they are based on tap dance and Irish Step dancing mixed with a contemporary style. The flexed feet and hands, and contractions and releases of the spine, have a Martha Graham look. The dance here is concerned with the longings and memories of a village community as they reflect on their homeland across the sea, and the folky feel of the steps is very appropriate to the atmosphere.

Elevation

Elevation involves rising from the floor, in a jump or in relevé on a half-toe or en pointe. This is an exciting part of any choreography.

> Here we are again with both feet planted firmly in the air.
>
> (Hugh Scanlon, British Trade Union leader)

Figure 3.3   *Notation for Task 4*

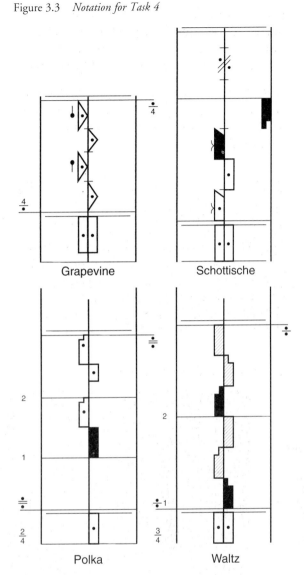

Grapevine   Schottische

Polka   Waltz

TASK 4

1 In Figure 3.3, a number of folk steps are shown in Labanotation. Read and then dance the scores.

2 With a partner, compose a short duet which uses a variety of contacts – e.g. ballroom hold, link arms, hold waist, hands on partner's shoulders. (Music suggestions: Cajun music by Balfa Brothers' *Arcadian Memories*; Malcolm Arnold's *Dances*.)

BAD Dance Company in full flight in The MAD BAD Line

Every human movement has three phrases:

1 preparation
2 action
3 recovery.

These are particularly clear in the action of jumping:

1 Preparation: bend knees; lift centre, rib cage and head.
2 Action: extend feet and legs strongly and suddenly to take off – lifting arms may assist upward thrust; breathe in; lift focus.
3 Recovery: for safety and the protection of the Achilles heel, always land 'through the foot' – i.e. toe-ball-heel to floor; bend knees; maintain alignment and lift from centre on landing.

As noted in Chapter 1, sometimes beginners, in an effort to take off, over-contract the muscles of the body, and a 'bucking' effect is seen in the air. Encouragement to *relax* in the air is needed here.

Jumps can be identified by whether the take-off and landing are on one foot or both. You only have two feet, so clearly the permutations are:

- *hop:* take off from 1 foot, land on the same foot;
- *leap:* take off from 1 foot, land on the other foot;
- *jump:* take off from 2 feet, land on the 2 feet;
- *sissone:* take off from 2 feet, land on 1 foot;
- *assemblé:* take off from 1 foot, land on 2 feet.

TASK 5

1 Notate the above five jumps, and label them by name.
2 Compose a phrase of movement which contains these five jumps in any order. Add steps and repetitions as desired.

Other details – like rotation of the legs, the use of the free leg(s) in the air, flexed or extended feet, the arm position, turning, travelling and so on – give jumps endless expressive potential. Jumping can skim the floor, burst upwards suddenly, propel powerfully forwards or sideways. A jump may soar, like leaps arcing through the air, or use arms swinging in opposition to enhance the effect of suspension in the air. When combined with runs, the leap has a spectacular look. Landings can differ too. A rebound into *another* jump gives a bouncy effect and expresses something quite different from just falling to the floor on landing. (What might the latter type of landing express to an audience?)

In *Nympheas* (1976) by Robert Cohan, 2-foot-to-2-foot jumps with deep pliés on landings are used effectively in one section danced by the men, and give the impression of frogs springing between the pads of waterlilies. In *Troy Games* (1974) by Robert North, there is a duet in which the dancers remain on one leg throughout. A great deal of hopping is obviously used in this sparring bout, and of course makes great demands on the dancers' stamina.

TASK 6

1 ▽△ Combine lively jumps with travelling close to the floor (crawl, roll, slide, knee walks etc.) to create a short solo of surprises. Try to incorporate sudden changes of level and attitude. (Suggested music: *The Mission*, Ennio Morricone, CDV2402 – various tracks.)

2 ▽△ Combine your solo with those of two or three other dancers to make a short trio. Ask spectators to describe what they see and to suggest titles.

Turning

Turning is almost a dervish exercise with the world going around and you feeling calm and quiet.

(Hanya Holm in The Vision of Modern Dance, 1979)

The belief in the power of turning in the Sufi religion of the Middle East is so great that the dervishes' hours of spinning, they feel, connect their being to the heavens and the earth, centring them and empowering them to overcome any dizziness. This is, as such, a strong element for expressive movement. Turning strictly refers to rotating the whole body around with a change of front, or a full or multiple rotation. *Twisting* is also rotation, but is different because only *one part* of the body turns around whilst the *other* part remains still. There are many different types of turn: full, half, quarter, multiple, inward and outward, jumping, travelling, on- and off-balance, pivot, spin and so on. These all require good placement and alignment to avoid a loss of balance or orientation. When beginners first start, they may feel as if their whole universe is moving, and this can cause great insecurity. Constant practice is therefore required.

The eyes must focus straight ahead, not downwards, for balance. In classical ballet, 'spotting' is often used. This involves fixing the eyes on one spot for as long as possible and whipping the head round as quickly as possible. This helps to avoid dizziness. Modern and post-modern genres sometimes deliberately remove spotting, and the skill of retaining orientation then becomes internalised, not unlike the whirling dervishes. A practical example is

Helter-Skelter Hove and Brighton Youth Dance in full spin

barrel turns, which in ballet are performed outward, leaping sideways around and spotting on a centrally placed barrel. Originally a favourite of sailors, this is an exciting explosive jump to watch. The post-modern version may be performed inwards, with less sudden upward feel and more skimming in soft curves along a straight pathway. The deliberate removal of spotting gives an even, lifting quality.

Turns can also start in different ways. Lifting the weight onto a half-toe rise (relevé) or en pointe allows the body to easily rotate around the axis. This may be continued in multiple by using the free leg to extend and flex in retiré (drawing the leg up in a bent position so that the toe touches the inside of the support leg) to give added momentum on each 360° turn. The weight of *throwing* an arm, leg or head may also initiate turning. In the romantic classic *Giselle* (Coralli and Perrot, 1841), Giselle rises from her tomb and spins into life to enter the spirit world of the *wilis*. And the post-modern work *Rotary Action* (Arnie Zane and Bill T. Jones, 1985) makes a clear use of cartwheels, rolls, turning around a partner, and the rotating of hips and shoulders in a simple but effective interpretation of the title.

TASK 7

Choreograph a trio/quartet using the idea of transport. With turning as your dominant movement theme, ideas which may be useful for improvisation will include: the wheel, the Highway Code, traffic control, behaviour behind the wheel, bicycles, trains and the behaviour of passengers in train stations or at bus stops. (Suggested music: 'Whirling', from *Contemporary Dance Rhythms*.)

Gesture (isolation)

Graham's knee comes up to her chest, her back curves slightly forward, and now her leg, knee leading, juts inward, circles out, in, out again, while her arms swoop through the air like a bird's wings. ... Graham speaks of the turbulent emotions lying deep within Judith's body.

(Elinor Rogosin in The Dancemakers, *1980)*

The powerful language of gesture is all around us everyday. Waving goodbye, folding arms, pointing figures, raising eyebrows, a nod and a shake of the head are ordinary body language which we all use to accompany speech. These everyday forms of movement are a rich source for choreography – as we note in the quotation above, where the gestures tell of the deepest vengefulness and passion. Gestural movement does not involve any transference of weight. Gestures are usually movements of single parts in isolation, and the *rotation* of the joints can here play a significant part in subtle communication. In Labanotation, the facing of a palm on the hand is as shown in Figure 3.4. Similarly, rotation of the legs in the hip sockets in turn-out, parallel or turned-in (see

Figure 3.4   *Notation for palm facings*

Figure 3.5   *Notation for leg rotation*

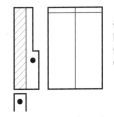

an open-facing palm looks generous and offers support

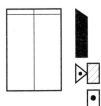

arm slices down to deep forward left diagonal, with the cutting edge

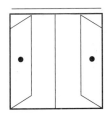

inward rotation

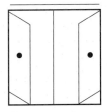

turn-out

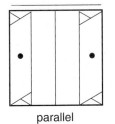

parallel

Figure 3.5) opens up a range of expressive possibilities from humour to lyricism.

Bharata natyam from India uses a large amount of hand, arm and facial gestures called *mudras* in a complex language to tell rich narratives of myths and stories. Elements of this genre are visible in the work of post-modern choreographer Lea Anderson for The Cholmondeleys and The Featherstonehaughs. Anderson also uses sign language to give her work a characteristic quirky, detailed look.

> I became riveted by a single striking resemblance, which was simply their extraordinary range of gesture and facial expression. Their hands ... seemed to have a life of their own tracing elaborate, decorative patterns in space or spinning memories; ... while their faces had an even more eloquent repertoire of pouts, stares ... and glances.
>
> (*Judith Mackrell in* Dance Theatre Journal, *1986*)

Mimetic gestures are used in classical ballet to tell stories and make clear the relationships between characters. Jean Georges Noverre (France, 1727–1810) describes his thoughts on reform for ballet in his *Lettres sur la Danse et sur les Ballets* (1760):

> ... study how to make your gestures noble, never forget that it is the life-blood of your dancing ...
>
> (*Cyril Beaumont in* Dance Horizons, *1966*)

The Cholmondeleys in The Cholmondeley Sisters

Later, in the nineteenth century, Marius Petipa (1818–1910) used long passages of mime, and sometimes as a kind of sign language so that obvious meanings were clear. For example, shaking a fist meant anger, while placing the hand on the heart meant love. Other gestures were less direct, like pointing to the heavens to declare everlasting love, or circling hands and arms around each other and over the head to symbolise dance. This mimetic gesture is also

TASK 8 ▽

1 Using as many different parts of the body as possible, isolate and improvise with gestural movements. Some of these may be recognisable everyday gestures, others more quirky.

2 Select a few everyday gestures and a few less common to create a dance entitled 'For a small space'. (Suggested music: 'Ballet of the chicks in their shells' by Moussorgsky, from *Pictures at an Exhibition*.)

used a great deal in *Giselle* (Coralli and Perrot, 1841) by Giselle herself just before she shows off her dancing skills.

Stillness

Stillness is not an absolute point. It is an ever-receding depth of understanding.

(Mary Fulkerson)

Being still is an *active* process! It requires strong control. There is muscle activity in a pause, a feeling of ongoing energy. Stillness contributes to rhythm, acting a little like a full stop in a sentence, and it gives the onlooker a chance to reflect on what has just been seen. It may also act to highlight what is about to happen, and it is also often used as the ending for a dance.

The skill of balance may be involved if the body is being held still on a small area like the toes, and this requires strong control and co-ordination. The part on the floor pushes down whilst the rest of the body pulls upwards and sends energy outward to the extremities. This counter-tension outwards and towards your centre holds the body lightly over the base.

In Richard Alston's *Soda Lake* (1981) stillness is used extensively, and is clearly appropriate to his study of the vast open spaces of the Mohavi Desert in North America. The silent, motionless 'passive landscape' (as Alston described this desert in 1983 on *The South Bank Show*), as presented in a minimalist set, is a perfect vehicle for stillness. Alston chooses certain shapes and positions of rest for which the dancer in performance has to allow adequate time: holding such positions as 'the big bird' and 'the sentinel position' are demanding on a dancer's stamina and sense of timing.

TASK 9

1 ◿ In pairs, one person closes their eyes while the other makes a shape. Without opening your eyes, use touch to feel your way around your partner's shape. Your partner must keep very still. When you think you know the shape, make it yourself and then open your eyes to see how accurate your copy is.

2 ▲ ▲ ▲ Find prints of paintings by the Impressionist artist Georges Seurat — either *La Grande Jatte* or *Une Baignade* would be appropriate. In threes or fives, compose a short dance which uses stillness as a predominant feature to punctuate the movement. Convey a feeling of calm and heat. (Suggested music: Claude Debussy's 'Snowflakes are dancing', from *Children's Corner No. 4*, or 'Passepied' from *Suite Bergamasque No. 4*.)

Falling

In classical ballet, the *high level* predominates, while one of the aims of early modern dance, by contrast, was to *show* the effort of moving against gravity, not to hide it. This latter trend increased the use of *falling* and of low-level movement. I like to consider falling as the sixth dance action.

Doris Humphrey, one of the early pioneers of modern dance, regarded the struggle against gravity (suspension, fall and recovery) to be the very essence of life and action — 'The Arc between Two Deaths'.

Standing still before a mirror, I found that first the body began to sway. Then, letting myself go, three things happened. I began to fall, the speed increasing as I went down. The body made an involuntary effort to resist the fall ... I hit the floor.

(quoted by Ellfeldt *in* Dance from Magic to Art, *1976*)

Falling requires skill and coordination in order to be performed safely, and like all dance actions, it requires practice. There is a moment when the pull of gravity overtakes and the dancer 'intentionally' gives in to it. During this descent, the abdominal muscles must pull-up; and landing on the knees, elbows, shoulder tip or sacrum should *always* be avoided. There are two types of fall:

1 a *collapse*: a relaxed, successive giving-in which happens over the centre of gravity and tends not to rebound.

2 an *off-balance fall*: the centre of gravity shifts off-centre, making falling unavoidable.

Various actions may pre-empt a fall – jumps, swings, turns – and at the end of the fall action phase, recovery may involve stillness, a roll or a rebound to continue.

TASK 10

1 Explore the feeling of walking, falling and recovering. At the ends of falls, try out different techniques: stillness; rebound; rolls. In addition: falling in different directions: forwards, backwards, sideways and diagonally; try out both *collapses* and *off-balance falls* (see above); and try adding jumps and swings into the falling. After 5 or 10 minutes, join up into a large group.

2 Continuing to explore the above themes, select some of the more successful ideas, whilst also copying the variety of tempos, falls, shapes and rolls that the other dancers are doing.

2 Using landing/gymnastic mats, try to teach each other any falls and rolls which someone may have learnt in a martial-arts class – like a judo or karate session – or in a gymnastics class.

Lea Anderson, in the 1992 *Perfect Moment* video (directed for Channel 4 by Margaret Williams), used a section involving fast and furious falls and rolls with a rough-and-tumble judo-like look. The *political* combat between male and female was ritualised in this head-on collision between the Featherstonehaughs and the Cholmondeleys.

Falling was used for more comic effect by Christopher Bruce in *Sergeant Early's Dream* (1984). The section entitled 'Peggy Gordon' reveals drunken young men lamenting their love for Peggy. She looks on, little impressed by their cavorting drunken stupor, as they, hardly able to stand, lurch from one forlorn moment to the next.

TASK 11

From a standing position, transfer your weight simply, smoothly, gradually and safely to the floor until lying flat. Then roll to stand. Practise until the phrase is very clear, and then notate it, showing clearly which parts of the body (see Figure 3.6) contact the floor in which order. Make sure weight transference is smooth throughout.
Notate a simple score showing which parts of the body take weight in the descent.

Figure 3.6 *Labanotation signs for parts of the body*

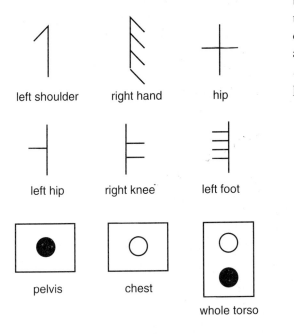

left shoulder	right hand	hip
left hip	right knee	left foot
pelvis	chest	
	whole torso	

The six dance actions of travelling, elevation, turning, gesture, stillness and falling, which are the foundations of choreography, are further developed by using a variety of other considerations, namely the *where*, the *when* and the *how*, which will form the focus for the next part of this chapter.

The space component

'No room! No room!' they cried out when they saw Alice coming. 'There's plenty of room!' said Alice indignantly.

(From Alice in Wonderland *by Lewis Carroll)*

Designing a dance in space helps the audience to understand it; and any dance must be organised in space in a way appropriate to the chosen idea or theme. Dancers work *in* a space – i.e. a studio, gym, stage or whatever – but they also dance *with* space: it is alive, like an active partner. Mary Wigman (1886–1973) was a German early-modern dance pioneer famous for the way in which she used space as an active element. Rudolf Laban (1879–1958) classified dancers by their preferences for moving on a certain level, high, medium or low.

PERSONAL AND GENERAL SPACE

The space that lies around you as far as you can reach without moving off the spot is your own personal space bubble. In *Embrace Tiger, Return to Mountain* (Glen Tetley, for the Rambert Company, 1968 – see p. 80), the dancers are placed bubble distance apart and go through ritual t'ai chi meditations. Later on, duets bring them into very close contact with each other, with touching and shadowing, and there is a feeling of agitation as their personal bubbles are invaded. Moving out into the larger space beyond your bubble opens up many spatial choices and possibilities.

Embrace Tiger, Return to Mountain *by Glen Tetley (a) to show dancers within their own space bubbles (b) later in the dance the dancers begin to overlap*

(a)

(b)

FLOOR AND AIR PATTERNS

As they gradually reveal themselves to an audience, the *patterns* created by travelling on the floor (see Figure 3.7) and by gestures made in the air, be they curves, straight lines, circles, zig-zags, spirals or squiggles, will provoke different responses. Although it is difficult to pin down any exact responses, some generalisations may be made. Curving patterns are lyrical, gentle and continuous, whereas straight ones tend to come over as bold, more formal and strong.

Figure 3.7   *To show notation of floor pattern*

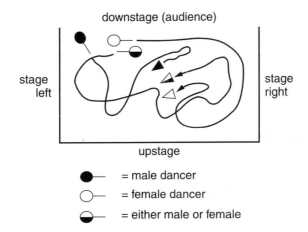

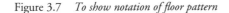

downstage (audience)

stage left

stage right

upstage

●— = male dancer
○— = female dancer
◐— = either male or female

DIRECTIONS

As with different patterns, different *directions* – forwards, backwards, sideways, circular, up, down – may also provoke different reactions. Advancing forwards is positive, assertive and authoritative, whereas the backwards retreat possibly more defensive. Jumping up is lively, while there is an opposite feel to the falling down. Sideways may be seen as sneaky.

TASK 12 ⧖

Use the words below to create short phrases of improvised movement which use direction, pattern in the air and on the floor, and personal/general space in a way appropriate to the meaning of the words.

- Up one minute, down the next.
- Far-reaching effects.
- Neither here nor there.
- On the straight and narrow.
- Draw the line.
- At loose ends.

DIMENSIONS AND PLANES

Movement can be described in three dimensions:

- *height:* up and down (rise/sink);
- *width:* side to side (open/close);
- *depth:* forwards and backwards (advance/retreat).

When two dimensions are joined together, *planes* are produced:

- the *horizontal plane* (also called the *table plane*): joins width and depth;
- the *vertical plane* (also called the *door plane*): joins height and width;
- the *saggital plane* (also called the *wheel plane*): joins height and depth.

Movement which emphasises the width dimension can appear flat, perhaps mechanical or puppet-like. This kind of movement would be appropriate when dancing in a *mask*, because of the inhuman, two-dimensional look which, like a mask, it conveys. The opening of

Ghost Dances (Christopher Bruce, 1981) uses the width dimension to great effect. The dancers' tilting head gestures, sideways leaps and extensions into stillness create an unreality in our minds. They place hands on each others' shoulders and move in unison in a side-to-side folky step, presenting an image of power which is ominous and threatening to us mere mortals. These movements also serve to emphasise the death masks and the body paint which create the effect of flat skeletons hanging in the gloom. As soon as the mere mortals enter, we are drawn into the latter's more 3-dimensional world – and into their vulnerability – by the way they travel slowly along the depth of the diagonal (up stage left to down stage right). By adding depth to the original movement, Bruce places these mortals in a more real, human world. The audience is drawn into a place where two worlds meet, and an accompanying sense of danger is conveyed.

LEVELS

Levels are an aspect of the height dimension. In classical ballet, the emphasis is often on the high level, whereas the low floor level is a feature of modern and postmodern dance. Martha Graham's earthy relationship with gravity was also a feature of the work of Doris Humphrey; and we also see it today in the post-modern work of Lea Anderson, for the Cholmondeleys – in 'Knees', the end section of her 1989 work *Flesh and Blood,* the dancers seem earth-bound, weighty.

From the vertical to the horizontal, from standing, kneeling and lying, her cast explore the different levels between high and low, as if making contact with the unknown.

(Ann Nugent in The Stage, *1989)*

The middle level is our everyday one. Falling out of or rising above this level offer obvious expressive possibilities for choreography.

To show use of varied levels: BAD Dance Company in The MAD BAD Line

THE SIZE OF MOVEMENTS

Tiny hand gestures, large sweeping arm gestures, a single step, travelling all around a space – these movements will communicate different sensations to onlookers; and the contrasts involved here should be explored by all choreographers.

Again, this factor is shown clearly in the work of Lea Anderson in *Flesh and Blood*. The small movements of eyes, noses, fingers and heads which draw the letters J, O, A and N in the air are later developed by *enlargement*. they travel and transform into arm gestures in the second section, 'Movement choir'.

TASK 13

In groups of four or five, find as many objects which can be used to place dancers on a high level – e.g. chairs, ladders or stage blocks – as you can. Use movements which emphasise the difference between high and low levels, and explore the possibilities individually – include the simple lifting and lowering of each other.

Experiment also with moving the objects so as to change the way in which planes and dimensions are used – you may prefer, at this stage, to stand out in turns and *observe* the resulting changes.

Finally, add the option to use *tiny* and *large* movements which others can pick up on by copying you close by or far away, by using large gestures to 'involve' other dancers across the space, or by travelling together.

This improvisation does not need to produce a finished dance, but it is advised to use outside onlookers to give feedback on the results.

THE FOCUS

This constituent feature of a dance composition can mean different things at different moments during a dance. Indeed, it can involve any of the following:

- *where* the dancer is looking: up or down; at a part of the body; at another dancer; at the audience;
- which way the body is *facing*: for example, does a certain shape look better facing on a diagonal or flat to the audience than it does facing sideways on?
- the performing skills of a dancer: these may have to do with facial expression, or with the dancer's attention to how to perform a certain movement (e.g. which part of the body to focus on in order to create a full expression). This factor, which will be dealt with later, is of concern to choreographers, because it is they who are trying to bring such skills out of their dancers.

These are important considerations when composing dances. A dancer looking inwardly, on the self, will clearly convey a different image from one focusing on the far distance, on an object or on another dancer on the stage. Choosing an appropriate focus for dancers is therefore vital.

In *Sergeant Early's Dream* (1984), the dancers' focus is often thrown out to sea which is painted on the backcloth. This draws the attention of the audience to the dancers' longing for their original homeland which is full of memories and nostalgia. In other sections where humour or tragic loss is required, the focus is often instead on the *other dancers*.

BAD Dance Company showing the use of focus

SHAPE AND VOLUME

The body can create a variety of shapes – curled, straight, wide, twisted and so on – and the spaces *around* and *between* bodies also need to be sculpted. In visual art, this latter space is often called the *negative space*. In dance it is seen during stillness, but also in the transitions from one shape to the next, and when it is enclosed by boundaries, it creates a feeling of *volume*. For example, when a dancer places the arms in front of the body, as if curving them around an imaginary beach ball, the sensation of volume is clearly felt.

Different shapes have different expressive potential. In classical ballet, it is so often *curving* lines which are used. These have a sense of the lyrical and the romantic, and an ongoing flow and grace. In contrast, the harsh angular and straight lines of early-modern dancers are hard-edged, tough and strong, and these have held the potential for expressing the social upheavals of their times.

> The modern dance as we know it today came after the World War. This period following the war demanded forms vital enough for the reborn man to inhabit ... All life today is concerned with space problems, even political life. Space language is a language we understand. We receive so much of sensation through the eye.
>
> *(Martha Graham in* The Vision of Modern Dance, *1980)*

Similarly with *symmetrical* and *asymmetrical* shapes: the former giving impressions of regularity and stability, and the latter coming over as more unpredictable and insecure.

> If symmetry should be used sparingly in choreography because of its calming effect, then asymmetry, which stimulates the senses, is the area to court and understand for dancing.
>
> *(Doris Humphrey in* The Art of Making Dances, *1959)*

Further consideration about the use of space is to be found in later sections. In Chapter 4, which deals with the physical setting, there is an analysis of how to use a stage space, and of how different physical settings affect spatial design. The arrangement of groups of dancers in space is examined under a separate section in Chapter 6.

TASK 14

1 ⧗ Individually, choose four contrasting body shapes.

- Place them in an order and link them up with movements.
- Find a way, whilst holding each shape, of making it turn or travel, or both.
- Experiment with giving the shapes different facings so that an audience sees them from different angles – e.g. above, sideways etc.
- Experiment with changing the focus of the eyes during both stillness and travelling – e.g. moving from a focus on different parts of the body to a focus on the room around you.

2 ▽ From the above, choose movements to create a short solo piece entitled either:

- 'Distortions', or
- 'No way out', or
- 'Metamorphosis'.

(Recommended music: *The Big Blue* film soundtrack, by Eric Serra.)

As we move through space, we also, of course, move through *time*, and this will be the next constituent feature of dance that we will examine.

The time component

'If you knew time as well as I do' said the Hatter 'you wouldn't talk about wasting *it*. It's *him* ... I dare say you never even spoke to Time! ... Now if you only kept on good terms with him, he'd do almost anything you like with the clock.'

(Alice in Wonderland, *by Lewis Carroll*)

Time can seem to have a life of its own. We have all experienced waiting for the kettle to boil, and how, when we are in a hurry, it seems to take longer. As choreographer, you may alter how an audience perceives time by the way that you yourself manipulate it. Like design in *space*, time plays an intrinsic part in the organisation of movement for choreography. It orders and measures, but it can also be a slippery customer, so, as the Mad Hatter cautions, it is advisable to be on good terms with it.

Patterning movement in time gives it form and makes it interesting for the onlooker; and the performing dancer, on their part, requires an accurate feel for the *temporal* boundaries of the choreography. This will be analysed further later in the book. Similarly, the analysis of time and rhythm in music will be examined in more detail later. Here, we will be concerned only with the more simple aspects of time as a constituent feature of dance composition.

SPEED AND DURATION

Dance is concerned with a single instant as it comes along.

(Merce Cunningham in *Dance from Magic to Art, 1976)*

Sudden or sustained, and fast or slow, are the two most simple ways of analysing a movement, in terms of how much time it actually takes. Sudden movement can produce a sense of urgency in the onlooker, in contrast with an indulgent, gradual feeling that a slower and more sustained movement can create. If you compose a 3-minute dance which is made up of 12 slow movements, it will have a leisurely feeling. Pack it with 200 movements, on the other hand, and the onlooker will feel rushed along at a breathless pace.

As choreographer and dancer, you need to build up your sensitivity to the duration of movement. Merce Cunningham and others often work with a stopwatch, which allows the speed and duration of a movement – which, after much rehearsal, always stays accurate – to be measured independently of the tempo of the music. One of his dancers, Karole Armitage, once said that he had taught her to recognise exactly how long a movement takes.

In composing dances, it is likely that you will mix slow and fast speeds. The way that you mix these will reflect your personal sense of time.

PHRASING

Single actions joined together make up *phrases*. Finding your own inner rhythm that will guide you to form phrases is an ongoing process which itself may take a long time. Phrases usually have a feeling of unity, logic or completeness about them. Each is a simple unit with a beginning, middle and end. The individual parts have a physical logic which connects them and makes sense. Phrases are grouped together, and build up into longer units and sections. In this way, their individual and group timings give a dance its *form* and allow the audience to find a visual sense. Unphrased movement is like a blurred photograph: very difficult to make sense of or to watch for any length of time. Phrasing occurs naturally both in life itself and in other art forms like music, poetry, painting and film.

In technique class you will learn phrases which, by challenging your physical skills as a dancer, contribute to your dance training. These are not necessarily of the same kind as phrases found in choreography which has as its main aim *expression to an audience*. It is important that you, as a dancer and choreographer, learn to be sensitive to the differences between these two kinds of phrase.

Phrase length

> Phrase means length in time. Breathe length if you're angry, it's a short breath, it's a short phrase. If you are in a love scene, like Tristan and Isolde, it goes on forever, you're in a l-o-o-ng phrase.
>
> *(Martha Graham in* The Dance Makers, *1980)*

A phrase may be of any speed or duration, and there will be a mix in any one dance. When music is being used, the phrases are usually based on the underlying beat or musical form. Finding a movement's natural timing/phrasing allows you to alter it to suit whatever the expression demands. As Graham points out, breath can be a strong influence in phrase length – a forceful, sudden exhalation or panting, for example, will produce its own kind of phrase length. Increasing the depth of your breathing can give you a strong sense of where the phrase begins and ends. Each deep breath is a short phrase.

- inhale: rise, expand;
- hold: suspend, high point;
- exhale: fall, collapse, release into an action.

The length of a phrase is determined by its *content*. If a short punchy effect is required, the phrase will be a corresponding length.

TASK 15

Watch, on video, *Waiting* (Lea Anderson for Channel 4's *Tights Camera Action*, 1994, 3 minutes). Watch once, then a second time, and then give short answers to the following questions (you may even choose to watch a number of repeated viewings):

1 There are three phrases filmed front on. How are they similar? (2 marks)
2 Why does Anderson choose these similarities? (2 marks)
3 What effects are created from the use of the cigarettes and the wigs? (2 marks)
4 Where does the middle section start and end? (2 marks)
5 How are the phrase lengths different in this section, and why? (2 marks)
6 How do you know, at any point, how much time has gone by in the video? (4 marks)
7 What is the significance of the final 'wrinkle or tear'? (1 mark)
8 What is characteristic of the work of Lea Anderson in the way that the passing of time is treated in this videodance? (2 marks)
9 What makes a videodance different from a live stage performance? (2 marks)
10 In what ways does Lea Anderson exploit the possibilities of videodance in *Waiting*? (6 marks)

Total: 25 marks – answers are at the end of this section, on p. 89.

Phrase shape

The content of the phrase determines not only its length but also its *shape*. Our breath phrases, for example, will differ in shape. The deep breath has a clear high point, but the panting phrase is less shaped, with no real high or low points. These latter, more even phrases have their place within any dance composition, as they can give a sense of preparation for the more intense moments.

The shape of a phrase is mapped according to where its low and high points are. These may occur at the beginning, the middle or the end. The high point may be structured through an emphasis on any aspect of space, time or dynamics. It may be faster or stronger, or more expansive in space. And these changes can come about gradually or instantaneously.

Stillness may also be used in shaping. A catch of breath or a moment of hesitation or anticipation may provide time both to reflect on what has just happened and to heighten the impact of what is *about* to happen. A pause or a longer hold can help both to capture the attention of your audience and to increase their interest in your composition.

Time affects the dynamics of any movement. If you change the time taken by a movement, you change the *quality* of that movement. And furthermore:

Accuracy of time is necessary to maintain the desired space. Change the space and the time changes, unless the speed of the particular phrase changes in order to keep the time the same. Change the time and the space and the movement changes.

(Carolyn Brown in Merce Cunningham, *1975)*

TASK 16

Using sudden and sustained speeds, stillness, and different levels and sizes of movement, make three phrases of different shapes using the following words as guides:

- melt, float, collapse;
- erupt, crawl, pulsate;
- sparkle, float, fade.

Use breath as an accompaniment when possible – it may add to the shaping of the phrase.Improvise individually on this task.

(Recommended music: *Diva* film soundtrack.)

ANSWERS TO THE TASK 15 TEST ON *WAITING*

(Answers similar to those below are also acceptable.)

1 They are all of the same length, and they all use small gestural movements and facial expressions.

2 The repetitive feel conveys an atmosphere of time passing very slowly, restlessness, tedious waiting, fidgeting.

3 The cigarettes burning down show time passing. The wigs floating in slow motion convery a moment 'suspended' in time, a moment which last forever. This effect is enhanced when the wig continues to move even when the rest of the body has stopped – i.e. when the time of the phrase is *extended*.

4 It starts after the first overhead shot when all-over body movement begins, the camera shows more varied angles and the dancers start to change places. It ends just before the shots, taken from below, of the individual dancers.

5 The phrases are *longer*, because the all-over body movement requires more time to perform. The greater amount and size of movements in this section serve to build the dance up to a climax and to hold the viewers' attention.

6 A few seconds, 24 hours or a lifetime, depending on your point of view! The clock in the video starts and finishes almost at the same time.

7 There is some difference of opinion here. It could be a tear, because one of the dancers has fallen off the set. Or it could be an *ageing* of the skin, as would happen during a very long wait.

8 Anderson has an interest in how things change and transform – as seen in the 1993 *Precious*:

Like alchemists striving to turn metal into gold, the dancers sought to realise their dreams through a process of altered states and changing perspectives.

(from notes in The Cholmondeleys educational resource pack)

9 A videodance allows an opportunity to show things that are not possible in the real world. In stage performance, one limitation to the dancer's physical capabilities is the pull of gravity. Such limitations do not exist for filmed dance.

10 In the use of various camera and editing effects: dressing dancers identically in order to assist continuity; cutting in slow motion

to give an enhanced feel of suspension in time and space; using overhead shots to exploit the variation of motifs and add to distortion for interest; using distorted angles (particularly in the middle section) to create a feeling of uncertainty about whether what one is waiting for will ever actually happen. These techniques also make for a more surreal atmosphere, as in a Dali painting with people flying, walking on vertical surfaces and so on.

The dynamic component

Every moment varies *dynamically* along a range from light to strong. The dynamics and textures of a dance are like the colours of a painting. They create interest and contrast, as well as conveying much of the choreographer's intentions. In classical ballet, especially in the romantic tradition, the dominant dynamic is that of the sustained and the effortless. The tradition of modern dance, by contrast, emphasises heavy falls and suspended recoveries. Whichever tradition is being used, the choreographer needs an understanding of the terminology and analysis involved in the dynamics of dance.

Energy is the potential for action which gives the 'Go!' In dance training, finding the right amount of energy to perform a movement efficiently is a priority. In composing dances, the task is to find out how to use energy in a way that is most appropriate to whatever it is that is being expressed.

Energy remains neutral until a *force* is applied which *releases* it. Depending on the intensity of the force applied, the resulting movement will vary in its *weight* from strong to gentle. 'Weight' is a term used specifically by Rudolf Laban in his analysis of *effort*, but it is also a term used in the dance world generally.

When force and time act together, *dynamics* result, and there may be a sudden *strong* dynamic or a sudden *light* one. Some dynamics are quite specific and have their own names – like a swing, a collapse, a vibration or a percussive (sudden, strong, sharp, staccato) movement.

Laban defined a wide range of specific qualities which he called *efforts*. These are described by the way that space, time and weight are combined – see Table 3.1. In Laban's analysis, space refers to the pathway of a movement through the air.

Table 3.1 *The Eight Basic Efforts*

Effort	Time	Weight	Space
Punch	sudden	firm	direct
Float	sustained	light	flexible
Flick	sudden	light	flexible
Dab	sudden	light	direct
Press	sustained	firm	direct
Glide	sustained	light	direct
Slash	sudden	firm	flexible
Wring	sustained	firm	flexible

The broad spectrum of dynamics which is available for choreography should be explored to the full. In *Nympheas* (Robert Cohan, 1976), sustainment and suspension are first emphasised. Impressions of waterlilies floating and of the gentle movement of the water are conveyed. Contrast is then provided in the storm scene when the dynamic becomes more sudden, wild and free. And there is also a bouncy section for the male dancers suggestive of frogs hopping and jumping on lily pads.

The range of dynamics can also be used to portray *character*. Even in the world of classical ballet, with its dominance of smooth effort-lessness, subtle changes can still be used to great effect. In Sir Frederick Ashton's *The Dream* (1964), the characters are identified by the individual dancers' own inherent dynamic qualities. The original Puck, danced by Keith Martin, has robust, bouncy, driving character, well-suited to the impish spirit.

BAD Dance Company in In A BAAAAD WAY, by Linda Rickett. Try to describe the contrast in dynamics in these two photographs

TASK 17

Individually improvise to create a phrase which presents images from the landscape of a rainforest. These images may include: the sun rising above high mountains; waterfalls crashing down into a calm pool; rare orchids opening, and humming birds darting and hovering around them; the tilt of the high, cool mountain peaks; the sway and swing of a tree canopy; bathing and floating in the cool river; the crash of destructive bull-dozers. Make sure the phrase has a clear length and shape, and a variety of dynamics. (Suggested music: *Spirit of the Rainforest* by Terry Oldfield, New World.)

MOVEMENT COMPONENTS – CONCLUSION

The movement tasks outlined above have given ample opportunities to use a variety of stimuli as starting points for improvisation, composition and analysis.

In all aspects, the movement components involved in dance – as analysed above – are only as effective and expressive as the *dancers* who perform them, and it is with this point in mind that the next section of this chapter examines the choice of dancers and the demands placed upon them in performance.

The dancers

CHOOSING AND WORKING WITH DANCERS

We may wonder why certain dancers are chosen for a particular company or dance. There are a number of basic factors which we can pinpoint that influence the choreographer's choice:

- the number of dancers required;
- the particular role they are dancing;
- their physique;
- their gender.

Each of these will be considered in turn.

A choreographer ... has no way of expressing himself but through movements which he must implant in the muscles of other dancers.

(David Lichine in Ballet, *1947)*

Alvin looks for dancers who will bring some special quality and who can make a strong statement on stage. He is really quick to see if somebody's personality is the kind of personality that will give ... Alvin has a good eye for how we'll all look together.

(Elinor Rogosin on choreographer Alvin Ailey, in Dance Makers, *1980)*

That's why Balanchine is such a marvellous choreographer. He has a concept of his dancers ... he knows each of them so well that he can propose something for them to try that they might not be aware they can do.

(Twyla Tharp in Dance Makers, *1980)*

The statements above reflect various opinions about the choice of dancers and how a choreographer may work with them in order to draw out their best. Most professional choreographers have a large number of dancers to choose from, and they will choose the ones which most suit their own personal style. This may mean that certain dancer's *physique* will be right for a particular kind of technique; for example, Balanchine was famous for choosing very thin dancers in order to show off the classical lines that he required. Other choreographers may choose dancers for their *inner qualities*; for example, Lea Anderson prefers dancers of all shapes and sizes, but is concerned that they also be *thinking people*.

When you're doing lots of tiny movements that need to be linked or performed in such a way that the dancer looks as though they know why they're doing everything. Each movement has a reason behind it ... I'm constantly looking for things for dancers to be thinking on stage.

(Lea Anderson in interview)

In a similar way, choreographer Murray Louis is also concerned about this:

> There is a line in the film *The Turning Point* that made me cringe ... the abstract choreographer insisted the dancer bring no emotion to the movement. 'Just do the steps' ... I thought 'what every abstract choreographer wants is that his dancers invest the movement with what the movement requires without the overlay of extraneous emotionalism.'

(Murray Louis in Inside Dance*, 1976)*

When choosing dancers, you need to be clear about how they can enhance your dance, and you need also to be able to *show* them what role it is that you want them to bring to life. In dance companies, this is done over a long period of time, and it is unlikely that you, as a student, will have such a luxury. Your task is instead to achieve as much of a rapport with your dancers as possible in the short time you will have available. But the basic approach is the same: one of communication to and from dancer and choreographer – sharing information, questions and problems, and gradually building the common ground and the common understanding necessary for the dance to be shaped.

> Alston admits, 'I really like to establish an ongoing relationship with dancers.' ... he is constantly feeding the dancers he works with. Watch him in rehearsal and you see someone who isn't just telling the dancers what to do, he's advising them how to do it and explaining why it's best, easiest or most efficient to do it that way.

(Allen Robertson in Dance Now*, 1995)*

There are examples of choreographers in ballet and modern dance who have struck up special relationships with individual dancers. These are those rare occasions when a dancer and a choreographer act as a mutual 'spark' for each other. Richard Alston and Michael Clarke

worked together in this way in various works including *Soda Lake* (1981) and *Dutiful Ducks* (1982). Clark's training in ballet and in the Cunningham technique equipped him with fast foot work, an ability to change direction quickly and an open torso which curved with ease and fluidity. All these technical strengths suited Alston's style perfectly. Sir Frederick Ashton and Dame Margot Fonteyn had one of the longest working partnerships in ballet history. As with many of these relationships, however, the path was not always a smooth one. At first, Ashton found her difficult, imprecise and not able to use her body properly. He recalls:

> When I finally created for her the role of the bride in *Baiser la Fée*, I felt great frustration in being unable to mould her precisely as I wanted. Her performance needed to be much more precise. I got very cross with her at times and went on and on at her relentlessly. One morning after I had been particularly severe, she suddenly rushed and threw her arms around my neck and burst into floods of tears. I knew that I had won the battle; that I would be able to work with her.

(Keith Money in The Art Of Margot Fonteyn*, 1965)*

This confrontational working method would not suit all tastes, and indeed in later years it has had many critics. In the world of 1970s post-modern dance and British New Dance, a very different approach was adopted:

> From Ballet all the way to Cunningham technique, the dancer's body has been at the disposal of the choreographer to produce the desired effect. A technique equal to that was, and is, required ... The dancer was becoming more responsible; their direct contribution as themselves was more pertinent.

(Claire Hayes in New Dance*, 1987)*

Improvisation is used as an exploration into movement possibilities focusing on specific problems, which form the central point of the choreography. The dancers have the responsibility of discovering their own movement and energy level with the outer structure of the dance.

(Rosemary Butcher in New Dance*, 1977)*

This more collective way of working represented a shift of concern away from traditional working methods to those which held more holistic principles. The concern for the dancer *as a whole human being* is now the priority.

The number of dancers

The *number* of dancers that is chosen should be appropriate to the choreographic idea. A large corps de ballet is clearly going to have different visual impact from that of a trio or duet. Nineteenth-century ballet works usually involved large numbers of dancers at the end and soloists in the middle. In modern dance, by contrast, the groups tend to be smaller, and the performance of the group as a whole tends to be just as important – if not more so – than that of a soloist in any given piece.

Generally speaking, the more dancers there are, the more dramatic possibilities there will be. In a duet, the possible relationship – or conflict – is 1 vs 1. With four people, there are five possibilities:

- 1:1:1:1, or
- 2:1:1, or
- 2:2, or
- 3:1, or
- 4 together.

The possibilities do not end here, however, because *different* dancers may, at *different* times, act as the odd one out, and that increases the number of possible relationships again. In total, there are *15* possible combinations for a quartet.

TASK 18 ▼

In fours, read the notation placings in Figure 3.8. Decide together on the order in which to make these group shapes, and link them up with simple walking and running. Can you now find what the 15 different permutations for a quartet are? Add your findings to the original 5 shapes.

Bearing in mind how complex the possibilities are, it is thus especially advisable to ensure that the number of dancers be appropriate for a particular choreographic idea. If your starting point is a large painting with lots of action and figures, it may be appropriate to have 5, 6 or more dancers. And for a poem or story with a certain number of characters, the number of dancers needs to be the same.

In Robert Cohan's *Hunter of Angels* (1959), the choice of a male duet was ideal to tell the story of Jacob and Esau. It offered an opportunity to show the struggle between the twins, and it cleverly and economically involved one of the dancer's playing a *dual* role as both Esau and the angel which visits Jacob. The transition between these two characters was accomplished smoothly and convincingly.

Figure 3.8 *Notation showing placings for Task 18*

Pierrot Lunaire *by Glen Tetley*

The idea of a trio is, like that of a quartet, to weave the dancers together, as in Glen Tetley's *Pierrot Lunaire* (1962), where a couple is broken up by a third person (this work explores the classic story of relationships to its maximum). In full-length ballets like Sir Frederick Ashton's *The Dream*, 1964 and Glen Tetley's *The Tempest*, 1979 the Shakespeare stories hold many opportunities for different size groups to be used in the various dramatic situations, and for the different characters. Again, choosing the correct number of dancers is crucial to revealing the narrative. Later in this book, more attention will be given to timings for and the staging of groups.

Role

Choosing those dancers who are appropriate for a specific role has already been mentioned in the previous section on dynamics. An individual dancer may have natural tendencies towards certain qualities and specific technical abilities which make them ideal for certain roles. In classical ballet, this may often be the case with characterisation – Anthony Dowell as aristocratic Oberon in *The Dream* works well because of his natural elegant line. The same principle applies to post-modern works, but may not be so obvious. Speaking about the choreographer Rosemary Butcher, critic Stephanie Jordan points out:

> Her works, physically simple as they might appear, demand fine, experienced dancers and can be extraordinarily diminished in their absence.

> (*Stephanie Jordan in* Striding Out, *1992*)

Other post-modern choreographers like Bill T. Jones choose total 'non-dancers' as well as those with superb technique. In his *Still Here* (1994), Jones used people whom he had met through a therapy workshop for those who had lost loved ones through AIDS and other long-term terminal illnesses. Their taped testimonies, together with their role as actual performers in the piece, made the work 'undiscussible' for some critics (Arlene Croce in the *New Yorker*).

Physique

The dance world seems to have a predominance of *ectomorph* body types, perhaps especially in ballet (as already noted in Chapter 1). However, for performing lifts in pas de deux, a body strength in the legs and upper body is required which would seem to suggest the need for the more robust *mesomorph* body type. Similarly, in the post-modern genre, where responsibility for lifting is often shared equally throughout the group, suitable physiques are more likely to make for safety and injury prevention, and the dance itself should also ultimately look better for the audience as a result.

The choreographic demands of the corps de ballet are such that a uniform physique is a prerequisite. This may also be observed in some mainstream modern dance companies. By contrast, in the post-modern genre we see the most diversity in physiques, as in The Cholmondleys, The Featherstonehaughs, Bill T. Jones's company and so on.

Gender

A not dissimilar situation exists in choosing dancers for their gender. Certain roles in classical ballet demand specifically male or female performers, according to conventional stereotyping, and this may also be the case, of course, in some modern dance choreography. Take, for example, Martha Graham's 1944 *Appalachian Spring* work which uses the heterosexual role model, with her as bride and Eric Hawkins as groom (Hawkins went on to become her husband in real life). Merce Cunningham's works, by contrast, tend to be rather more *androgynous* in that his parts seem able to be interchangeable between males and females. This is a feature which we also notice in the work of post-modern choreographer

Richard Alston. In *Soda Lake* (1981), Alston states quite clearly that it is a solo for either gender. Although originally choreographed for Michael Clark, in its later revival for the Rambert, it was danced sometimes by Mark Baldwin and sometimes by Amanda Britton. The nature of the movement is such that it has a gender-neutrality. It is the fact that the dancers have a similar training in Cunningham and ballet techniques that is the main reason for choosing them.

Post-modern choreographer Mark Morris also uses androgyny in his work, not through the gender-neutrality of the movement but by smashing the accepted norms of classical ballet and deliberately swapping roles around. This anarchic attitude to tradition and to gender stereotyping is best seen, perhaps, in his version of *The Nutcracker*, called *The Hard Nut* (1993). In the dance of the snowflakes (a section well-known to ballet-goers), the stage is filled with dancers dressed uniformly, moving in unison en pointe and so on. Nothing unusual you may say, until you notice that these accomplished dancers are a mixture of men and women all executing the same movement, albeit with differing aplomb. The different qualities of the different genders render the movement a new richness and excitement. This tendency in post-modern choreographers to reject traditional gender stereotypes reflects a concern for political correctness in sexual politics. Choreographers like Lloyd Newson, with his company DV8, are concerned with such issues as homophobia, and he casts the dancers appropriately. For example, in *Strange Fish* (1992), the opening image is a naked female Christ on the cross. Similarly, Lea Anderson has a concern for breaking down traditional stereotypes:

> The way I choose to show people is very conscious. I choose not to use very stereotypical role models and I choose very carefully what gender does what. It is deliberate. I'd never show a bloke chucking a woman about ... I've seen enough of those. ...

> *(Lea Anderson in interview, educational resource pack on Flesh and Blood)*

Strange Fish *by DV8 Physical Theatre*

There are many moments in Anderson's choreography where alternative gender values are presented. In *Birthday* (1992) – later to become a video dance *Perfect Moment* (1992), director Margaret Williams – three couples are kissing in unison. The audience is challenged by the choice of mixed genders to work out which of the dancers make up which of the couples.

Put at its simplest, there are two possibilities when choosing dancers. You could first choose the dancer and then build the choreography around their individual characteristics. Or you could choose a dancer whose style, physique and personality already suits your own choreographic idea.

References and resources

BOOKS

Crisp, C. and Clarke, M., *Making a Ballet*, London: Studio Vista, 1974.

Ellfeldt, L., *A Primer for Choreographers*, London: Dance Books, 1988

— *Dance, from Magic to Art*, Iowa, Wm C. Brown Company, 1976

Hay, D., *Lamb at the Altar* (the story of a dance made with trained and untrained dancers)

Humphrey, D., *The Art of Making Dances*, New Jersey: Princeton Book Co., 1991

Klosty, J. (ed), *Merce Cunningham*, Clarke, USA: Irwin & Co. Ltd., 1975

Morrison Brown, J. (ed), *The Vision Of Modern Dance*, London: Dance Books, 1979

Rogosin, E., *The Dance Makers*, New York: Walker & Co., 1980

VIDEOS

Ballet Rambert, *Different Steps: Three Approaches to Choreography*, Rambert Dance Co., tel.: 0181 995 4246, 1985

The Royal Ballet and the University of Surrey, *The Dream*, available from the University of Surrey's Dance Studies Department, tel.: 01483 300 800, 1994. Also, an accompanying information pack

DV8 Physical Theatre, *Strange Fish* and *Dead*

Dreams of Monochrome Men, from Dance Videos, tel.: 0171 836 2314, 1995

The Kirov Ballet, Polygram 079 206 3. Includes excerpts from *Petrushka, Chopiniana, Adagio* (Barber), *Le Corsaire, The Fairy Doll, Markitenka, Paquita*

Lea Anderson, *Waiting* from *Tights Camera Action*, series II, Channel 4, 1994, used in Task 15

MUSIC

The following have lots of tracks between 2 and 3 minutes long:

Morricone, E., *The Mission*, Virgin Records, CDV 2402-257994, 1986, recommended for Task 6

Malcolm Arnold, *English and Irish Dances*, Polygram 425 661 2LM, 1990 recommended for Task 4

Contemporary Dance Rhythms, 1996 available from John Jalib Millar at Shamal Studios,

65 Bayham Street, Camden, London. Tel.: 0171 388 8205, recommended for Task 7

Tomita, I., *Pictures at an Exhibition*, by Moussorgsky (electronic version), RCA ARL1-0838, 1975, recommended for Task 8

Serra Eric, *The Big Blue*, soundtrack to the film *The Big Blue*, Gaumont/Virgin CDV 2541, 1988, recommended for Task 14

Soundtrack from the film *Diva*, Discovery Label, CD950622 recommended for Task 16

Terry Oldfield, *Spirit of the Rainforest*, New World, NWC 195, recommended for Task 17

chapter four
THE CONSTITUENT FEATURES OF DANCE: THE PHYSICAL SETTING

The movement and dancers are a main consideration, but of course, the complete picture also includes the choices of:

- the performing space or venue;
- the set;
- lighting;
- costume;
- props.

These will be the focus of this chapter.

The performing space

The type of space that a dance is performed in will affect the design of the choreography. The dancers themselves will also need to relate to the environment in which they are dancing. With both the dance and the dancers actively relating to the performing space, the audience should have a clear view of the performance in all its aspects. The following quotation makes this clear.

> My first piece *Tank Dive*, was made for a small room ... that is actually a little auditorium ... and the whole piece is predicated for that space; I mean one of the walls was curved, so a lot of patterns had to do with that. It has very much to do with site lines.
>
> *(Twyla Tharp in* The Dance Makers, *1980)*

Although we usually expect to see dance on a stage, nowadays choreographers work in many different types of venue. Dances can even be seen in enormous outdoor spaces – such as in Twyla Tharp's *Medley* which was designed to be visible 300 yards away. In the post-modern era, dancing in airports, tunnels, art galleries, museums and gymnasiums, and on rooftops and beaches, have all been considered to be suitable for performance.

THE PROSCENIUM STAGE

When you go to the theatre, the picture-frame *proscenium* stage is the traditional set-up. This is the one most often used for classical ballet, and it offers rich possibilities for showing things clearly if it is used correctly.

The historical context

In the fifteenth century, Italians staged lavish indoor spectacles. Theatres dating back to 1580 can be found in Italy. There would be a raised stage framed with a proscenium arch.

These were fairly open so that the performers, often courtiers, could move easily from the auditorium to the stage. Sometimes, the *audience* would perform too.

The placement of dancers

Placing and moving dancers around on such stages must take into consideration the fact that different areas have differing degrees of *power*. Dancers placed upstage will appear *distant* (in space *and* time) for the audience, whereas downstage has a feel of more intimacy, and can be used for comic effect. The stage is divided into named areas as shown in Figure 4.1.

To show a stage from Florence 1616

Figure 4.1   *To show stage areas and their possible uses*

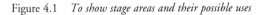

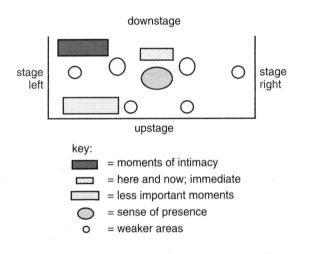

The picture-frame stage is a very specialised place. Hot spots and cooler areas, as seen in Figure 4.1 are of paramount concern when deciding where to place certain characters. In the classic romantic ballet *Giselle* (Coralli and Perrot, 1841), it is noticeable that Hilarion, the gamekeeper, uses the downstage area more than the other characters. His rage and suspicion and the confrontational nature of his character are enhanced by the nearness to the audience. Giselle herself dies centre stage (dead centre!). This makes the denial of her life appear totally tragic to the audience. The fairy king Oberon's first appearance in Ashton's

The Dream is placed far off in the distant upstage. The effect here is to make him all-powerful and not of this earth, in control of the fairy kingdom from on high.

The movement of dancers on pathways in the stage space

Similarly, the *diagonals* on the stage are very powerful. According to Doris Humphrey, if a figure walks down from upstage right to downstage left, this action:

> … will clothe this figure with heroic strength, all made merely by the use of architecture of stage space.

> *(Doris Humphrey in* The Art of Making Dances, *1959)*

On this pathway, the dancer will pass through weaker and more powerful points of the stage space – not least of which is centre-stage, where the presence will be at its strongest. Approaching downstage, the dancer will then become more human, someone we care about. This device is used in *Giselle* when Hilarion is being thrown into the lake by the *wilis*. Starting downstage left, bottom corner, Myrtha, Queen of the wilis, seals his fate by ordering him to his watery grave, the lake. He is propelled along the line of the corps de ballet stretching the whole length of the diagonal to the far upstage right corner. The other dancers seem almost invisible, their fine arm gestures, so effortless, stirring the air as he is blown along. Then, he finally exits. Gone from the human world, he is now forever in the distance of time and space, in the immortal world.

There are always exceptions to the rules, however, and choreographer Merce Cunningham, although acknowledging the stage space as such, chooses to ignore the above considerations. He makes it the responsibility of the *audience* to decide what to select to watch in dances that scatter over the space like leaves blown by the wind. There is *no* central focus of power. This is particularly noticeable in his dance *Tread* (1970). The electric fans, designed by Bruce Nauman, are regularly spaced across the front of downstage, causing not only an interruption in the audience's sight lines but also a breeze in the first few rows. This puts the viewer in a situation where, as in real life on the street, you must make choices as to what to watch and when. You could focus on the entire stage, or on just one small area between two fans, or on Cunningham's interrupted journey across the stage. It is almost as though the picture frame has gone and the stage is filled with dancers in any number of places, all of equal importance. Cunningham's attitude to space is similar to that of American modern painters of the 1960s and 1970s, like Jackson Pollock whose technique of dripping paint randomly onto canvas gave the effect of a continuous flow through the space.

> Cunningham inherited a stage space … a formula of perspective unchanged since the Renaissance. As a result, stage space implied a class society in which centre stage was regal. … The sides, the back and corners? Strictly plebeian, home of the brave corps. … There is no *best* spot on a Cunningham stage. … The stage is not merely decentralised, it is demagnetised.

> *(James Klosty in* Merce Cunningham, *1975)*

When working in venues with an audience on two, three or four sides, Cunningham would give different dancers different fronts. This would create more of a 3-dimensional look – one well suited to the next physical setting which we are looking at.

IN-THE-ROUND: THE CIRCULAR STAGE

The 'in-the-round' physical setting, which dates back to the ancient Greek chorus set-up, and even before that to circles in ritual dances, alters our whole attitude to – and concept of – design; and even nowadays, it is difficult for some to make the adjustment to the circular setting. Consideration must here be given to a *3-dimensional* design in the choreography – particularly in the placing and facings of the dancers. This, as just mentioned, would pose little problem for a Cunningham choreography – unlike for most ballet and modern dance works, which may have been framed for the proscenium stage.

Obviously, circle patterns and circular group shapes will work well, and this makes for many possibilities: to face the centre and give a feel of a magical magnetic centre; to spiral around to and from the centre, like the Snail formation in a mediaeval *Carole* (line dance); to place the dancers' backs to the centre and acknowledge the outside space; to proceed around the edge of the circle in a ritualistic manner, to crisscross the circle with other geometric formations like triangles, squares, lines or less formal clusters of dancers. Acknowledging the power of the circle can lead to much choreographic interest. Using it in an uninformed way, on the other hand, may lead to a drab design which does not allow the audience 'in', either because it comes over as 2-dimensional or because too much use is made of inward/centre facings. (It is interesting to observe how young children's or beginners' first attempts at choreography often involve working in an inwards-facing circle. All that the audience can then see are their backs, obscuring any interesting movement which may be happening.)

To show use of circle formations: Nureyev and Fonteyn in La Bayadere

In Robert North's *Troy Game* (1974), the circle is used to emphasise the amusing atmosphere of sparring and competition between soldiers. The group travel around the circle in a motif which allows them to acknowledge the audience, the centre of the circle and each other. It has an alive, 3-dimensional quality.

By manipulating the turns and the timing, they rotate and try to catch each other out by a sweeping leg gesture, rather like a football tackle to the opponent's lower leg. Each soldier jumps over this tackle just in time. Thus, the circle continues to 'hypnotise' and to amuse the audience simultaneously.

TASK 1 ▽▼ ▽▼ ▽▼ OR ▽▼

In groups of 6 or 8, work together to compose a dance entitled 'Black holes, shooting stars, the planets and their spinning moons'. Choreograph it with a view to performing it in-the-round. (Suggested music: 'Alienscape' on *Dancetechnic*, by David Harry, 1992, available from Primrose Studio, Lancaster.)

OTHER STAGES

As well as the performing settings mentioned above, there are others which also require consideration about the placings and spacings of dancers in choreography. Although similar to the proscenium stage or in-the-round, they each have their own individual characteristics:

- *End stage:* there is no frame or arch, and the stage and the auditorium continue into each other.

- *Apron stage:* part of the stage projects into the audience.

In any of these, *where* the audience is seated – in terms of above or below the stage – will affect what they see. If they are lower than the stage, then the front vertical lines will be emphasised. On the other hand, the movement in the horizontal plane, the floor pattern and the formation will be stressed if the audience is seated above the stage.

THE SITE-SPECIFIC PERFORMANCE SPACE

We may think that dance performances out-of-doors are something quite avant-garde and post-modern, but before the courts of Europe introduced the proscenium stage they held spectacles of quite a different type: the wealthy Italian aristocracy of the High Renaissance held spectacular pageants out of doors as well as inside the palaces. Centuries later in the 1960s, dancers and choreographers returned to outside settings as an alternative to the theatres. They also looked for alternative indoor venues in which to present dances which used their environment as a rich source of stimulus

for the imagination. And now, dances are performed anywhere and everywhere. The choreographer Lea Anderson – in the 1990s – and Rosemary Butcher typify the attitude of choosing unconventional performing spaces.

These more informal environments pose very different problems for choreographers. As Rosemary Butcher became aware, in her out-of-doors work, the dance can tend to get lost in the surrounding architecture, or amongst passers-by. For this reason, she later used the perspectives and distances of specific sites to

BAD Dance Company on outdoor location

To show outdoor spectacles of the Renaissance, Alcina's Island, 1664, in the grounds of the Palace of Versailles. It uses the lake as part of the set. The island in the centre back was burnt in a huge firework display. The wings are supported by guy ropes

her advantage. In *Passage North East* (1976), Butcher first placed the dancers in the distance: on the far side of the harbour to the Arnolfini Gallery, Bristol. Then, they crossed by boat to end up dancing to the audience in front of the gallery. In North America in the 1960s, many other artists also experimented with these more informal settings, both indoors and out. One such artist was Anna Halprin. Halprin was part of the Judson Group, New York (started 1962), which comprised dancers who were working as a cooperative. This set a trend later in the UK when X6 set up a similar group in London in 1986.

> We don't accept the theatre as a conventional place where the audience is here and you're there, but it *is* a place. ... You don't have to be on the stage separating here from there. ... Everything we do is dance somehow...
>
> (*Anna Halprin in* The Vision of Modern Dance, *1980*)

Such informal indoor and outdoor settings offer different ways for the audience to relate to the choreography. In X6, choreographers like Madee Dupres experimented with how she could build an easy relationship with the audience in these settings. Her audiences were asked to comment or even to take part sometimes. In *Choice and Presence* (1977), they were invited to make noises of their own choice when she raised a foot. Thus, the audience was involved not just visually but also audibly and sometimes physically. In the same piece mentioned above, they would also raise and lower blinds as she improvised the dance. Clearly, this way of choreographing is *not* concerned with the rules and sight lines of the picture-frame proscenium stage!

TASK 2 ▽ OR ▽▽▽

Walk around your campus and find a place you feel that you could dance in. Spend some time there, and discover what parts of it draw your attention – a space between the buildings, a tree, a staircase, a bench ... Watch, and listen. What type of people use this space? Do they leave certain energies behind them that may add atmosphere to your dance?

Gradually add things to this place – in movement, or in objects, costume etc. – that make clearer the special qualities of the place. They might echo the buildings, shapes, light, sound, memories evoked. Develop movements which draw attention to your discoveries about this place. What is special about it? Is it dangerous? Is it fun? Is it busy or calm? It is a place for travelling or waiting? What makes it different?

The basic physical setting may be transformed by whatever a choreographer may choose to place in it. This will be the next aspect of the physical setting to be considered.

The set

In the outdoor environment, of course, 'set' is often already present, and the choreographer may choose merely to add to it. On the stage, however, the choice of set is individual to each dance and to each choreographer, and involves anything from leaving the stage plain and bare to covering it with plastic carnations or dead leaves as Pina Bausch did in *Carnations* (1982) and *Bluebeard* (1977). (The trampling of the flowers under the dancers' feet is Bausch's way of telling us that people often crush each other in their relationships; and the dead leaves similarly remind us of a couple whose romance is gradually fading.)

The history of ballet shows how sets gradually evolved alongside the development of technique and choreography.

THE HISTORICAL

By the sixteenth century, the set began to become important. The theories of Roman architect Vitruvius were revived, and three types of stage set emerged:

1 *scena tragica*, showing objects suited to monarchs;
2 *scena comica*, showing ordinary houses;
3 *scena satyrica*, showing pastoral scenes.

These would underline the messages which the entertainments contained. This is particularly clear to us when we notice the use of complex machinery to make gods and heroes appear from the heavens. Note that at the time of the Renaissance, amazing the audience was the stamp of authority of the ruling families. It would function to enforce their power over others. It was also an acceptance of Aristotle's belief that theatre existed to release the emotions. As the sixteenth century progressed, backdrops became interchangeable through a variety of ingenious devices, and it was at this time that the proscenium stage first appeared. The use of perspective to add to the illusion gave events like *Le Ballet Comique de la Reine* (1581) a focal point in the auditorium – which is where the royals would sit, centre front row. This has influenced the design of proscenium stages in theatres ever since.

By the seventeenth century, wings had also been invented, and theatres now sprang up – particularly in Italy. The proscenium became properly established, and a splendour of machinery, colour, light and dance exploded.

In the eighteenth century, luxurious Italian and French spectacles were set against meticulously painted backdrops of staggering architectural realism. These larger-than-life sets marked the pinnacle of neoclassical theatre dance in the late eighteenth century and early nineteenth centuries. Respect for order, antiquity, heroism and nobility were the characteristics of theatre design, particularly in Italy. People like Sanquirico designed sets with perspectives painted with mathematical precision, giving an ordered appearance. The French Rococo design was particularly outstanding at this time, and there was also a growing taste for the exoticism of China and the East – as seen in *Les Fêtes Chinoises* (1754) by Jean-Georges Noverre in Paris. This fashion was combined with a move away from seventeenth-century formality in favour of a more natural look. This was in the context of a growing curiosity about freedom of expression both in society and in the other arts generally.

The rebellion against the cold logic of neoclassicism, which itself was a reaction against the more frivolous Rococo style, finally resulted in the great era of romanticism in society and all the arts. Revolution in *society* was a main influence here. The French Revolution was about to explode, and with it the ordinary people were to become leading lights in society, replacing the European aristocracy in the bid for power. As such, they became part of the romanticist backdrop from which writers, musicians and painters could choose elements when telling stories.

Ballet was a late arrival to the romanticist movement. In 1820, at the Paris Opera House, ballets were finally produced outside of the operas themselves. The writings of Victor Hugo and others began to influence ballet. The breakthrough came with *La Sylphide* (1832). With Marie Taglioni in the lead role and designs by Ciceri, an atmosphere of magical moonlit forest glades and floating sylphs was created. In the nineteenth century, the painted backdrop of the romantic ballet – with its realistic trees and even *real* plants, and its mirrors placed to look like lakes, as in the original *Giselle* – became the new fashion.

The decline of this burst of freedom of expression in the middle and the end of the nineteenth century affected the design of sets as well as the standard of dancing and choreography. Set designs now became largely mindless and decorative, with little meaning or originality. Only in Russia were standards upheld, and even there tradition was becoming stale. However, it was from here that ballet was to be reborn in glittering glory, like the phoenix rising from the flames, when a rich Russian patron of the arts, Sava Mamontov, commissioned painters to design sets for his private operas. From this, Serge Diaghilev was inspired by the painters Bakst and Benois to go on to found the Ballet Russes, which became a

hot bed of innovation. The closeness of designer, composer and choreographer, insisted on by Diaghilev, led to explorations into creative new ideas and ideals for all aspects of the ballet. Diaghilev employed names like Picasso (*Parade*, 1917) and Tchelitchev (*Ode*, 1923) – the avant garde of European painters. Thus, ballet began to look forward once more. Gone were the weary, worn pre-war images.

Europe was in post-war turmoil, and in this context the Ballet Russes took on the break with the past, as did cubism in painting and discord in the new music of such composers as Stravinsky and Satie. It was a meeting point and a melting pot for ideas which struck out in new directions. Consequently, stage design took on many different functions and identities: the humorous novelty of moving skyscrapers in the cubist *Parade*, where costumes became so extreme that it was difficult not to see them as sets rather than as dancer's clothes; or the then daring and sensual evocative colours of the Bakst design for *Schéhérazade* (1910). In *Ode* (1923), the revolutionary use of phosphorescent costumes, neon lighting, puppets and film to tell the story of eighteenth-century Russian court spectacles and revels was astonishing to audiences of that time. The Ballet Russes, from its Monte Carlo theatre, was touching base, and in Russia the new politics of communism interested Diaghilev. Along with this went artistic developments like constructivism. This movement was influenced by cubism but focused on making constructions which explored space and form for their own sake. The famous constructivist Gabo designed the set for *La Chatte* (1927). The transparent mica sculptures on a black floor and backdrop were uniquely original in that time.

La Chatte, *designed by Naum Gabo*

THE PRESENT DAY

Some modernisation of the conservative painted backdrop is now common, and the tradition of commissioning contemporary artists continues. One such designer who worked closely with Sir Frederick Ashton was the Russian born Sophie Fedorovitch. Her design for *La Fête Étrange* (1940, London Ballet, by Andrée Howard) combined the traditional with a sense of simplicity and economy which are more modern in style.

Simplicity and paring things down to their very basics was one of the innovations of the hard-hitting modern dance works of Martha Graham in the 1920s and 1930s. Talking about the difference between traditional painted backdrops and modern dance decors, she says:

... basically a painting enlarged for the stage ... at best can only be an *accent* for the dance. ... Dance decor can ... serve as a means of enhancing movement and gesture to the point of revelation of its content.

(Martha Graham in The Vision of Modern Dance, *1980)*

In her collaborations with the Japanese sculptor Isamu Noguchi, in dances such as *Frontier* (1935), the set became integrated into the choreography and served to enhance the meanings in the movements. In *Frontier*, a six-minute solo, Graham appears as a young woman living in the wild western lands of the USA. The set is a section of a fence, from which two large ropes fly out and upwards like the railway track disappearing into the vast open spaces which surround her home. The dance is about the North American pioneering spirit on one level, but it also touches on how the space makes the woman feel. She marks out a square pattern on the floor – almost like the fence bordering a ranch – using tiny steps.

From this point onwards, a rich variety of set designs opened up. Merce Cunningham's collaborations with famous avant-garde painters has produced some intense and remarkable moments of choreography. In *Rainforest* (1968), the dancers moved among helium-filled silver pillows designed by Andy Warhol. This is typical of the unpredictable element in Cunningham's work. The design, music and dance are all independently created, only coming together in performance. This is designed not only to surprise the audience but also to add to the environment in which the

dancers are performing. The dancers in *Rainforest* move around and between the pillows with ease and with little concern. The dance and the pillows may be connected or not: the decision lies with each dancer and with each member of the audience. This is a very different attitude from that of Martha Graham whose sets are there to support the symbolism and emotional meanings of the choreography.

In Britain's New Dance movement, post-modern choreographers were exploring the set as a part of their overhaul of the values and strategies of dance. Choreographer Rosemary Butcher, with her parallel interest in the visual arts, has often collaborated with sculptors, architects and visual artists. In *Five-Sided Figure* (1980), the shapes of the geometric structures created by artist Jon Groom were either matched or contrasted in the choreography. Lea Anderson, on her part, rarely uses sets in her work, but in 1994 motorbikes *were* used in

RainForest *by Merce Cunningham*

Metalcholia, and in 1995 *Car* featured a silver Saab 9000. The choreography here is in, on and around the car, which is driven on and off throughout the three sections of the piece.

The role of the car as an icon in our lives is torn apart – from political assassinations to film, from a sexual object to a simple power statement. Cars will never be the same again.

(In a programme note for Go Las Vegas, *1995)*

Anderson is always probing and questioning our acceptance of many social values. We are challenged, questioned and open to uncomfortable scrutiny.

TASK 3 ▽

(Extra time is also needed to collect the boxes.)

In a large group, collect as many different-sized cardboard boxes as possible. Mix them with blocks, chairs, ladders, benches and any other structural objects to hand, and arrange these in unexpected angles to create an environment. Explore ways of moving under, over, around and through the structure.

Compose a movement around ideas selected from the following:

● restriction
● shape
● escape
● change
● hide and seek.

A given set may enhance choreography by reinforcing the images which are being used or by acting as a complementary dimension in time and space. Or it may act simply to accompany the movement as an independent element on the stage. Whatever its function within the dance, the set may itself also be changed and transformed by the use of different *lighting* effects. This other aspect of physical setting is the next one which we will look at.

Lighting

From minute to minute in our everyday lives, we respond to changes in the light around us. This is a natural reaction exploited to the full in the theatre. From the earliest days of classical ballet, through the discovery of the use of ether for stage lighting, to the spectacular possibilities of today's lasers and other forms of technology, the use of changes in light has served to influence the audiences' reactions massively. As Lois Fuller discovered:

Notre Dame! ... what enchanted me more than anything was ... the rays of sunlight that vibrated in the church, in various directions, intensely coloured, as a result of having passed through sumptuous windows.

(Lois Fuller in The Vision of Modern Dance, *1979)*

A change in light triggers an automatic response in us. It attracts our attention, and it defines space. Atmospheres of warmth, danger, isolation and fear are here all possible.

THE HISTORICAL CONTEXT

During the Renaissance, and up until the middle of the seventeenth century, candles and daylight would have been the only source of lighting for any performances. With the invention of oil lamps and candelabra, however, more elaborate lighting effects became possible. These were then added to by the use of reflection in mirrors, and simple projection was also introduced. Fireworks displays further became common. But it was the invention of gas lighting in the 1830s which was to make a real difference. The romantic ballet could now be danced in a convincing moonlight. The gas itself, *ether*, became a source of fantasy for writers and poets of the day. Its effect on the mind was to produce hallucinations of mystery, and the word 'ethereal', meaning 'beyond the real, in the supernatural', was born. The ethereal included anything weird and wonderful. Spirits roaming in the dark, deepest forests, not unlike vampires, ghosts or ghouls – anything strange and exotic was the fashion.

In 1831, a designer named Ciceri staged *Robert the Devil* at the Paris Opera. The moonlit cloisters, where white-veiled nuns emerged from their stone tombs, marked the beginning of many such scenes in the romantic ballets which followed. The famous Act Two of *Giselle* must have been a revelation for the audiences. Ciceri's forest glade was both dark and light but with a ghostly supernatural moonlight, and here the spirits of maidens who were abandoned on their wedding night roamed, vengefully seeking out victims, without pity for any man who may wander their way. In the gaslight, the wilis – as they were called – must have seemed to have been floating off the ground.

THE PRESENT DAY

Before going on to look at the modern-day use of light in dance, it is first of all worth considering a few technical aspects about lighting.

Different sorts of lights

- *Floods:* these give a general wash, or light the *cyclorama* (the back wall – usually white).
- *Battens:* these are rows of lights.
- *Spots:* there are two kinds: one gives a softer look – a *fresnel*, while, on the other hand, a *focus* gives a harder edge – i.e. a sharply defined beam. Both of these can have attachments which restrict the size of the circle of light: an *iris diaphragm*, and *barn doors* which reduce the spillage of light into unwanted areas.

Boundaries between areas can be established. The use of projected slides, film and video can add to the technical effects.

- *Gels:* these can be slid into frames and fitted onto the front of the lights to give colour. Warm pinks and ambers, cooler light blues and steel or intense greens and deep reds and blues are all possible. Generally, the deeper the gel the dimmer the light will be produced. Mixing gels will give other tints, like yellow (red + green) or purple (red + blue), but this will dim the brightness of the light.

When using lighting, the colour of the costumes must be considered. Costumes will usually look better if lit by a mix of pale, sympathetic tints. Blue light on red fabric will make the red disappear. The choice of light colour can change the mood, create images and add a symbolic meaning to enhance the dance.

The *direction* from which the light shines is another important consideration. In dance, a side light at the body level works well because it gives depth and moulds well to the flexible body of the dancer. Overhead light is the one most used.

It is always advisable to *cross-light*, that is, light an area from more than one direction. Large amounts of light from front-of-house above will give a stagey look, whilst light shone from a low level only can create eerie shadows.

The *intensity* of light can also vary to give effects like – at the end of a dance – a slow fade-down or a snap blackout. Similarly, at the start of a dance, the scene may gradually become visible, or figures may first appear just as silhouettes or as lit figures in general darkness. A *cross-fade*, where some lights fade up as others fade down, may be used to change from one scene to another – changing the atmosphere from, say, daytime to night.

Effects such as *gobos* (cut-out patterns placed in front of a light) can create patterns for dancers to move through – such as a forest glade. This can also be done by the projection of cut-out designs, a device which can distort the bodies of the dancers. Flashing lights, in turn, can give a lively, disco feel, and strobes and colour wheels can be useful too.

The work of Alwin Nikolais is renowned for its stunning and elaborate blend of light, slides and effects. Nikolais transforms the human shape of his dancers, makes them disappear, and then makes them reappear in kaleidoscopes patterns of colour. His *Somniloquy* (1967) makes use of a slide projection onto a gauze curtain, in a setting like the mouth of a cave. Dancers appear behind this curtain, their faces lit by hand-held torches. When they shine the torches onto the gauze, they make patterns on it. The projections change colour many times: blue, green, red, purple, silver. Finally, a projection of many *white* dots places the dancers in a snowstorm. Nikolais' concerns

in his choreography are with the environment that we all live in. It changes, and *we* too change in a constant battle for survival.

In almost total contrast, the dance *Soda Lake* (Richard Alston for Michael Clarke, 1981) is daring in its simple use of plain white light. This post-modern solo is danced in simple black costume, accompanied by silence and by minimalist sculpture for the set. Such a paring-down of the physical setting to its bare minimum is a characteristic of a particular kind of postmodern approach.

Siobhan Davies' *The Glass Blew In* (1994) explored the differences between *human* qualities and those that have to do with shape and texture. The lighting was designed by Peter Mumford, and the original programme note says it all:

> The piece is a sensuous, poetic interplay of colour, pattern, dynamic and sound . . . Mumford has marked out the stage with a rectangle whose floor is at different times, a wash of green violet or magenta. . . . It gives full rein to Davies' fascination with borders. She presents her dancers not only inside the rectangle, but also on or outside its demarcation.

(From the original programme for The Glass Blew In *by Siobhan Davies, 1994)*

The closeness of the dance and its lighting design is seen at its most intense here. Not only does the light support the mood, it also defines the actual space environment in which the dancers move.

In Lea Anderson's *Go Las Vegas* (1995, lighting by Simon Corder for the Featherstonehaughs), the audience itself contributed to the lighting. On entering the theatre, they were provided with small torches, and instructions were given in the programme, and verbally by one of the dancers, on exactly when and how these were to be used. At a signal, the torches are shone onto the dancer's phosphorescent silver suits, so that these light up whilst the dancers' faces and hands remain in blackness. The suits thus dance as if they have a life of their own. It is a fitting finale to a dance which has shredded the glitz and glamour of faceless showbiz – another direct hit at an aspect of our society which Anderson scrutinises, turns on its head and leaves well and truly deconstructed.

They're a pack of good time anarchists who take on the dance establishment with rambunctious glee.

(Review of Go Las Vegas *in* Time Out *magazine, 1995)*

TASK 4 ▽

From the list of dance titles below, choose one and describe how you would light it. Make clear how it would start and end. Describe any changes which occur during the dance. Keep it simple.
Be sure to include notes on colour, direction, intensity, special effects.

- 'The corridors of power'
- 'Water scene'
- 'Silent movies'
- 'What goes around comes around'.

You may not have access to lights, but when next at the theatre or watching dance on video, be sure to keep an eye out for how the lighting is used to enhance the dance.

Costume

Any costume can be worn in relation to a dance. One can make the *most* of its restrictions, or one can use it to enhance both the general visual design and the particular ideas/concerns of the dance. In this sense, it is like choosing the right sort of lighting: it should be appropriate to, and should enhance, the overall purpose and expressivity of the dance. The following are the most basic considerations in the choice of costume:

- shape
- colour
- material.

THE HISTORICAL CONTEXT

In the spectacles of the late sixteenth and early seventeenth centuries, costumes were highly theatrical. Rich fabrics and fantastic designs were often used to enhance character. Some designs were grotesque and evil, others were harmonious, and the animal world was represented by the decoration of animal skins, the use of parrots and so on. Mortals and immortals mixed together in a world of magic and illusion.

To show Berain design 1616, Habit d'Africain

Habit d'Africain

By the middle of the seventeenth century, the world of fashion and very expensive clothes were a priority for the courts of Europe. The professional dancers of the court ballets had to dress elegantly and stylishly. The costumes were decorated symbolically so that the story was clear to the monarch and the court. After all, the ballets were usually about them, and so court dress with some decoration suited the occasion. According to the etiquette of the court, a dancer representing the monarch would be presented on stage for the monarch himself to admire! The way a man bowed or received bows told everything about him, and the audience too understood the symbolism of the costumes and choreography. The court life was thus presented in dance, and everything was done to support the power of the monarchy. Often, the ruler would be shown in the finale as the god Apollo or as the Sun, the supreme being within his domain. It must have been a

fine line between who was just a performer and who was part of the *real* court, and hence the entertainments could make both political and imaginative statements at the same time.

The male dancers' designs allowed freedom of movement, but the females' skirts had to reach the ground. Masks were popular to show stylised characters such as sweet nymphs or hideous demons.

Gradually the court ownership over the theatres of Vienna, Milan and Paris weakened, and a more independent, professional dance tradition emerged. At the Paris Opera in the early eighteenth century, ballet became free as a performing art. The success of *Les Fêtes Chinoises* (1754, Jean-Georges Noverre), revealed a new interest in the foreign and exotic. The rigid rules of costuming according to prescribed characters were less important, and as the need to move took priority, skirts shortened. In the 1730s, Camargo shortened her skirts from floor level to a few centimetres above the ankle. This enabled her renowned *entrechats* – the crossing or beating together of the feet during a leap in ballet – to be seen by the audience. In the writings of Noverre in the early eighteenth century, the major changes that were happening in ballet were clearly stated in his comments on costume.

Obstinacy in adhering to outworn traditions is the same in every part of the opera; it is monarch of all it surveys. Greek, Roman, shepherd, hunter, warrior, faun ... all these characters are cut to the same pattern and ostentatious display rather than good taste has caused them to be spattered at caprice. Tinsel glitters everywhere. ... I would banish all uniformity of costume. ... I should prefer light and simple draperies of contrasting colours worn in such a manner as to reveal the dancer's figure. ... I would reduce by three-quarters the ridiculous paniers of our danseuses, they are equally opposed to the liberty, speed, prompt and lively action of the dance.

(Jean-Georges Noverre, Letters on Dancing, *1930, translated by Cyril Beaumont)*

Noverre was against warriors who were dressed in their Sunday best, and he rejected masks as artificial. He was then moving towards greater natural design.

Around the corner lay the French Revolution and the new romanticism. Adoration of the exotic, peasant life and local colour, mystery and the supernatural was seen in Marie Taglioni's *La Sylphide* (Paris Opera, 1832). The design, by Ciceri, included romantic, moonlit forest glades into which the white *tulle tutu*, fitted bodice, flowery crown and pink tights fitted perfectly. The invention of the *pointe shoe* allowed ballerinas to float over the earth, spirit-like. Costumes now also conveyed national identities from far-flung places – Scotland, Bulgaria, India.

Ida Rubinstein in Scheherazade; *costume by Bakst*

The influences of the artists Leon Bakst and Alexandre Benois produced a revolution of design and colour during the rebirth of ballet in the Diaghilev era at the start of the twentieth century. In the costumes for *Schéhérazade* (1910), there was a startling new use of intense, sensuous and powerful colours. The whole look was daring, vibrant and fantastic.

This taste for the shocking and avant-garde reached its height in 1917 with Picasso's humorous, absurd and modern designs in *Parade*. The movement of the Managers – the characters who ran the travelling show – was impeded under the heavy wooden frames of their skyscraper costumes. The dancers themselves were often a secondary consideration to the design.

THE PRESENT DAY

Shape

Costumes can often make life difficult for dancers (as we saw in *Parade*). Dancers usually rehearse in their most comfortable clothes, and when suddenly dressed in an unfamiliar costume, their whole sense of the movement may change. Costumes should move *with* the dancer, so that the dancer feels able to move with all the fullness required. Frederick Ashton had a favourite designer in Sophie Federovitch. He said of her:

> She believed firmly that nothing must hide the dancing or impede the dancers, and that the background should not distract.
>
> *(Sir Frederick Ashton in* Making a Ballet, *1974)*

Costumes for ballet tend to be more traditional in style than those for modern dance companies, and they usually flatter and enhance the dancer's classical lines. However, more adventurous attitudes to design for ballet costumes are perhaps more common now than they used to be. A modern dress version of *Giselle* was recently staged by English National Ballet Company, with Charles Cusick-Smith the designer. It is set in the 1920s, with images of film stars and swish hotels. There is a clash of style, however, when a sword, such a crucial element in this ballet, appears. This is an anachronism: a gun would have been more likely in those times; and this is a problem also often presented with modern-dress versions of Shakespeare. In this instance, the sword is, however, essential for Giselle's suicide. The design for Act Two then brings us not a corps de ballet but instead an evil, undead, vampire-like hoard – truly romantic in its chilling horror and supernatural mystery.

Sir Frederick Ashton's *The Dream* (1964), by contrast, clearly reflects the influence of the romantic traditional shape in the costumes of the fairies – in particular, in wings and knee-length tutus. The human characters too are set in a time gone by, with three-piece suits, wigs, frilled shirts and neckties for the men of a Victorian era.

A costume may be chosen deliberately to *distort* the lines and shape of the body. Alwin Nikolais combined this idea with his extraordinary lighting effects:

> In this piece a faceless trio, entirely covered by sacks, comes to life through various patterns of body pulsations. ... They remind me of a collection of potato sacks pulled up over a mound of bubbling rubber.
>
> *(Elinor Rogosin in* Dance Makers, *1980)*

Nikolais is concerned with imposing *limitations* on the dancers, and with the way that this reflects the problems that humans have in

Five Brahms' Waltzes in the manner of Isadora Duncan *by Frederick Ashton; dancer Lucy Burge, costume by David Dean*

managing their own environment. He rejects the Graham interest in Freudian psychodrama, heroines and national pride in favour of the relationships between human and nature. The question of the role of technology and a 'green' focus moves him to create, on stage, other worlds for our contemplation.

Colour and materials

After the 1920s, there was a reaction against the opulence and excesses of the Diaghilev era for some time later. Designers restricted their use of colours to a more austere range, and shape too became pared-down. There was still fine traditional design for the world of ballet, but now also forward-looking designers for the new choreographers who formed the rebellious movement in modern dance. Isadora Duncan was the first to make a real impact, choosing to wear flimsy fabrics in the style of a Greek tunic – shocking to many at that time. This was beautifully reproduced in the tribute work *Five Brahm's Waltzes in the Manner of Isadora Duncan*. Danced by Lynn Seymour and chore-

ographed by Frederick Ashton in 1975 (and later revived for Lucy Burge by Ballet Rambert in 1976), it too used the free, floaty fabric that had made Duncan famous. The material enhanced the freedom of the movement and its energetic patterns through the air.

Such partnerships as Merce Cunningham and Robert Rauschenberg also pared down costume and rejected decoration. Simple, all-in one, tight-fitting leotards, often in plain pastel shades of colour or – as in *Summerspace* (1958) – painted to match the background with tiny dots or soft sprays (design Rauschenberg), were now used. These costumes would make the dancers appear not as if they were *in* space but as if they themselves *were* space.

The dance of Martha Graham was for austere times, and to be taken in a serious mood. Graham often designed the costumes herself, and these were often dark and almost puritan, and frequently inspired by the movement itself. Take Martha Graham's solo *Lamentation*

(1930) where the intense repetitive rocking and sorrow was moulded into the tight-fitting sheath. New fabrics like stretch jersey were now used for the first time. This use of costume enhanced the main idea of the dance.

The post-moderns of the 1960s onwards produced an enormous range of ideas on costuming dance. At first, they rejected all the achievements of their forerunners in modern dance.

> No to spectacle no to virtuosity no to transformations and magic and make believe no to glamour ... no to style no to camp.

These are the words of iconoclast of the 1960s Yvonne Rainer, and natural everyday movements and simple street clothes were the final product. The dancers of New York, and later the UK, were working on shoestring budgets, and this factor had a significant influence on the look and values of dance.

From a choice of the dullest, most insignificant rehearsal clothes, we move to the imaginative designs of present-day French choreographers. Regine Chopinot and Philippe Decouflé. In Chopinot's *KOK* (1990), the costumes are designed by Jean-Paul Gaultier, the king of French avant-garde fashion. The final result is stunning and chic, with rich colour and pattern, as well as upfront sexuality. In the film *Codex* (1986), shown as part of the *Tights Camera Action!* series on Channel 4 in 1994, we see a design treat. The dance explores two different patterns, one regular and the other not. With the dancers dressed in all-in-one suits, with frog-like flippers on their feet and matching hats, a total illusion of 'real and yet not real' is created. Add to this an easy, zany humour and eye-catching movement, and Decouflé's aim to create a total spectacle is attained. This effect was also seen in his work for the opening of the Winter Olympics in Albertville, 1992.

In present-day Britain, costume design takes many and diverse forms – from the cool, simple cut of the Siobhan Davies company, as seen in the jeans and denim shirts of *Wyoming* (1988), to the leather jackets of the Cholmondeleys in *Metalcholia* (1994) or the long silver dresses made in the new Liquid Jersey in *Flesh and Blood*. The dress in Martha Graham's *Frontier* (1935), in its homespun heavy fabric, reminds us of who she is, and of the time and place of her life in the Wild West of the USA. In *Flesh and Blood* (1989/1993), Lea Anderson's choice of the metal, fluid, reflective fabric similarly *reminds* us of the chainmail of St Joan. Depending on the light, this latter fabric would change colour and texture during the various sections of the dance. This effect was also seen in Robert Cohan's work *Nympheas* (1976) for the London Contemporary Dance Theatre. Sections of Monet's impressionist painting of waterlilies were painted onto all-in-one leotards. The colour of the paint changed with the lighting, so that typical impressionistic changes in light and weather were reproduced on stage – from a calm blue summer's day to the sudden dark of a passing storm, the deep brown and greens soaking into the costumes.

In Richard Alston's *Wildlife* (1984), the sharp zig-zags of Richard Smith's set of moving kites are echoed in the strident designs and vibrant colours of the painted leotards. The dancers are in some imaginary deep forest, and their sharp, angular movements, enhanced by the costume and set design, convey moments of animal instinct and their struggle for survival. There is an image of the broken lines of camouflage of animals in the undergrowth.

Even by the simple addition of a hat or other accessory, the dancer is transformed into any strange being or character you may choose. In Siobhan Davies' *Carnival* (1982) for Second Stride, the various animals – which are brought to life by the music of Saint-Saëns – are depicted by the delightful addition of hats

Wildlife by Richard Alston, design by Richard Smith

and scarves – and even spectacles for the ageing and engaging elderly tortoises.

Masks and body or face paint offer other possibilities. These were particularly well-used in *Ghost Dances* (1988) by Christopher Bruce for the then-named Ballet Rambert. The ghosts of South American myth appeared ghoulish and sinister in body paint which emphasised their skeletons, and in white eerie masks which hid any signs of mortality or human feelings. Similarly, in Glen Tetley's *Pierrot Lunaire* (1962), the sad, pathetic lead is the white-faced clown, danced by Christopher Bruce – a character very vulnerable to people of lesser compassion than himself.

We can say here, in summary, that costume may enhance the intentions of a dance by doing one of a number of things:

- emphasising the mood by choice of colour, shape, fabric, texture;
- enhancing the formal properties of movement through certain lines and shapes;
- clarifying character and story.

TASK 5

Fill a box with as many items of clothing and fabrics of different texture as possible. Place it in the centre of the room and let dancers take turns at 'Lucky Dips'. Whatever is pulled out of the box gives to movement ideas which everyone copies. The dancer passes on the item to another dancer who continues to improvise with it before abandoning it and dipping in for another. This idea can be further developed by making deliberate choices instead and then working in small groups to form short dances using the clothing chosen as a main source of movement ideas.
Props may also be added to the box if desired.

Props

As with set and costumes, props are an integral part of a dance. When used thoughtfully, they will not only serve as decoration but will also serve to enhance the intentions of the dance and so add to the audience's appreciation.

Props may:

- enhance a character;
- have symbolic meaning;
- add to the movement itself;
- in the case of very large props, become almost *the set itself* as well.

Looking at a few examples will help you to understand the power of props.

PROPS WHICH HAVE SYMBOLIC MEANING/ENHANCE CHARACTER

The magic myrtle flower wand of Myrtha, Queen of the Wilis, in Act Two of *Giselle*, is *symbolic* of her all-powerful presence. In the Kirov version of the ballet, the wand actually explodes as she condemns Albrecht to dance himself to death, and it also moves of its own accord, thus adding to the narrative. And in Act One, the sword which Giselle throws herself onto (although not in many present-day versions) is symbolic of the sign of the cross. In committing suicide, Giselle places herself out of the protection of a grave within the churchyard. Hence, she is doomed to become one of the undead wilis. This is a custom which would have been well-recognised by an audience in the 1800s.

Martha Graham is once again not to be overlooked, in her collaboration with sculptor Isamu Noguchi and the innovations which it produced. For them, sculpture coming to life on stage is part of the whole ritual, and it enhances both the meaning of the movement and the audience's emotional response. In *Night Journey* (1947), a rope binds together Jocasta and her son Oedipus. The rope is a symbol both of the umbilical cord and of sexual love. This Greek myth of doom and destruction is powerfully told from the women's point of view.

Following in the Graham style, work like that of Robert Cohan for the London Contemporary Dance Theatre in the 1970s and 1980s produced some delights, like *Waterless Method of Swimming Instruction*, 1974, where, in one section for the men only, huge rubber rings take on lives of their own, providing boats for the dancers to row and, when piled up on top of one dancer, completely entrapping him.

In Christopher Bruce's *Sergeant Early's Dream* (1984), the section entitled 'Geordie' uses the lyrics of a song which tells of a woman's lament for her hanged husband. Her scarf becomes the symbol of the hangman's noose in the final image of the dance, reinforcing the characters and the narrative of the song and dance.

Twyla Tharp's production of *The Catherine Wheel* (1983) reveals a dysfunctional family fighting itself. Often, the greed and self-obsession of the family members takes the form of an unhealthy interest in material possessions, and most of all in a large and rather sinister pineapple. This prop features as a symbol of all that is negative in the world. Its very shadow is a weapon of destruction, like a hand grenade or a nuclear bomb. At one point, it even becomes the apple which Eve used to tempt Adam. The heroine of the dance, St Catherine, was martyred when she was burned on a wheel, hence the name of the firework; and it is no coincidence that when a pineapple

Waterless Method of Swimming Instruction *by Robert Cohan*

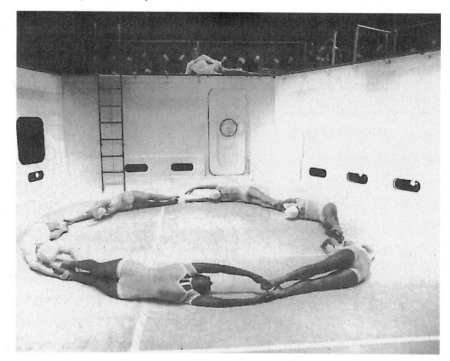

is cut into slices, it resembles a wheel. This is a prop which is totally central to the meaning of the whole full-length dance work.

THE PROP-SET

In 1928, the Russian artist Pavel Tchelitchev combined an innovative range of elements in his stage design for the Ballet Russe's *Ode*. This presented a modern view of the festivities of the Russian court of the eighteenth century. The dancers were covered entirely so that they became anonymous figures. They held cords which wove a web over the stage and were connected to lines of dolls at the back of the stage. Such were the interconnections here that it seemed difficult to know where the costumes ended and the props or set began. This kind of distortion also features in the later work of Alwin Nikolais where again props are simultaneously costumes, and it can be difficult to know whether or not they are also part of the set.

Similarly, Georges Balanchine, in his design for *Orpheus* (1950), chose a white silk curtain to fall in a dramatic swirl like lightning, and a rope which, although a part of the costume of the Dark Angel, *also* became an integral part of the movement.

An early work of Robert Cohan, *Hunter of Angels* (1954), used a huge ladder which was both set and prop at the same time. This was moved around with great skill (considering its size and weight) to become the wings of an angel, a womb, a labyrinth and Jacob's ladder to heaven. In this way, it was, at different times, both an extension of the dancers' bodies and a set to be explored in countless ways for movement possibilities.

Study the photograph of *The Tempest* on p. 123. How does the set add to the story?

A prop-set in Glen Tetley's The Tempest; *design by Nadine Baylis*

PROPS WHICH ADD TO THE MOVEMENT

In a Graham-style work, the costumes, set, props and music are all integrated with the movement in a deliberately orchestrated attempt to reinforce the meaning of the choreography. This is not so for ex-Graham dancer Merce Cunningham whose approach is to make each element of the production a *separate experience* – as, again, in *Rainforest* (1968), where the helium-filled silver pillows, designed by Andy Warhol, are met by the dancers in an unconcerned way.

In Richard Alston's *Wildlife* (1984), the set comprises a collection of huge 'kites' (designed by the artist Richard Smith) suspended above the stage. These angular mobiles are connected to electric motors which enable them to move around and up and down, enhancing both the movement of the dancers and the zig-zag energy of the music.

Sometimes a prop can act as both a set *and* a costume. In a post-modern work of Steve Paxton's called *Music for Words*, a transparent 12-foot-square room was deflated around him until it became his costume.

Choosing a diverse range of objects and then allowing improvisation with these to lead to performance is a common approach for postmodern choreographers. *Stories* may grow from these objects, or the objects may change the way that you *move*. The only limit is the imagination.

Rosemary Butcher's collaborations with visual artists have led to some surprising results. In 1981, in *Spaces 4*, the artist Heinz-Dicter Pietsch improvised with polystyrene as he watched the dancers. As the dance progressed, he built various objects which captured the *spatial* qualities of the dance, and the dancers in turn connected their movements to the installation, echoing corners and rough edges, or confirming boundaries. Following on in 1987, his props for *Touch the Earth* were metal rods which were *carried* during the dance. The dancers gently marked out their homelands which were reminiscent of various locations which Butcher associated with the plight of the native American Indians and the loss of territory. The poles are images of teepees or farming tools, and the movement is deeply reflective of a community in a state of sharing and supporting.

In *De Gas* (1981) by Ian Spink, towels, jugs, towel rails, bowls and fans fill the space. There is a particularly clever trio where three male dancers move through a loop involving covering, uncovering, falling and throwing and catching the towels. It is a slick sequence, beautifully timed to end with one of the dancers seated with their feet in a bowl of water. The subject of the painter Degas' female nudes and their vulnerability is turned around here so that the washing, drying and combing of hair is carried out by men. The exploration of gender and of our expectations of stereotyping is presented to the audience for consideration.

The dance production now only requires one other constituent feature to complete the picture: the accompaniment or aural setting. This is an area full of possibilities and choices. What the audience *hears* also needs to be appropriately chosen to support your movements, sets, lights, costumes and props, so that what is heard and what is seen can be combined into an understandable whole for and by the onlooker.

TASK 6

Select a number of objects as props, such as:

- a pillow
- an umbrella
- a large pole or stick
- a large hoop
- a feather
- a picture frame
- a balloon
- a newspaper
- a doll
- a cardboard tube
- a large piece of silk or chiffon.

Experiment with how the object affects the way you move when, for example, you carry it or attach it to you. Let the objects become something *other* than what they are. For example, if they are heavy, let them become light, or if they have an obvious use, use them for something else totally different.

Finally, choose one object and let it lead to a dance; *or* arrange a few of them around the stage space and create a story or landscape or 'scene' with them. (Suggested music: *Underneath the Bunker*, by The Orb.)

References and resources

BOOKS

Au, S., *Ballet and Modern Dance*, London, Thames and Hudson, 1988

Bentley, T., *Costume by Karinska*, USA: Abrams, 1995, well-illustrated, and includes costumes from Ashton and Balanchine

Clarke, M. and Crisp, C., *Ballet: an Illustrated History*, London, A. & C. Black, 1973

Cohen, S. J. (ed), *Dance as a Theatre Art: Source Readings In Dance History From 1581 to the Present*, New York: Princeton Book Co., 1992

Kirstein, L., *Dance: a Short History of Classic Theatre Dancing*, Dance Horizons, 1969

Moss, K., *The House: Inside the Royal Opera House*, London: BBC Books, the book of the TV series

Sorrell, W., *Dance in its Time*, New York: Columbia University Press, 1981

Spencer, C., *Leon Bakst & the Ballets Russes*, UK: Academy Educational, 1995, well illustrated

VIDEOS

Soda Lake, by Richard Alston, available from the National Resource Centre for Dance, University of Surrey, tel.: 01483 259 326

Hunter of Angels, by Robert Cohan, ISBN 0 946 48391 4, 1984, as above for address and telephone number

The Catherine Wheel, by Twyla Tharp, the National Video Corporation Limited, Castle Hendring, HEN 2 148. From Hendring Ltd, 8 Northfields Prospect, Putney Bridge Road, London SW18 1PE, 1982

Ghost Dances and Journey, by Christopher Bruce, the Houston Ballet

MUSIC

Dancetechnic, by David Harry, available from Primrose Studio, White Cross, Lancaster, 1992, tel no: 01524 849622, recommended for Task 1 – This tape has many tracks which are useful for improvisation

Underneath the Bunker by The Orb, Polygram Island label IMCP219, 1996

chapter five
THE CONSTITUENT FEATURES OF DANCE: THE AURAL SETTING

Accompaniments for dance

There are many types of accompaniment (aural setting) to choose from for dance. The most obvious one, music, is often chosen, but it must be stated loudly from the start that it is also worth trying out others. The list of choices includes:

- silence
- the voice
- sound (both natural and found sound)
- music.

The final choice must be one selected, like the movements themselves and other constituent features, with great care. In the end, both what the audience receives *visually* and what it receives *audibly* should be compatible in some way, even if this is because these aspects are very *different*: the differences here may create interesting contrasts and clashes.

SILENCE

The early German expressionist dancers, like Mary Wigman at the start of the twentieth century, often chose silence as the accompaniment to their dances.

> Nearly all her most original dances are unaccompanied by music ... music is secondary, almost superfluous.
>
> (*Herman Ould in* Dancing Times, *April 1926*)

Without any sounds to hide behind, a dance must be clear, strong in content. It must have its own vibrant internal rhythms and form. Silence is the equivalent of the spaces in visual art or the stillness in dance. The apparently negative aspects of any art form are just as important as the obviously positive ones. They exist woven together: you can't have one without the other.

All kinds of movement and atmospheres are possible in silence.

Water Study (1928) by Doris Humphrey is an outstanding example of the use of silence.

> ... the dance without music ... increases concentration and attention onto movement to an astonishing degree. ... 'Water Study' ... was composed for fourteen girls whose bodies rose and fell, rushed and leaped like the various aspects of water, the only sound being the faint thudding of feet in running movements, reminiscent of surf.
>
> (*Doris Humphrey in* The Art of Making Dances, *1959*)

The use of silence in Richard Alston's *Soda Lake* (1981) enhances the complex rhythmical changes in the movement. There are sudden changes of speed, from quick allegro footwork to prolonged stillnesses. The enormous empty space of a *real* desert landscape exists in a vast silence, and in this work, the overall bare, minimal look is similarly well-balanced by an accompaniment of silence. There is a real atmosphere of quiet openness and solitude where the dancer performs.

Sometimes, a few seconds of silence at the start or end of, or during, a dance can add contrast and avoid predictability. It may also serve to highlight moments of greater importance by allowing the onlooker's ear to rest and thus to appreciate the movement more.

VOICE

When people move, they often accompany their movements with voice, in song or in words, quite naturally. Or there may be another person doing this, or it could be on tape. The accents and types of sounds could blend smoothly with, or they could act as a contrast to, the movement. The voice may use words, human sounds like giggles, sighs and so on, or song. The choice is wide-ranging, and involves the inner world of the dance. The speech may also be distorted, and it does not have to make sense. For example, it may sound like a rap with a repetitive rhythm (in the original, the words may not have been repeated, and consequently, the sounds become like a musical score). *Dutiful Ducks* (1982), a solo for dancer Michael Clark by Richard Alston, used a sound tape (text score by composer Charles Amirkhanian) which repeated a few rhythmical phrases of words, like: 'Dutiful, d-d-d-d dutiful ducks, dutiful ducks ... in double LA Tree tops sway.' The phrasing, rhythm and accents of the movements all matched those of the text score. The sources of voice in text may be found in poetry, stories, diaries, newspapers and magazines.

Longevity (1990) by Gary Lambert is dedicated to the North American civil-rights leader Martin Luther-King who was assassinated on 4 April 1968. The accompaniment comprises both silence and his famous 'I have a dream...' speech, and the movement not only follows the rhythm of the words but also, in places, uses some of the words' literal meanings.

John Cage, composer and long-time collaborator with Merce Cunningham, would use many types of sound in his scores for choreography. Like other constituent features of Cunningham's work, the sound is treated as a separate entity in itself. For *How to Pass, Kick, Fall, Run* (1965), Cage read short stories from the side of the stage. *Canfield* (1974) used communication between walkie-talkies which also made static and other electronic noises. It was later reported that Cunningham had imagined the radio sounds of the astronauts' moon landing as his choice of accompaniment for this dance.

TASK 1 ▼

Choose a short fairy story. Photocopy it, and cut it up into separate phrases that make sense. Let each dancer choose at random one or two phrases and improvise them, saying the words at the same time as moving. Show each other the results.

Discuss how the phrases may be put together into a group dance using silences, repetitions of phrases and an understandable narrative. Try to add humour and drama so that the story becomes more than it was in the original version.

SOUND

Non-human sounds from nature and the environment can be very appropriate for some dances. The sounds of wind, water, storms, street activity, railway stations, birds, football crowds or telephones are just some of the possibilities. You could sample some yourself by taking a portable tape recorder out and about and making recordings. In Robert Cohan's *Forest* (1977), the sounds of wind, running streams, thunder, rain, bird calls and a wolf howl are mixed with an electronic score to create a forest atmosphere. The dance movement mixes images of the animals who inhabit the forest with their calls which ricochet around the space. When dancing in an outdoor location, the *found* sound can become the accompaniment itself. For example, the sound of passing traffic can draw attention to desired issues in a dance that is concerned with environmental pollution.

To John Cage, any sound or noise is music. He has given piano concerts consisting of sitting and not playing for twenty or so minutes, thus forcing the audience to listen to the everyday sounds around them. In his view, this is a way of experiencing the environment. The high level of technological advances now means that the dancers themselves can create their own aural settings as they move. In *Variations V* (1965), the dancers' movements activated antennas on stage which sent signals to the orchestra pit. Triggered by light intensity, the antennas set off tape recorders, radios, and so on, to make electronic sound. In this way, the dance was not at all dependent on the accompaniment – rather, the score depended entirely on the *movements*.

The sounds the dancers themselves make can often serve as the accompaniment. Stamping, clapping and breath sounds all provide possible aural settings. Tap dance, Indian and flamenco all use the sounds of the feet and hands to enhance the rhythmical experience for the audience. Metal taps on the shoes and heels, bells on the ankles and wooden castanets in the hands all serve to emphasise the aural aspect of the movement.

In Christopher Bruce's *Swansong* (1987), the idea of the interrogation of a political prisoner in a South American jail is cleverly brought to life. The feet of the interrogators and the prisoner tap out and shuffle question-and-answer conversations. Claps and finger clicks are also used. All of this is mixed into a sound and musical score that heightens the intensity of the plight of the tortured prisoner. They play cat and mouse with him, and in a macabre setting of red noses and music-hall song and dance, we feel that his fate is sealed.

MUSIC

The most obvious thing to do is to set movements to music, but this is making the dance totally reliant on the aural setting. It is the movement that should be the main concern of the dance. As George Balanchine once remarked, the audience should see the music and hear the dance. The relationship of dance to music is discussed in greater detail later in the book. What we are concerned with here is choosing music that has a positive influence on the dance. The dancer should feel able to be 'inside' the music, as if the air is full of it.

Choosing music

A poor choice of music can ruin a dance. Ideally, the dance and music should *support* one another. There are a number of things which should be considered when choosing music:

1 *Balance.* A piece of music which has large numbers of instruments or a rich production quality may not be entirely suited to a solo dance. On the other hand, some music is sparse in its style and so may not be ideal for a large group dance.

2 *Avoiding the obvious.* Music from the Top Ten, or old favourites which you enjoy listening to, are *not* always the best for dance. Similarly, some well-known classical music or hits from West End shows can also prove difficult because people know them so well that they already have their own set ideas about them, and this may mean that your choreography will be overpowered by their preconceptions. Often, much of this type of music is the wrong length anyway, and cutting it is not only illegal but also unartistic. After all, how would you feel if a musician cut off the last minute of your dance because it was too long to fit to the music? This shows a lack of respect for the artistry of the other artist.

Of course, there *are* always exceptions to the rules! Michael Clark used the well-known song *Shout* by Lulu to great success. This can be seen in Charles Atlas' film about Clark, and in Clark's work called *Hail the New Puritan* (1986). Clark followed the simple structure of the song to the note. It was the unorthodox choice of movement style, involving his typical fast classical footwork and flexible torso combined with a sharp, clean execution in the dynamic range, that made for the success. Clark's highly technically accomplished dancers held their own with the music. The *contrasts* between the visual and aural aspects served to hold those two aspects in balance. Furthermore, the use of humour or satire in a dance may be enhanced by choosing music which holds within it many known clichés.

It is your responsibility as a choreographer to research the availability of music. These days, there is a massive range of music available. Explore this by visiting your local music library, and try listening to things with names on them that you may have never heard of. In this way, if you find something, you can buy it without having wasted money on a blind testing. There is no excuse for not finding the wildest wackiest of music for your work.

3 *Quality.* Whenever possible, it is important to use top-quality recordings. It is best to make a rehearsal tape, and not to use the original all the time but to save it instead for performance. Recordings full of scratches and jumps, or that are hardly audible, are unacceptable unless that particular effect has been chosen for a special reason. For example, if you wished to create the feel of an old black-and-white film, it may be appropriate to choose such recordings.

4 *Style.* Music set in a particular country or period of history needs careful handling. It is possible to mix and match modern music with, say, that in an Indian style – as Shobana Jeyasingh frequently does – but it requires sensitive handling. On the whole, the overall styles of the dance and music need to be *matched.* Scottish, Spanish, Irish, African, Renaissance, mediaeval, impressionist, romantic, neoclassical and jazz styles are all useful if handled properly. If these labels are unfamiliar to you, then perhaps a little research into music would be helpful.

5 *Live music.* Ideally, live music should be used whenever possible, but of course access to this is not always possible. You may know other students who study music and who may be willing to play for you. You will need to provide them with copies of the score, and it may help to make a recording of their playing for you for rehearsal periods. There may even be some who can compose, and this could be very exciting. Improvising together can be great fun, and very productive. Using percussion instruments, dancers too can accompany each other in improvisation. It is important to let dancers and mu-

sicians *take turns* in leading. In the final choreography, the musicians may play an equal part in the performing. This is seen in Ian Spink's (1981) *De Gas* where the cellist is an integral part of the whole performance. He is seated with his feet in a bowl of water throughout.

Using music

There are a number of ways that a dance may be formed with music:

- dance and music composed together;
- dance created first, then music composed for it;
- compose music first, then dance to it (most common);
- a dance sketched in, then either music composed for it or suitable music is found;
- music and dance composed separately, only coming together in performance.

When a piece of music is chosen first, you need to do a number of things to prepare for the creation of the dance:

- Listen to it over and over again, carefully.
- Improvise to it.
- Develop an understanding of its feel, form, meter, tempo, instrumentation and so on (use written notes to help your memory).
- Decide how the dancer's counts work into the music.

Remember, music and the dance do *not* have to match exactly. The dance needs a rhythmical life of its own which is not dictated by the music.

Abstract dancing is analogous to abstract music. The same three elements are there – the tone, rhythm, melody and harmony, with the addition of the kinesthet-ic appeal only possible in the dance. This means that to a sensitive onlooker there is a constant stream of primitive excitement going on inside . . .

(Doris Humphrey in The Art of Making Dances, *1959)*

The more complex the musical scores, the more demanding it is on the choreography. Thus, music by Schoenberg would be more demanding to choreograph than a simple piece of Mozart or a short country and western song by, say, k d lang. One way of overcoming the difficulties involved is to use *dancer's counts*. These are not necessarily the same counts as the music, but are determined by the *phrasing* of the movement within the music framework. For example:

- Music: 8 phrases of 4/4 played fast = 32 counts.
- Dancer: 4 phrases of 6-6-8-12 = 32 counts.

In this way, the counts grow organically from the demands of the movement, and are thus more in tune with the needs of the dance and the dancers. This makes working with difficult – or for that matter *any* – music easier. Ideally, it should be possible for each dancer in a group to have *different* sets of counts to the same piece of music, and yet for all to finish with the music at the same time as each other. Doris Humphrey did this in *New Dance* (1935). The music played 6 phrases of 4/4 whilst the dancers moved on phrases of 7-7-10. The sum of both is the same. It is a satisfying moment visually and aurally for the audience, as both meet at the end after having had their independence.

The tasks below allow you to try new approaches to accompaniment and music that you may not have considered before.

TASK 2

1 ▽▽▽ Find a copy of 'The Jabberwocky' by Lewis Carroll. Select certain key
▲▲▲ words and phrases which may be spoken by a narrator or by the
dancers themselves. Decide on an overall format for a group of 5 or 6 dancers which
is not too literal but may use certain atmospheres, moods, moments and meanings.
The monster might be made up of many individuals and not just one. Also, the
fighting scene could involve all the dancers fighting an invisible Jabberwocky.
Notice here too the form of the poem itself, in that the first and last verses are the
same.
Find some music or sounds which the text can be easily woven in and out of. It may
be music that creates a general atmosphere of fear and mystery without a particularly strong beat. (Suggested music: the soundtrack of the film *Diva*.)
Using text, music and silence, compose the group dance.

2 ▽ Using percussion instruments for an accompaniment, make three dance
▲ phrases of 5-5-8 counts. Dance them whilst accompanied by the group playing 6 measures of 3/4 in a steady tempo, accenting count 1 of each bar.
Take it in turns to dance and play.

3 ▽ Using K. D. Lang's song 'Big love' (from *Absolute Torch and Twang* Sire
▲ 7599-25877-2). Listen carefully to it, then write down the number of beats
and measures in the verses and chorus. Make movement phrases which have irregular counts that are not the same as the music but that add up to the same total at
the end of each verse or chorus.
Practice until the two fit together. Start or finish with a silent section of movement.

Later in this book, there will be more detailed information on musical terms and analysis. Dancers need to know how to analyse musical structures in order to be able to compose dances creatively and appropriately.

A sensitive and appropriate choice and use of music is seen in Siobhan Davies' *Carnival of the Animals* (1982). Not typical of her usual work, it is a humorous piece mixing images of animals with human characteristics. The original score by Saint-Saëns, *Carnaval des Animaux* (1886), is not followed slavishly, although the overall structure, form and expression of the music does support that of the dance, and vice versa. In the section 'The swan', the cello sounds are echoed in the swan-neck, cello-shaped motif, and the lyrical sound of the music is also softly reflected in the dynamics of the movement. In 'The cuckoo', a dimension of humour is added as the bird is depicted as a forlorn suitor of a very superior female. His repeated sad heartbeat arm gesture echoes the music on nearly every 'cuckoo' sound. It is even funnier when he misses one.

Leaving the final word to a well-known and highly respected choreographer:

> I listen to a lot of music and I love it, but I don't often work with it. Or rather I work with it 'in private' in that I get many ideas about time, rhythm and time

structures from music. ... I found at one time if I used music that I really liked I ended up creating something that was very enjoyable to do, but the movement tended to be banal and very simple, getting into nothing but steps, running around on the beat. ... I began working with ideas because body rhythms are different from musical rhythms.

(Richard Alston in Making a Ballet, *1974)*

References and resources

MUSIC

K. D. Lang's song 'Big love', from *Absolute Torch and Twang*, Sire 7599-258/7-2, 1989, recommended for Task 2

Soundtrack from the film *Diva*, recommended for Task 2

chapter six

FORM IN DANCE

Tis to create and in creating live
A being more intense, that we endow
with form.
Our fancy, gaining as we give the life we
image.

(Lord Byron)

In Chapters 3, 4 and 5, the basic building blocks – the constituent features – of dance were analysed, and we considered how to make appropriate choices of such constituents when composing dances. In giving dances a choreographic *form*, the movement components, dancers and physical and aural settings have all now to be woven together into a tight web.

The work as a whole must be one of stuff, as an emerald is all emerald – crush it to powder, and each tiny pinch of that powder will still be an emerald.

(Ted Shawn in The Vision of Modern Dance, *1979)*

It is the overall *unity* of the dance which the audience sees and hears in performance:

If you look carefully at *Scènes de Ballet*, you will see that there isn't a single step in it that doesn't relate to the structure as a whole. This is equally true of unassuming ballets like *Les Rendezvous* and *Les Patineurs*.

(David Vaughan in Dance Now, *1995)*

This chapter examines how the various constituent features are organised so as to produce the final 'look' of the piece.

Form

Form, in its raw state, is all around us in the world we live in. Morning, afternoon, night, the four seasons, birth, life and death are all universal forms which everyone recognises. In making dance, music, poetry, painting or film, we take our sense of order and recreate it in an *imaginary* world.

Form is the shape of the content. Form without content becomes form for the sake of form. ... The form should contain the original impetus out of which it was created.

(Hanya Holm in The Vision Of Modern Dance, *1979)*

Form can thus put across *content*, like the meaning in the dance of Martha Graham, or it can be the message itself: the overall simple feel of the movements can themselves be the expressive content of the dance.

In rehearsal, the choreographer will be working around some basic ideas for the constituent features and for what the overall look may be. A gradual process of developing and structuring the materials – including, of course, the dancers themselves – eventually leads to a cohesive dance form which must satisfy the choreographer's own needs but also be clear to the dancers, and to the audience.

The ways in which the movement is manipulated, and the way in which the various constituent features interrelate throughout the dance, make each dance unique. As well as using intuition during the creative process, the choreographer needs knowledge about certain possible *procedures*. As in music composition, there are certain useful traditional devices and structures in choreography which comprise the skills of the craft, the tools of the trade. Like the physical skills involved in the training of a dancer – skills which add to the dancer's resources – these technical skills will increase the choreographer's own range of abilities. And again, as with the dancer's training, it is the physical *doing* which is crucial. *Participation* in the solving of choreographic problems, and in improvisations and compositional exercises, is the way to develop a wider range of choreographic skills.

Once experience and understanding is increased, these 'rules' will add both depth and a wider range of choice to the process of composition; and of course, they may be broken where justifiable. Without a knowledge of such choices, the choreographer may be stuck only with what they already know, plus what they have learnt through trial and error, and this situation may well narrow the individual's range of expression rather than enhancing and fine-tuning it. Practical experiences in the following categories are necessary:

- compositional devices;
- compositional structures;
- the relationship of the dance to the accompaniment;
- the organisation of groups in space.

The final finished dance should have a natural, organic feel. Each part of it should grow naturally, almost *inevitably*, into the next just as a seed grows into a flower.

Compositional devices

Motifs are a single movement or a short phrase of movement which embody the *style* and *intention* of the dance. They are repeated, varied and developed by *manipulating* the movement. These manipulations usually involve some change in the movement components of action, space, time or dynamics (see Chapter 3).

Below is a list of ways in which motifs can be developed:

- Use different parts of the body.
- Alter the basic body posture, say from standing to lying, sitting, upside-down or twisted.
- Add or change the action.
- Change the size.
- Change the level.
- Alter the focus.
- Change the direction, dimension or plane.

- Alter the air or floor pattern – make the air pattern into the floor pattern, or vice versa.
- Increase or decrease the tempo – augment or diminish, i.e. make slower/faster.
- Vary the pattern of the beats of the rhythm.
- Change the accents.
- Retrograde it – reverse the order of the movements.
- Change the dynamic or quality.
- Fragment the motif – use only one part repeatedly or some parts only, or change the order of the parts.
- Alter any of the aspects of the physical setting.
- Mix bits from different motifs together.
- Combine any of the above.

(There are added considerations in motif development when dealing with group dances, but these are dealt with later under a separate section.)

Motif development is a way of producing a lot from a little, while also avoiding too much repetition – which may be boring for the audience. The phrases involved will also tend to lengthen into whole sections and organically provide a logical development, contrasts and eventually *unity*. We all know those awful moments when inspiration just is not happening! Once, after much practice, you are able to do it spontaneously, motif development will help you to avoid drying up.

Figure 6.1 *Notation for motif development exercise in Task 1*

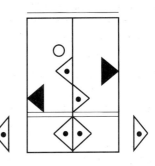

TASK 1 ⧗

Dance the motif from the notation given in Figure 6.1. Develop the motif as follows:

1 Repeat it.
2 Add an arm gesture as you sway.
3 Add another action on so that you now have 3 parts: the sway + arm gesture + another action (turn, travel, jump, fall or stillness).
4 Repeat just the sway.
5 Reverse the order of the 3 parts – i.e. retrograde.
6 Fragment the 3 parts by changing the order.
7 Dance all 3 parts, but add a new detail – i.e. embellish it.
8 Repeat one part 3 times.

Practice this whole sequence 1 to 8 until it is memorised.

⧖ Write a notation score for your developed version. You can continue to develop in your own way from here. (Suggested music: *Strike the Gay Harp* by The Chieftains, 3 Claddagh Records.)

A similar manipulation of motifs is called *theme* and *variation*. This, however, is more of a recognised structure in music *composition*, and so it will instead be dealt with later, in the section on compositional structures.

CANON

The device of canon involves two or more dancers dancing one or more motifs at different times. It therefore only applies to duets and group dances. Motifs are here danced in succession. This may give rise to relationships between dancers of: leading and following; question and answer; cooperation and confrontation. In music, canon is seen as a pre-set structure, but in dance it is more usually used as a device for developing motifs. Thus, the group movement becomes organised in time.

Dancers moving in *unison* may do one of the following:

- the same movement at the same time;
- similar or complementary movements at the same time;
- contrasting movements at the same time.

Similarly, there are different types of canons:

- A *simple canon* will be in strict order. Each dancer dances an entire motif, then keeps still while another dancer takes over. This is the simplest type of canon, and it may be made more interesting by allowing the dancer's timings to *overlap* so that the dancers are always a few counts behind each other. This places demands on the dancers' skill at dancing in *groups*, for it requires sensitive timing with, and an awareness of, others.

- A *simultaneous canon* involves dancers doing the same motif at the same time but starting from different points in the phrase. So, Dancer 1 may do counts 1 to 8; Dancer 2 may start at count 6, dancing 6-7-8-1-2-3-4-5, and another dancer may start at 4, dancing 4-5-6-7-8-1-2-3; and so on. This creates a dense, coherent and interesting look.

- A *cumulative canon* is just what it says: cumulative. Each dancer joins in with the lead dancer at various stages during the dancing of a motif, and they all finish at the same time. This gives a look of an increase in force or power through an increase in emphasis on the movement.

- *Loose canons* offer more opportunity for the manipulation of a motif. There may be a use of different levels, facings or placements in the stage space. Adding stillnesses is also effective, as may be varying the dynamic or rhythmic elements.

TASK 2

Take a short phrase you know well from technique class. In threes or fours, try the various canons in the list above. Be as accurate as you can throughout, and use your 'radar' (sense of timing and spacing) with the others sensitively.

CONTRAST

Contrast introduces new material which is noticeably different from anything so far seen in the dance. As already stated, using motif development will naturally include the use of contrast. This can be introduced suddenly or gradually. For example, a light, slow motif can be contrasted with large fast jumps, and this can be done by gradually increasing the tempo and strength, or by switching from one to the other in an instant. In *I am Curious Orange* (1988) by Michael Clark, there is a clear use of contrast when a slow, balletic, lamentful solo is immediately followed by the dancer tearing off her pointe shoes and performing a frenetically fast dance. Similarly, the bright and dark characters in ballets such as *The Nutcracker* and *Sleeping Beauty* create dramatic tension in their conflicts. In Sir Frederick Ashton's *Cinderella* (1948), considerable skill was needed to combine the lyrical with the comical while keeping the feel of a complete whole. The contrast between the two was so well-woven that in spite of their obvious differences, the two aspects nonetheless held the story together:

> The fun of the farce keeps relaxing the hold of the central story and in the story the dances don't try for intensity and fail … The spell it creates doesn't crystallize in a climax or a specific dance image but no mean gesture breaks the continuity of it. … To keep in a three act ballet such tone, to sustain it without affectation or banality, shows Ashton's power, and he shows this in doing it as simply as possible, by keeping the dancing sweet.
>
> *(Edward Denby,* Dancers, Buildings and People in the Street*, 1965)*

Similarly, in Ashton's *The Dream* (1964), the humour of the pas de deux between Titania and the ass Bottom is such a contrast to the later harmony of the duet when Titania is reunited with the fairy king Oberon in mutual love, that it strengthens the sense of climax in the whole ballet.

HIGHLIGHTS

Highlights will maintain the interest of the audience and draw attention to particular features or images that the choreographer may wish to emphasise. Usually, a dance has a few moments which the audience remembers the most vividly. These therefore function to make clearer the *meaning* or *intention* of the dance. Highlights inject *pace*. As the audience is swept along in the stream of consciousness of the piece, the highlights enable them to maintain a grasp on its overall direction more easily, and this clearly heightens their enjoyment, understanding and appreciation.

There are a variety of ways of creating highlights. One approach – similar to that found in the development of motifs – is to manipulate a movement component. One obvious technique here is to make use of rhythmical and dynamic accents. Highlights can be created by using a stronger dynamic, but they can also arise from emphasising a softer, gentler dynamic. A prolonged stillness, in anticipation of something happening, is also effective in creating tension and interest.

Expectancy and the unexpected are both attention-getters, and the skilful uses of each are unbeatable.

(Doris Humphrey in The Art of Making Dances*, 1959)*

For dramatic and narrative structures, the creation of tension and pace is vital, and highlights can be useful to do this. One method used by choreographer Ian Spink in *Further and Further into the Night* (1984) was the repetition of motif. This dance is based on Alfred Hitchcock's classic thriller *Notorious* (1946). It is a story of romance and intrigue. Many of the motifs relate to movements from the film, so that everyday movement is used a great deal. At one point, the gestures involved in serving a drink are repeated over and over to various dancers. This creates humour and also tension.

An increase or decrease in the *numbers* of dancers may draw attention to themes like isolation, rejection or celebration.

A change of set, costume or light, or a prop placed carefully in anticipation of its later use – any of these alterations in the physical setting may cause various moments to be highlighted.

In a dance entitled *Perhaps: the Study of Doris, a Confused Sender and Receiver of Love Letters* (1995) by the author, the setting of the pink boudoir to a variety of Doris Day love songs about letters was the introduction to the dance proper. At the same time, babe cherubs gave the audience pink, heart-shaped marshmallows and love hearts. In this way, there was a highlight before the main body of the dance began, which allowed the audience time to anticipate the intentions of the dance. In contrast the actual dance was accompanied by live music ('Sanatinetta' by Brian Israel, played by Modern Box Co.), thus using the unexpected to catch the audience's attention.

Similarly, in the *accompaniment*, a sudden unexpected silence is as effective as a whole outburst of heavy rock music.

CLIMAX

There may be several highlights in a dance, but there is only one main high point: the *climax*. The dance should be organised to gradually build towards this, making it seem inevitable, organically right. This again involves a crucial pacing of the constituent features. Pacing is a balancing act which requires a delicate and subtle treatment of all the interconnected layers of the dance. It follows the logical progression and direction of the piece, whilst also continually providing enough interest and even diversion, so that the climax happens at just the right moment. When the final climax happens, it should confirm what the audience has expected and yet also provide a certain element of *surprise* so that it is not too obvious. It should sum up everything that has happened before it. The climax might be a fast and furious outburst of energy and action, or it could fade away to a gentle quiet, or it may be marked by the end of a particular story. Or, it may well be that the climax does not come at the end of the dance.

The actual ending of the dance is, however, the last thing that the audience will see, and they will remember it the best, and so it must be memorable – it must not disappoint or puzzle, or leave the audience uncomfortably up in the air not knowing whether or not to applaud. It is noticeable that the endings of Lea Anderson's works are often glitzy and fast. We see this, for example, in the shiny phosphorescent suits of *Go Las Vegas* (1995). And in the ending of *Precious* (1993), which depicts the process of alchemy turning base metals into gold, the dancers realise their dreams by changing their perspectives and states of being. Finally, they achieve the golden state of equilibrium, and the movement's pace increases to a furious tempo.

There is a similar ending in Twyla Tharp's *Catherine Wheel* (1983). The final section is entitled 'The Golden section'. In response to the music (written by David Byrne of the band Talking Heads), the dancers move in highly energised unison and canons. The choreography of this finale section is accompanied by the lyrics '... and they're enjoying themselves. Movin' in every direction with their eyes wide open.' The cascading movement is effervescent, and like a firework display it explodes and glitters all over the stage. It expresses the optimistic conclusion of the dance's theme. Even though people can be destructive to each other and their environment, there is hope that they can learn to share and celebrate their individual strengths and differences. And the image of the Catherine Wheel, which was originally used to martyr Saint Catherine, becomes a positive symbol of a brighter future.

But not all endings need to be razzle-dazzle. The recent *Movements in 8* (1995), danced by the Phoenix Dance Company and choreographed collaboratively by Maggie Morris and Gary Lambert, has a dazzling climax where individual soloists jump, turn, fall and shift through space with breathtaking energy. But the end itself is a return to the soft, internalised style of the beginning. The dancers seem to be meditatively centring themselves, and slowly they exit, melting into the red sunset. There is a real feeling of the passing of a dancer's day: waking into the day's activities, performing in the evening, and slowly calming down into slumber. The exit of the dancers at the end leaves only the musicians on stage, and the ringing of a large gong finally resolves the whole dance.

It is clear from both of these examples that it is not only the movement components that are manipulated to achieve climax and the end but also the other constituent features of the physical and aural setting. The *imagination* is used to create a spontaneous fusion that feels organically inevitable.

TASK 3 ▽▽▽

'Surprise me!' Ensuring that you use contrast, highlights and climax, compose a duet which has a surprise for the audience. (This was set as a choreographic task by Robert Cohan in 1986 at the London School of Contemporary Dance. It proved to be very testing for all the choreographers present.)

BALANCE

The proportions of the sections of the dance need to be appropriate to the individual movement phrases and how they relate to each other. Each movement must be given the full amount of time that it needs to be seen in its entirety. As phrases develop and lengthen, they become whole sections, and each must be an appropriate length for its movement to be appreciated fully. Similarly, if there is a *meaning* in the movement, enough time is needed for this meaning to be put across to the audience.

In rehearsal the choreographer will be making spontaneous and intuitive choices about how single movements grow into phrases, and about how long those phrases are, and how long the sections are that are the *sum* of those phrases. These are delicate decisions which will give the dance its final overall form. Throughout the creative process, the choreographer will be *organising*. As movement is developed, the process of giving the dance a balanced structure is occurring simultaneously. Sometimes, the order and length of motifs, longer phrases and whole sections is obvious early on in rehearsal, but at other times it may require some experimentation. Finally, the choreographer decides what is, for them, a sensible and appropriate ordering and length for all the parts. This will amount to the final balance and proportion of the dance.

Forest (1977) by Robert Cohan provides a good example here. The dance is based on three simple motifs:

1 the 'calling' motif;
2 the 'prowling' motif;
3 the 'pairing' motif.

Through repetition, variation and development, they combine in numerous ways to create the form of the dance. Several sections become obvious to the audience as it watches. Many short sections overlap by means of frequent entrances and exits, making their beginnings and ends clear. The dance has 9 sections which fall into 4 main parts (ABCD) during which various different moods are expressed: slightly romantic; the darker menace of a pack of prowling predators; calmness; tense nervousness.

In an interview, Cohan once spoke about a dance performance which involved the on-the-spot choreographing of a new dance for each new day in the presence of a public audience. This nerve-wracking process produced a dance of continual highpoints which did not allow the correct sequencing or pace that the sections of dance needed for a full development and life of their own. Cohan stated that he would not attempt that process again.

TRANSITION

Transitions are the links between movements, between phrases and between sections of the dance, and as such they are an integral part of the dance. As one movement or phrase grows into the next, the organic and logical progression should also flow.

Transitions can differ in:

- length – gradual or abrupt;
- complexity – as simple as a plié for a jump, or involving a whole phrase of movement.

Transitions usually *correspond* to what they are linking, so that a transition between whole sections may be more complex than that which connects two simple actions. In *Septet* (1953) by Merce Cunningham, the dancers' exits and entrances at the end of each section use everyday movements like hand shakes, nods and waves. This draws attention to the gaps between the sections, making the transitions as important as the dance itself. In Robert Cohan's *Waterless Method of Swimming Instruction* (1975), the transitions between the various sections use simple ideas of entering the water as entrances and exits. This not only makes for an easy integrated feel but also adds to the meaning of the dance.

LOGICAL SEQUENCE AND PROPORTION

Sequencing a dance logically involves organising the natural progression from start to finish. Part of this process includes a consideration of the individual proportions of the beginning, middle and end sections. The final chosen order and length of the sections and their constituent features must give the appearance of a unified whole. It should also amount to the most expressive sequence and proportion for the corresponding expressive intentions of the choreographer.

The proportion of the beginning, middle and end not only of the whole dance but also of each individual section is also vital to correct pacing and the expression of the intent. For instance, a long, gradually building opening section leading to a shorter middle section and an abrupt end may well be suited to some dances. In other instances, a dance may be more suited to a fast short opening section, a long middle section of some complexity, and a gradually winding-down ending. The task below gives your a chance to work on these ideas.

TASK 4

1 ⧗ Look at the titles below and choose appropriate proportions for their beginning, middle and end sections. Write these out in table form. Give brief descriptions of the length of sections and the general motifs and images used.

- 'The rebellion goes up in smoke'
- 'The river from source to sea'
- 'Obstacle race'.

2 ⧗ In groups of 4 or 5, choose one of the themes above and improvise around the chosen sections. (Suggested music: Side 2 of the Penguin Café Orchestra's *Broadcasting from Home*, EGDC 38.) As you work, select the most appropriate track for your needs.

UNITY

No matter how complex the form of a dance is, it must still work as a whole unit. Too many unrelated components or ideas will be too confusing for an audience to comprehend. The flow of the piece, its peaks, troughs and conclusion, is what gives the piece its unity or overall form. The central concern of a dance helps to maintain the flow, giving it coherence. This may involve either a particular meaning or a concern with the movement for its own sake. The central theme is selected, then the process of manipulating and selecting appropriate constituent features follows in rehearsal.

Contrast and variety are a part of the overall unity, and they too must be selected in a way appropriate to the central concern of the dance. Sometimes, even the most unlikely and incongruous ideas can work if these fall within the main purpose of the dance. Then, by their very differences they enhance the central idea and help the onlooker to grasp the main mood, meaning or inner vision of the dance.

TASK 5 ▽▼▽▼▽▼

Allow at least three 1-hour sessions for this task.

- Look at the pictures below. Use them as a score for a dance.
- Improvise and select short phrases/motifs for each.
- Memorise these, and teach them to 3 or 4 dancers.
- Randomly choose which order they appear in, asking the dancers to perform them so that you can observe. Continue to do this until you are able to select one or two of the orders as the most successful. Note that this will involve making transitions if there are sticking points.
- Gradually, by careful observation:

  - develop and extend the motifs so as to make sections;
  - decide on the length of the beginning, middle and end sections;
  - give consideration occasionally as to the climax and the end;
  - consider if there is enough suitable contrast and variety.

- At any point, you may like to consider trying out different accompaniments as you work, until you find one which is most appropriate.
- Give the finished dance a title.

The above task should produce a dance which could, after rehearsal, be performed, and it should have overall form and unity, the central concern here being the photographic images. The organic structure of the dance will have grown through the gradual manipulation and selection of movement and the use of choreographic devices.

Alternatively, choreographers may look to structures which are *pre-set* and are often derived from music or art or literature. In the next section, these structures will be examined in detail.

Compositional structures

Compositional structures are traditional frameworks which have set patterns. These frameworks are often found in music, literature or art, and fit into one of the following three categories:

1 sequential
2 contrapuntal
3 episodic.

SEQUENTIAL STRUCTURES

These contain themes which progress in a definite order. Letters of the alphabet are used to label each theme or section. The simplest sequential structure is AB. Choosing the structure which best expresses the dance idea is essential. Unity is still necessary between the themes A, B, C etc. – again, they have to have something in common, even if it is through contrast. The themes also have to be linked with appropriate transitions. In songs, a transition is often called a *bridge*, and it is usually an instrumental.

Sequential structures may contain movement which has been developed using choreographic devices like motif development. These structures are set, but may be applied creatively to become organic wholes – for example, to become the framework for one section or for the entire dance. A dance may even involve a mixture of different choreographic structures, and this may lead to overall structures which again are more organic. The arrangements are freer in style, such as AABCDAD, and will respond to the dance idea. This is a more intuitive way of working, and is probably the one which you will use most. Trying new approaches and structures like the ones listed below may be difficult at first, but they will help you build greater skill in your choreography.

The AB structure – binary (two-part)

This is the simplest form, like a verse and a chorus of a song. It is typical of many folk dances and songs. A and B are repeated many times and in any order: ABBAB, ABAB, AABA, ABAAB etc.

The ABA structure – ternary (three-part)

This is a form which is very comfortable to watch because of its feeling of completeness. A is the unifying theme and the centre of interest, then B gives contrast. The original A returns either as an exact repetition or in an easily recognisable variation or development. It is important that A and B be linked by *transitions*, and these may become important in their own right as they mix together features from both A and B. This allows B to grow *out* of A and then to flow easily back *into* A. The sections are still independent, but also connected. This again gives balance and unity.

Many popular songs use this structure: the chorus A, a verse B, and a repetition of the chorus which is often augmented or elaborated in some way to give emphasis to the idea of the song.

TASK 6 ▽▽▽

Listen to 'We got the beat' by The Go-Gos (1994, IRS 7243 8 31756 2 8). Analyse the music using A B C etc. When you are satisfied with your analysis, compose motifs which fit with the music structure. The movement may, however, be of a contrasting and unexpected style – e.g. balletic vocabulary with a strong, fast, dynamic quality.

ABACADA structure – rondo

Here, the basic theme A returns after each contrasting theme. A must appear at least three times, but it can itself be varied. Indeed, the variations of A will maintain interest in the theme. The other sections should be individual and different, but should also be linked with appropriate transitions to provide continuity for the audience.

The rondo structure was popular in Europe in the eighteenth and nineteenth centuries as a lively round dance. A would be danced by everyone, and the B, C and D sections by individual soloists.

The Martha Graham solo *Frontier* (1935) is in rondo form. In a series of scenes from her life on the frontier of the Wild West, Graham is first seen against the fence looking out across the vast plains. After each exploration away from the homestead, she returns to the fence in a clear rondo.

Theme and variation – A1, A2, A3, A4 etc.

Varying a motif is a real test of compositional skill. A must be sufficiently interesting to keep the attention of the audience. Unlike develop-ing a motif, varying it involves keeping the original order of the movements the same. The variations then take the form of subtle adjustments in dynamics, space, style, mood and tempo.

The *Nympheas* (1899–1926) paintings by impressionist artist Claude Monet show a single scene at different times of day and in different weather conditions. This idea was used by Robert Cohan in a dance of the same title. The scenes vary in energy from a calm, lyrical feel to a stormy, faster, wilder section. The lighting enhances the changes in mood through changes in colour and brightness. The music by Debussy, who was an impressionist composer, further emphasises the mood swings. And the feel of the impressionist style was completed by the dance itself, with its ever-changing suggestions of look and mood. A here is the scene, the motifs and the moods, and the constituent features pass through a series of variations to express the changes in the mood around this watery scene.

CONTRAPUNTAL STRUCTURES

The above structures give forms which are sequential, but there are also structures in which the main theme appears *throughout*. Again, these are musical forms also. Here, the main theme is seen/heard against itself, or against one or more *other* themes. This leads to a weaving of material, through which the main theme must be clear and strong enough to stand out from the complex structure. These structures are called *contrapuntal*, and in music, they create *polyphony*, that is a playing of two or more independent melodies heard together. The final effect is more complex and richer than each of the sequential forms. There are three different kinds of contrapuntal structure:

1 ground bass
2 round (or canon)
3 fugue.

Ground bass

Here, a single theme starts the dance and is repeated over and over all the way through the dance. This would be monotonous on its own, but other themes are danced at the same time. This structure offers good opportunities for groups to work either in contrast to each other or against a soloist. In addition, the dance idea should be one appropriate to this structure – say, for example, a dance entitled 'The inevitable is difficult to avoid'.

Round (canon)

This is like a song sung in a round, like 'London's burning'. The first dancer states the theme, the second enters at the end of the first half-phrase, the third enters at the start of the second phrase, and the fourth enters on the last half of the second phrase. The round ends in the same order as the last dancer finishes off the theme or movement.

The theme motif is often developed or varied as it is played off against itself. In this way, a simple type of *counterpoint* is involved here as one movement is seen simultaneously with another.

Fugue

> Four abstract themes, all moving equally and harmoniously together like a fugue.
>
> *(Doris Humphrey in* Shapes of Change, *1981)*

Here, the original theme appears and disappears in various developed forms throughout the dance. This makes for an irregular and complex structure, but one full of surprise and intricate interest. In music, the theme melody can be reversed, inverted, augmented or diminished, and movement motifs in dance can be treated in the same way. Sometimes, *counter-themes* appear with the main motif, and these may take over.

A fugue builds to a clear climax, then gradually winds down and may return, in a *coda*, to a softer repetition of the original motif. This can be useful for carrying dramatic ideas. *Fugue* (1988) by Ian Spink (and directed for television by Caryl Churchill) uses the formal pre-set structure to create dramatic tension. The accompaniment in part uses Bach's *The Art of Fugue*, mixed with text. The story is about a man's death and his family's way of coming to terms with it. The interest lies in Spink's use of formal structure to draw the audience's attention to the everyday. The dance uses the contrapuntal repetition of the main theme in numerous variations. Although it could appear to be yet another soap opera, the use of the fugue structure allows it to rise above that. In fact, there is an atmosphere of unreality because the audience are *equally* aware both of the narrative and of the structure. In a way, this makes the story even more moving, because the repetition here emphasises the strength of feelings as the family grieve. This is a typical post-modern approach to choreography insofar as it avoids cliché and provokes

EPISODIC STRUCTURES

Unlike the above, these are not musical forms. They are instead found in literature, as a story gradually unfolds. The narrative is told in connected and progressive sections, chapters, or – as in all good soap operas – episodes. Each section reveals more of the plot: A, B, C, D, E, F, G. Classical ballet often uses this form. *Giselle* (1841, Coralli and Perrot) and *Petrouchka* (1912, Fokine) are such story-type dances. Each individual section must have its own interest, variation and contrast. In *Giselle*, this requirement is helped along by the music by Adolph Adam which uses the technique, taken from opera, of *leitmotif*. Certain characters have their own musical themes, and variations reflect changes of mood or situation.

In Sir Frederick Ashton's *The Dream* (1964), the music by Felix Mendelssohn-Bartholdy contains themes for the fairies and a 'hee-haw' motif for Bottom. The score was arranged by John Lanchbery, and interesting problems were encountered in creating the narrative ballet. Ashton thought that the music could be mixed with other pieces by Mendelssohn in order to support the action, but Lanchbery was not prepared to do this, considering it to be unacceptable meddling with the original score. Instead, he pieced together only music which Mendelssohn had written for the story. In this way, the lengthy story was shortened to its essentials and made appropriate to be told through dance. The final film version of another in Ashton's story ballets, *Tales of Beatrix Potter* (1971), was criticised for its lack of a storyline.

> Some of the sequences don't bother to tell the stories, relying on instant recognition of beloved characters to do the work.
>
> (*David Vaughan in* Frederick Ashton and His Ballets, *1977*)

audiences into responding on a deeper, more thoughtful level.

The episodes must reveal the story, otherwise they are more of a mere collage of scenes with a unifying theme. This latter type of structure is seen in Christopher Bruce's *Sergeant Early's Dream* (1984). The different episodes in this work do not tell a story but present different scenes from one community. The scenes are linked via entrances and exits so that each flows easily into the next.

The story can also be enriched by adopting techniques used in films. Flashbacks or dreams take us out of real time and into memories, nightmares and fantasies. This adds a deeper psychological dimension – as seen in the work of Martha Graham. Graham's dance *Errand into the Maze* (1947) is based on the Greek myth where Theseus goes into the maze to battle with the monster, the Minotaur. The dance features the female character Ariadne as confronting the beast, and it creates a psychothriller. The sub-plot is the fear of confronting the fears that any of us may have on our journey through life. In a television interview, Graham refers to these fears which are featured in the dance as being in the front of both her mind and the minds of her dancers when they were flying through an electrical storm together on tour.

> Once again ... we see the Graham protagonist coming to terms with her psychological adversary, and beating back its advance with her own forceful action. Graham sees the woman who ends up in a subservient sexual relationship as either ... victim ... like Jocasta ... or outlaw ... like Clytemnestra. ... Her way of representing her position and the alternatives ... anticipated some of the most

radical feminist ideas of a generation later.

(Marcia B. Siegel in The Shapes of Change, *1979)*

The episodic structure is not only a straightforward story-telling tool: it can also have a wide range of subtleties and meanings.

OTHER COMPOSITIONAL STRUCTURES

Natural structures

As mentioned at the start of this chapter, form is all around us in the natural world. The seasons, life cycles and so on offer rich material for organic dance structures.

Collage

Sometimes, juxtaposing the unexpected can create a unity of its own. This is an approach used greatly in visual art. In the paintings of surrealists like Dali and Magritte, fantastic and absurd images are created which often result in surprises for an audience. The overall form remains a whole even though the content may be illogical.

The collage structure is a difficult structure, requiring careful and sensitive handling if it is not to fragment into an unconnected, discordant jumble.

Chance

The pioneers, in the early 1950s, of this type of structure were Merce Cunningham and the composer John Cage. They made detailed charts showing timings, spatial designs, sounds and movements. Then they would toss coins to decide on choices and the order of performance. This was how the dance *Suite by Chance* (1953) was composed. In 1969, different movements were matched to playing cards, and *Canfield* was the result. This method involves a detailed and careful choreography of the dance movements in-

volved, in order that these be secure in the dancers' minds: then, and only then, can they be performed in different orders and spatial placings.

The chance structure was the beginning of a post-modern approach which highlighted an interest in the creative process for its own sake. The idea of the content of a dance having a specific meaning was rejected in favour of *movement* being important for its own sake. This innovation was taken up in the UK in the early 1970s by alternative choreographers like Richard Alston. (Up until then, modern dance had been very much based within the technique and expressionist style of Martha Graham.) Cunningham himself visited the UK, as did others who had worked with him – like dancer Viola Farber. They all visited The Place, in London, which offered a staple diet of Graham tuition, but at the same time a great deal of experimental work was happening. It was at this time that dancer Siobhan Davies performed with the new company Strider. This was the brainchild of Richard Alston. The founder and benefactor of The Place, Robin Howard, encouraged all such experimental work.

Siobhan Davies became acclaimed as one of the UK's foremost choreographers of the 1980s and 1990s. Davies was trained at the London School of Contemporary Dance at The Place, and she went on to dance with the London Contemporary Dance Theatre, again based at The Place, under the direction of ex-Graham dancer, Robert Cohan. By the 1980s, she was making more independent work. One such work, which develops the chance-type structures, was *Plain Song* (1981). This is made up from seven complex phrases for seven dancers. Using a device introduced by Cunningham, she reshuffled the order of the parts of the motifs, changed their facing on stage, changed the dimension they were performed in, or developed them by adding lifts or falls. In this reordering, new phrases and motifs would also be created.

It would be fun for you to think up a system of your own that would enable you to create a dance-by-chance. You could use coins, dice, playing cards, or board games. Through the random use of the categories of action, space, dynamics and timing, movement phrases may be composed. Then, the order, place and time of their performance, on your own or in a group, may again be decided by a chance device.

TASK 7

1 △ Read the following list of dance titles and decide which of the above compositional structures would give it the most supportive form. (Answers on p. 149.) Explain briefly why you have chosen that structure.

(a) A dance to 'Chocolate (Spanish dance)', from *The Nutcracker* music by Tchaikovsky, 1 minute 9 seconds – recording by the Orchestra of the Royal Opera House, Conifer Records, ROH 002 (or similar recording).

(b) A dance entitled 'United we stand, divided we fall'.

(c) A dance entitled 'Mood swings'.

(d) A dance based on the story entitled *Amazon Sisters* which tells of a group of women in the Amazon who fought against a large electricity company building a dam because it would ruin the environment.

(e) A dance based on a collection of letters and images from a magazine.

(f) A dance entitled 'The planets'.

(g) A dance to 'Fishin' Blues' by Taj Mahal from *The Collection*, Castle Communication, CCSCD 180 1987.

(h) A dance entitled 'Random dance'.

2 ▲ ▲ ▲ Choose one of the above, and find a suitable accompaniment for a composition for 3, 4 or 5 dancers.

COMPOSITIONAL STRUCTURES – A CONCLUSION

Choosing and using these pre-set structures for your dances can be a helpful way to put your ideas in order. Again, try to use them in ways that are appropriate to what a particular dance is trying to convey. This may have a dramatic emphasis, or may be more involved with the movement content for its own sake.

ANSWERS TO TASK 7, QUESTION 1

(a) AB.
(b) Ground bass.
(c) Fugue.
(d) Episodic.

(e) Collage.
(f) Natural forms.
(g) Rondo.
(h) Chance procedures.

The relationship of dance to the accompaniment

When more is meant than meets the ear

(John Milton, L'Allegro *and* Il Penseroso,
circa 1632)

In the preceding sections of this chapter, the devices and structures which give a dance its overall form were examined, and by now you should have tried out many new ideas from which to start your choreography, or new ways to *organise* your ideas. You may have also read earlier about choosing from a variety of possibilities for accompaniments for your dances, and you now realise the wide variety of choices available to you. The most commonly chosen accompaniment (aural setting) is that of *music,* and so this next section of the book is going to look in some depth at this aspect. As well as an enormous range of choices for the style of music itself, there are also choices to be made about how the movement will *interrelate* with the sound. An understanding of these choices will help to make choreography interrelate with the music in more appropriate, varied and skilled ways.

Dancers and choreographers need an awareness of the structural elements in music. As we saw in the previous section, musical structure is rich and varied. This is similarly so for the elements which go to make up these structures. In dance, we manipulate the elements of action, space, time, dynamics and relationships. In music, composers are faced with similar factors.

This section will focus on:

● musical terms
● different possible relationships between music and dance.

MUSICAL TERMS

In the Schoenberg score there aren't any long phrases. He states his theme concisely. He uses little repetition, but there are extremes of sudden, fast tempos, and there are slow tempos that happen quickly, and then that rhythm's broken too. Another score like 'Voluntaries' ... one of Poulenc's best ... takes me to the opposite extreme. That's an inward score with a beautiful ... lyricism and a deep religious feeling.

(Glen Tetley in The Dance Makers, *1980)*

Could *you* be so specific in describing a piece of music? The description above shows a real understanding of music and its terms. Before

Rhythm

Rhythm is the basic pattern of sound and silence. It can be a steady pulse or beat, or it can be made up of regular repeated groupings.

> All Musick, Feasts, Delights and Pleasures, Games, Dancing, Arts, consist in govern'd measures.
>
> *(Thomas Traherne, 1657)*

During the classic and romantic ballet periods, most music was written in even rhythms: in 2, 4 and 8, or 3, 6 and 9. Rhythms can, however, be both even and uneven. An example of an even rhythm is 4/4 because there are always 4 units in one *bar* (or *measure*):

= 2 bars of 4/4, containing *crotchets* (or *quarter notes*)

After about 500 years of even rhythm in music, modern composers began to write in uneven rhythms – 5/4 or 7/4, for example. They also began to vary rhythms within one piece of music. This trend reflected the *social context* of the twentieth century, and of course affected modern dance choreographers like Martha Graham. Life in society was no longer so predictable or balanced. The uneven pulse of society was reflected in the uneven phrasing of sound and actions.

> One of the earmarks of the restlessness of our age is shown in our rhythmic groupings.
>
> *(Marion Bauer, in* Twentieth Century Music, *1993)*

An uneven rhythm combines notes of *different* values in one bar:

(a)   (b)

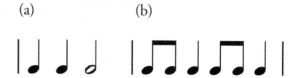

= 2 bars of 4/4 containing (a) 2 crotchets + 1 *minim* (or *half note*), and (b) 2 *quavers* (or *eighth notes*) + 1 crotchet + 2 quavers + 1 crotchet

It would be worth reminding you here of *dancer's counts*, which may be different from the musical rhythm:

Accumulative rhythm is where each new bar adds one extra count:

| 1 | 1 2 | 1 2 3 | 1 2 3 4 ‖

Subtractive rhythm is where one count is *lost* from each new bar:

| 1 2 3 4 | 1 2 3 | 1 2 | 1 ‖

> The use of percussion in Wigman's music was just wonderful, and I wanted some information about it for my own musical knowledge
>
> *(Alwin Nikolais in* The Dance Makers, *1980)*

TASK 8

In pairs, let one person play a drum while the other moves. The drum plays: Bar 1 12345-12345/123 Bar 2 45-1234/12 Bar 3 345-123/12 Bar 4 345-12/12345-1, and then play again in reverse order (retrograde).

The dancer starts on a low level, tightly curled up, then opens to full stretch on a high level, and then curls up again to the floor, alternating open-close with the rhythm of the drum. Then the rhythm is reversed so that it is accumulative, and the dance responds likewise.

Change round the dancer and player, and repeat.

Musical notation – the time value of the notes

As you saw above, musical notes have different *time values*. In the score example shown:

𝅝 = 4 counts (a *semibreve* or *whole note*)

𝅗𝅥 = 2 counts (a minim)

♩ = 1 count (a crotchet)

♫ = half a count (a quaver)

The time value of 8 quavers is the same as the time value of one semibreve.

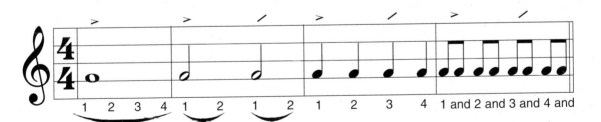

It is possible to divide a single note into *three*. So, one crotchet is equal to a *triplet:*

Accent

An *accent* is an increase in the stress on a beat, and is shown by the sign '>'. A less heavy accent is shown by '/'. This is seen in the score example shown. Shifting the accent away from the first beat in a bar creates a more irregular feeling in the rhythm. When this shift is set in a regular measured rhythm, it produces *syncopation*. Syncopated movement can be very exciting to watch because the accents fall in unexpected places and give an element of surprise. Here are some examples of syncopation.

The accent is usually on beat 1, but now is on beat 3.

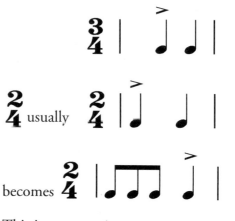

Missing beat 1 shifts the accent to count 2

This is a *progressive* accent:

TASK 9

1 ⧖ Syncopation can be easily felt by walking in regular 3/4, 2/4 and 4/4 rhythms and then changing to any of the above variations. As you move, feel where the *up-beats* (the weaker beats) and where the *down-beats* (the stronger beats) are.

1 ⧖ Take any technique exercise that you know well and alter the accents so that it becomes syncopated.

Dancers do not have to always stress the same beats as those stressed in the music. Indeed, the choreography can be richer and more interesting if the dancer's movement uses the *offbeat*. In this way, a feeling of increase in speed results, and this is called *double time*.

Clap this repeatedly:

Time signature

The *time signature* is a number which tells you the number of beats which make up a repeated group (i.e. a bar or measure). It is always shown at the start of every piece of music, and usually at the start of a dance notation score too. The time here is divided up by a regular accent or emphasis, and this gives the *metre*.

The number of beats in a bar (measure) gives the time signature. For example:

The top number shows how many beats are in one bar. The lower number shows what kind of note receives one count.

There are many common time signatures in music: 2/2, 2/4, 4/4, 3/4, 5/4, 7/4, 3/8, 6/8, 12/8. Each one has its own distinctive feel. For example, 2/2 can feel military and march-like, where 6/8 has a lively steppy feel. 3/4, in turn, is more lyrical and swing-like. The asymmetrical rhythms – like 5/4 – favoured by modern composers and choreographers may feel distorted and unstable for an audience. Actors using an uneven walk to enter into a scene know that the audience will respond by feeling an emotional disruption. Clearly, emotional responses of the dancer, the choreographer and the audience can all be influenced by the use of different rhythms.

TASK 10

Read the notation scores shown in Figure 6.2. Be sure to accent the time signatures correctly. Both tracks are features on *Moving in Time* by Parampara, 1992.

When two metres of unequal length and accent are combined, a *resultant rhythm* is produced. Combining 2/4 and 3/4 makes 6/4, 3/4 and 4/4 combined result in 12/4 as in the example shown.

TASK 11

1   Clap the 12/4 resultant rhythms in the example shown. Then, *walk* the rhythm clearly, showing the accents by stamping. Then, walk the rhythm *and* use other movements to show the accent – e.g. a jump, arm gestures, clapping or a change of level.

1   In trios, let one person move to the 3/4, another person to the 4/4, and the third person to the resultant 12/4, simultaneously.

Figure 6.2   *Notation for Task 10: (a) score from Syrtos Kephalinias, from the Greek Island of Kephalinia; (b) score from Lamita; add wild shouts during the gallops!*

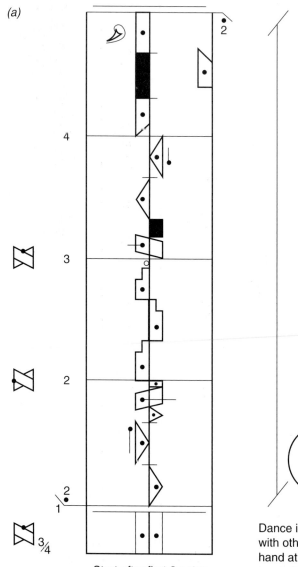

Start after first 3 notes

Dance in a circle, with others holding hand at hip level. Or dance alone.

(b)

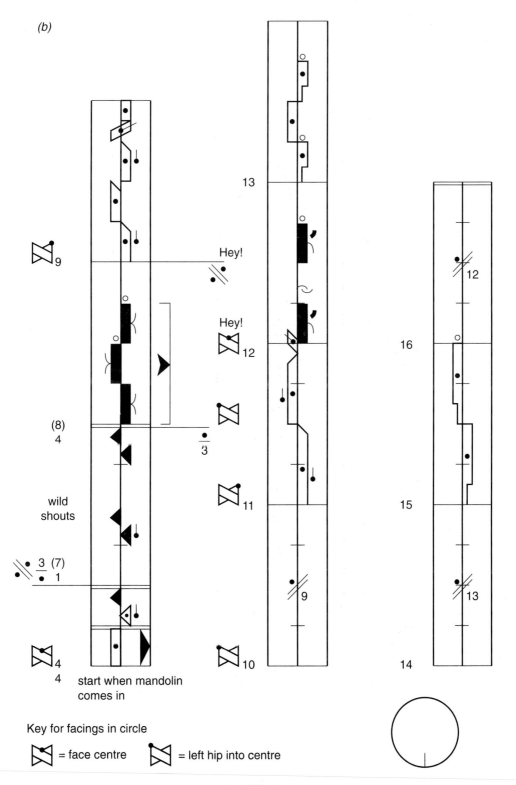

Hey!

Hey!

(8)
4

wild
shouts

$\frac{3}{1}$ (7)

13

12

11

10

16

15

14

Key for facings in circle

⋈ = face centre   ⋈ = left hip into centre

start when mandolin
comes in

A *mixed metre* is the result of mixing two time signatures which have different underlying beats. This results in bars with different time values – for example, combining 3/8 with 2/4, or – as shown below – 2/4 and 3/4:

Or, combining 4/4, 1/4 and 2/4:

Some metres mix more satisfactorily than others.

TASK 12

Find two or three metres which mix comfortably.

Tempo

The *tempo* is the *speed* of the beat. This may get faster or slow down. The tempo is usually shown at the start of the music score. Doing triplets travelling with clear changes of tempo is an easy way to experience this. As you move, there are clear changes in mood from the lyrical to a sense of urgency and directness. The *intensity* and the *dynamics* of the music is changed by changing the tempo.

The Italian terms that music uses to describe tempo are (from fast to slow): *presto, vivace, allegro, moderato, andante, adagio, lento, largo.* 'Allegro' means briskly and brightly, whereas 'largo' means very slow. The speed is measured by a metronome, so:

● Presto = approximately 180 beats per minute.
● Adagio = approximately 100 beats per minute.

If a tempo gradually increases, it is *acceleration*, and if it is gradually slowed down, it is *deceleration*.

The intensity of the music can also change if the *force* with which it is played alters. If the volume and force of the playing is increased, the music will rise to a *crescendo*. By *decreasing* the same, a *diminuendo* results, as the dynamics softens.

Ostinato

An ostinato is a musical idea (phrase) which repeats itself throughout a piece or a section of a piece.

As in dance motifs, musical motifs can be varies and developed. They may be:

- played faster;
- played at a higher pitch – i.e. *transposed*;
- inverted – i.e. played upside down;
- played backwards – i.e. *retrograde*;
- played with longer notes – *augmented* – or shorter notes – *diminished*;

or any combination of these.

Phrases

Phrases, as in dance, are units which may represent one idea. The music by Adolphe Adam for Giselle (1841) is a good example. The leit-motif here gave each character a theme; for example, Giselle's own theme was light, bright and full of steps for her dancing. The themes were varied, as in choreography, and Giselle's own theme, heard originally in Act One, was also played in Act Two but much more slowly and lamentfully to suit the change in mood.

Phrases usually occur in groups of two: two, four, six or eight bar phrases, and so on. When two phrases, or themes, are played *against* one another, it produces *counterpoint*. This can look very dramatic if used in the choreography.

The above terms are all connected with how time is divided and accented. There are other musical terms which relate more to the *pitch* of the notes – that is, to the highness and lowness.

Melody

Melody is a succession of notes, of differing pitch and with a rhythm, that results in a recognisable and repeated tune.

Polyphony

Polyphony is music consisting of two or more independent melodic lines which sound together and which counterpoint each other. This technique was used in the fourteenth century, and it produced a new element, harmony.

Harmony

Harmony results when a *succession* of chords is played. Chords are three or more notes that are played at the same time. In the romantic period, harmonies, like rhythm, were evened out so as always to be pleasing to the ear, and matched the 'happy endings'. This approach was challenged by modern composers, and the richness of dissonance gave music a new raw edge. Impressionist composers like Debussy and Satie worked in this way, as did Stravinsky later on to an even more extreme extent. Painters of the time like the impressionists Monet and Seurat experimented in similar ways in their use of paint: they broke up the colour rather than mixing it in the palette, and the viewer now had to make the mix for themselves. This too developed further in the shocking colours of Matisse.

So too in modern dance:

> ... the modern dancer has infused movement with that vibrant restless texture and that inner concentration typical of our psychologically oriented age.
>
> *(In* Modern Dance Forms, *by Louis Horst and Carroll Russell, 1961)*

The inward searchings of the works of Martha Graham into the new psychologies of Freud and Jung were the dissonance and discord of the modern dance world.

Different possible relationships between music and dance

Different choreographers use music very differently. Some stay very close to the score, while others may not even hear the music until the première. These are clear extremes of approach, but both of them have one thing in common: the *dance* is the most important element, and it is not a servant to the music.

> The new ballet, refusing to be the slave either of music or of scenic decoration, and recognising the alliance of the arts only on the condition of complete equality, allows perfect freedom to scenic artist and to the musician.
>
> *(Michel Fokine in his letter to* The Times, *6 July 1914)*

DIRECT CORRELATION

Here, dance and music work *together*, so that, for example, in quieter moments in the music, the dance also uses a softer dynamic. This may be the result of dance and music having been composed together. Marius Petipa, the ballet master of St Petersburg, Russia, worked with the composer Tchaikovsky on *The Sleeping Beauty*, 1890. This was a fine score, and it won over audiences. Petipa gave very clear instructions to Tchaikovsky in the form of a *libretto* (a text written for and set to music in an opera etc.). In this scenario, the full story is told and broken down in fine detail showing when each section requires musical changes. The final result was music which directly correlated with the action, mime and movement – as, for example, in the celebration waltz for the birthday party. The opening prologue serves wonderfully to introduce the characters. It involves variations for each of the fairies at Aurora's christening.

This tradition was continued in the Diaghilev

And so, also, for any other type of accompaniment.

It is common to think that the perfect relationship is one where dance and music support and enhance each other, whether through their similarities or through their differences.

The relationship can involve any one of the following:

- a direct correlation;
- a music visualisation;
- the showing or emphasising of character and narrative;
- a call and response;
- a mutual co-existence;
- a disassociation.

work of The Ballet Russes. Diaghilev was a catalyst in the close collaborations of choreographers, composers and artists. For the ballet *Petrouchka* by Fokine (1911), the score by composer Stravinsky was met measure for measure by the movement. The solos for the sad puppet who comes to life are movingly contrasted with the crowd scenes at the fairground. His failure in love is made to look even sadder by its juxtaposition against the gaiety of the carnival.

The work of Sir Frederick Ashton was also famous for its closeness to the music. The critic Alistair Macaulay reported about Ashton's *La Fille Mal Gardée*:

> ... never before had they seen ballet with the harmony, structure and fluency of music – that watching it was like reading a score.
>
> *(Alistair Macaulay, the* Financial Times, *1994)*

It may be worth finding a music student to collaborate with. There are no rules about how to start. It may be your idea or it may be the musician's. You may talk about what the starting point, images, structure, instruments and so on may be, and so arrive at the overall direction together. It is worth, indeed, trying to work as closely together as possible throughout the rehearsal period.

In the genre of modern dance, Martha Graham would usually commission the music for her choreography. Graham would supply the scenario of action, mood and timings of each section. She and the composer would then collaborate during the writing of the score, and the composer would be free to add detail. Once the music was written, she would start to choreograph. Often, the music was inseparable from the dance: she would work on the dramatic idea *during* the composing of the music, and so she did not then need to interpret the music because this already correlated directly with her choreography. In *Primitive*

Mysteries (1931), the rhythms, cadences and silences in the music are used to great effect. All the processions take place during the silences, conveying the ritualistic, spiritual feel of the religious event. At one point, a 5-count melody which had captured the dancers in a repeated back and forth motion changes to a 6, and the now even rhythm releases them into a jumping section. Their energy rises up towards heaven. Often the cadences draw attention to the main figure of the virgin. In one, she rises as the other dancers sink and fold in, bowing to her. In another, two women fall and she quickly stands up in a crucifix-like pose. The titles of two of the sections, 'Hymn to the Virgin' and 'Crucifixus', show of her intent to portray intense religious feeling, probably a result of her encounters with American Native Indians who had been converted to Catholicism. The music seems to drive the spiritual forces at work in the women. As dancers and characters, they seem possessed by the dance idea and the music simultaneously.

MUSIC VISUALISATION

> In my choreographic creations I have always been dependent on the music. I feel a choreographer can't invent rhythms, he only reflects them in movement.
>
> *(George Balanchine in* Dance From Magic to Art, *1976)*

The way of composing dance that Balanchine describes here results in dance and music appearing as one statement. Balanchine and Stravinsky – as already noted – once described their way of working as being able to *hear* the dance and *see* the music. Balanchine once wrote that everything the composer Stravinsky wrote could be choreographed, 'every note of it'. The final result is movement which has a life of its own and yet which subtly relates to the musical structure. Balanchine's earliest ballet *Apollo* (1928) is a fine example of this. The

Stravinsky music was finely interpreted by putting the movement in syncopation with it and shifting the accents into unexpected places. The story in the music shows the god Apollo with the muses of poetry, mime and dance. In a series of solos, duets, trios and quartets, Apollo gives each one creative energy before returning to the heavens. The typical clean, sharp lines of Balanchine's style are distinctive of his neoclassical style. Through the influences of society at that time, the modern and the traditional are brought together: the mix of the fashionable Art Deco sculptural shapes with the percussive hip isolations of jazz are blended with the classical technique. Together, they illustrate and visualise the music sensitively.

A similar combination of the classic and the modern is the theme of a contest in *Agon*

(1957). The movement evokes the sounds and sights of a modern city, powerful and beautiful in its architecture and pace of life. As the music by Stravinsky manipulates court dances into 12-tone sound structures, Balanchine modernises classical technique to a bare minimum. Neither the traditional ballet nor the modernism lose in the contest. The audience watch the two *co-exist*, and the contrast of their differences enhances the expressions of the dance.

> When I listen to a score by him (Stravinsky) ... I am moved ... to try and make visible not only the rhythm, melody and harmony, but even the timbres of the instruments. ... You hear a physical sound humanly organised, performed by people.
>
> *(Balanchine*, Dance Index*, vol. 6, nos 10, 11 & 12)*

Kenneth Macmillan and Sir Frederick Ashton are also choreographers who use this approach.

In the genre of modern dance, the work of Robert North is a good example of music visualisation. This is seen in his dance *Death and the Maiden* (1984). The dance takes the Schubert score of the same name, which is based on a story. In the Ballet Rambert video which features the dance, North states his belief that dance should fit the music exactly. North was artistic director of the Ballet Rambert company at that time.

SHOWING OR EMPHASISING CHARACTER AND NARRATIVE

This is more commonly used in the genre of ballet. In Adam's score for *Giselle*, as has been mentioned before, it is clearly seen. It was a first for the ballet in 1841, and the start of a tradition to be followed for a long, long time. This approach usually involves a mixture of music visualisation and direct correlation.

In John Lanchbery's score for Frederick Ashton's *La Fille Mal Gardée* (*The Unchaperoned Daughter*) (1960), the actions of the characters are clearly supported by the music. In the section entitled 'Lisa and Colas', the two lovers are involved in a flirtation. There is a romantic melody theme in the music which opens the scene over 5 bars as Colas approaches Lisa. Then, 9 bars of butter-churning music play as she ignores him and tries to look busy. The two themes are interwoven as he in turn tries to catch her attention, giving counterpoint. The music then changes to a polka as they play together. Similarly in his 1931 *Facade*, a whole range of music enhances

the variety of characters and shows off their individual characteristics with great clarity. There is the woman who rips off her skirt to dance wildly as the music plays the perfect whirling polka; a Charleston is played for a pair of 'flappers' (young unconventional women of the 1920s); and the final humour of the tango for a gigolo in pursuit of a not-too-impressed debutante uses the format of social dance to great effect. The whole affair is a witty parody of social dancing, with each tune and dance revealing a broad range of caricatures.

Glen Tetley made great use of the Schoenberg score of *Pierrot*. Tetley noted that the music had not stereotyped the character as a clown, but instead gave images of his dramatic highs and lows. The final dance *Pierrot Lunaire* (1962) successfully portrayed the many layers of Pierrot's character as heard in the music. The ups and downs here were clearly seen by the extreme and constant changes in the level of the movement, and the use of a scaffold as a set (by Rouben Ter-Aruntunian) increased the possibilities for this even more. Through a combination of the lifted style of classical ballet with the deep contractions of the modern genre (Tetley was trained in Martha Graham technique), the mood swings were succinctly expressed.

In the modern genre, Robert Cohan describes how Maderna's music for *Hunter of Angels* (1959) just happened to be absolutely right for the narrative of the bible story of the twins Jacob and Esau, conveying the conflicts of the twins and the angel's fight with Jacob. The final ascent to heaven in the epilogue was also suitably enhanced by the music.

In some instances, the narrative may not involve something as obvious as story-telling. Siobhan Davies is a case in point here. In her *Something to Tell* (1980, music by Britten: Cello Suite No. 3), the source is a text by Chekhov. A woman, lonely and isolated, is depicted in the various sections of the dance at different stages of her life. These show a number of her troubles and comprise less of a story and more of a description of her personality as she goes through a troubled and unsatisfying relationship. This was one of the pieces where Davies fitted the dance rhythms to the music. At the start of the dance, the music has phrases which alternate between a high and a low pitch, and this gives the dance an opportunity to explore the idea of a *conversation* in a duet between Davies and Robert North. Davies' style is less likely to respond to melody or rhythm. It will rather syncopate and counterpoint phrasings. This allows greater breadth and freedom of movement, but it still also supports the narrative in its broadest sense.

TASK 13 ▼ ▼ ▼

Use *L'allegro, Il Penseroso ed Il Moderato* by Handel, Part 1: 'Hence vain deluding joys' (53 seconds), 'Haste thee nymph' (solo and chorus, 2 minutes, 26 seconds).

1 Listen very closely several times until the structure and elements of the music become clear. You should have a pencil and paper handy to write down notes on the rhythms, phrasing, motifs/ostinato, repetition, variation and developments, metres, accents and lyrics (it would help to have a copy of the lyrics from the sleeve).
2 Consider the context of the music (consult the sleeve notes or information at the library), particularly how the poetry of Milton contrasts 'cheerful' and 'pensive' attitudes, and how this is reflected in the soprano, tenor and bass voices.
There are many images in the poetry which can give ideas for a group dance.
3 Compose such a dance for 4, 5 or 6 dancers which works either by directly correlating with, or by visualising, the music. You may choose to use the characters as depicted in the poem.

CALL AND RESPONSE

Indian and African genres often use this relationship between music and dance. The master drummer in African ensembles signals to the dancers when to change steps by calls on the drum. In Indian dance, the musicians watch the dancer and change when the movement does. In *bharata natyam*, the dancer is the choreographer. The dances tell classical stories, and there are abstract sequences. The dancer and drummer play off each other in improvisation, rather like in jazz. The aim is to explore rhythms. The dancer wears bells on the ankles, and the stamps weave with the beat of the drum. The syncopation looks and sounds exciting.

The modern dance choreographer Richard Alston (as already quoted earlier) describes his use of music as one involving timing in a 'conversational rhythm'.

In *Strong Language* (1987) by Richard Alston, the movement often has its own logic and independence, loosely working in response to the music. In the section named 'Strumming', the musical count is on 8, but the movement is counted 3-3-2. The effect is a resultant rhythm of shifting accents and metres which gives a look of music and movement being fresh and complementary. The mixed metre of the dance would also help to give an energised appearance, full of rhythmical delights for the audience. It would further help to avoid predictability, and yet still provide a very strong overall structure.

MUTUAL CO-EXISTENCE

The innovative choreography of Vaslav Nijinsky for Diaghilev's Ballets Russes was difficult for the audiences of the day who had been used to a direct correlation between dance and music. Nijinsky's ballets such as *L'Apres-midi d'un Faune* (1912) and *Le Sacre du Printemps* (1913) broke many rules. In *Faune*, the score by Debussy contained clear rhythms, but Nijinsky did not follow these. Instead, he used them almost as a background to give atmosphere.

The Stravinsky music for *The Rite of Spring* (1912) was in itself demanding enough for an audience unused to the discords that it contained. Faced with a combination of layers of counterpoint in the movement and a defiance of the rules of classical ballet in the *style* of the movement, the audience was unable to cope, and so it started a riot. The dance here holds its own identity strongly against what is regarded as a monumental piece of music capable of swamping the efforts of lesser choreographers. Indeed, it has done so on many occasions of attempted revivals. This is what *mutual co-existence* is all about.

Lea Anderson treats the music in a similar way, working closely with the composer on the overall structure. In her collaboration with Steve Blake, *Flesh and Blood* (1989), the *tempo* of the music rather than the phrases are her main point of focus for the movement. The dance and the music run alongside each other, sharing the interpretation of the mood, but they are not so concerned with sharing devices and structures. One critic wrote about *Flesh and Blood*:

> Everything this community of women do is authoritatively fitted to a live chamber systems-jazz score by Steve Blake, whose irony, fragmented, recycled melody and impersonal urgency catch Anderson's tone perfectly. The piece keeps changing, and achieves a sense of ritual and ceremony.
>
> *(Alistair Macaulay, the* Financial Times,
> *21 November 1989)*

There is an interesting comparison to be made here. Thinking back to Martha Graham's (1931) *Primitive Mysteries*, the relationship of the music to the dance could not be more different. However, the contractions and floor-work and the religious drive mixed with secular overtones are, elements that both dances have in common. This too was noted by the press in 1989.

DISASSOCIATION

Allowing both music/sound and dance to develop totally *independently* of each other was the innovation of Merce Cunningham and John Cage, and many others have since followed this approach. The strategy of bringing dance and accompaniment together for the first time only on the opening night itself gives both of these aspects its own separate value.

> It is hard for many people to accept that dancing has nothing in common with music other than the element of time and the division of time...
>
> *(Merce Cunningham in* The Vision of Modern Dance, *1980)*

Balanchine and Cunningham are thus almost opposites in this regard. For Cunningham, the only way to make the dance is to scrutinise the phrases of movement. It is from these phrases that the rhythms of the dance emerge. The Balanchine belief that a choreographer does not invent rhythm but only reflects that of the music has no place here. In his performances, the dance and the music live together, but their effects on the audience are *disassociated* from each other. For Cunningham, time is not beats to the bar. For him, 'Dancing is propelled by dancing.'

The early work of Siobhan Davies used commissioned music scores that were also created *separately* from the dance, with little direct relationship between the two. Often, the music served merely to set the mood or atmosphere – as in *Relay* (1972) where the musician improvised jazz piano. In her later work, Davies developed movement which responded more to the structure of the music in mutual co-existence.

The work of Rosemary Butcher reflects a similar development.

TASK 14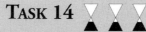

1 Use the group dance which you composed to *L'Allegro, Il Penseroso ed Il Moderato*. Dance it to the following pieces of music:

- *Purple Haze*, by the Kronos Quartet, 3 minutes;
- *Speaking in Tongues II*, by Sheila Chandra, 3 minutes 8 seconds.

The dancers will need assistance in making slight alterations in timing (perhaps in the transitions) to compensate for the very slight different lengths of the two pieces of music.

2 Assess the effects of the mutual-coexistence and disassociation approaches on the look of the dance. Did the contrast of the music with the dance emphasise and enhance features of the choreography? Was the disassociation uncomfortable but of interest for you as the viewer? Are you prepared to allow discord to be both interesting and challenging to the way you see things?

THE RELATIONSHIP OF MUSIC TO DANCE – CONCLUSION

It is a good idea to try to listen to as many different types and styles of music as possible and see if you can hear and analyse what the composer is doing with the sounds.

It is probably clear to you by now that the elements and structures of dance and music have a great deal in common. When the two come together in choreography, a whole Pandora's box of surprises, delights and troubles pops open! The relationship between the two aspects opens up many choices for the choreographer, and many skills are in turn demanded of the dancer. If appropriate choices are made, and if accurate performances are given, there may be many surprises for the audience.

The devices and structures presented so far are mostly involved with arranging movement for groups in time. However, the concern with design in *space* also requires attention, and this will form the final part of this chapter.

Organising groups in space

As seen in Chapter 3, the choice of dancers and the numbers of them are an important part of the choreographic process. In giving a dance a coherent form, organising their placement in *space* is another crucial factor.

A radical approach to this may be seen in the work of post-modern choreographer Trisha Brown. In her own words:

> *Walking on the Wall,* 1971, gave the illusion that the audience was overhead, looking down on the tops of the heads of the performers walking and standing below. It also showed what it was, the performance of a simple activity against the principles of gravity. The rigging and technical business of getting up there was in clear view.
>
> (*Trisha Brown in* The Vision of Modern Dance, *1980*)

This approach was extreme but effective in arranging the spatial relationship not only of dancer to dancer, but also of dance to location (i.e. the walls of the Whitney Museum), and of audience to dance. As Sally Banes describes it, the whole orientation of the audience was turned upside down, sideways, every which way:

> ... one has the distinct sensation that one is on a tall building, watching people walking back and forth on the sidewalk below. When they turn the corner on the walls, suddenly one feels as though one were positioned sideways, sticking one's head out of a window, perhaps, and seeing a sideways image of an upright person below.
>
> (*Sally Banes, in* Terpsichore in Sneakers, *1989*)

Of course, this was a highly unusual way of designing groups in space, and the usual scenario which you will be presented with is that of making movement for the *proscenium stage*. Placement on stages is described in Chapter 4. The concern here is with *arrangements* of groups of dancers, and this includes:

- group shapes/formations and their stage placement;
- spaces between the dancers;
- relationships between the dancers.

Helter Skelter Youth dance

GROUP SHAPES/FORMATIONS

The overall shape of the group involves a careful arrangement of the dancers that is appropriate to the content of the dance idea. There are many arrangements to choose from. Traditional lines and circles, as seen in folk dances, are often used to convey ideas like community, ritual, courtship, war, celebration and procession. These formations are often symmetrical, and if interest needs to be added, they may be placed off-centre in the stage space. Contrasting formations placed next to them will also add interest.

Formal lines like those of a corps de ballet – for example, in Fokine's *Les Sylphides* (1909) – are very different from the less regular formations of a dance like *Wildlife* (1984) where the concern is for the energy of zig-zags and for the angularity of shape.

Close masses and scattered groups convey contrasting expressions to an audience. Close masses include clusters of loosely arranged dancers and arrangements of dancers in more geometric shapes like triangles, wedges, squares and circles.

TASK 15 ▽▲ ▽▲ ▽▲

Look at paintings from different periods of history – e.g. primitive, mediaeval, Renaissance, cubist, surrealist etc. Find figurative paintings, i.e. paintings with people in them. Notice *how* the people are placed in relationship to one another – i.e. the groupings and poses. Choose one of the paintings and develop from it a series of group shapes that follow on logically from the ones in the paintings. Link the stillness with appropriate movements. Pay attention to the placement of the shapes in the space.
Pay attention to other details in the chosen picture, such as other objects or the scenery. Allow these to feature through the motifs when choosing actions, dynamics, the use of space, relationships.
Use the style of the painting to influence the corresponding style of movement you use. For example, a primitive-style painting may lead to a dance with an African feel.
Find an appropriate accompaniment for the dance.

SPACES BETWEEN THE DANCERS

If the dancers are placed close together, they will create a very different set of feelings in the audience than they will if they are scattered about. *Decentralising* the space and scattering the dancers is a characteristic of Cunningham work, and a similar aspect of the work of Sir Frederick Ashton was noted in the following critique:

> ... his use of space, especially in his purest dance works, *Symphonic Variations* and *Scènes de Ballet* and *Monotones*, was as unconventional as Merce Cunningham. Of *Scènes de Ballet* he said, 'I ... wanted to do a ballet that could be seen from any angle – anywhere could be the front, so to speak.'

> *(David Vaughan in* Dance Now, *Summer 1995)*

This is quite an unexpected use of the stage space in the context of classical ballet, which is usually designed for the proscenium stage.

Care must be taken, however, not to allow the dancers to be so far apart that the audience is unable to see the whole group. The most common fault of all is placing one dancer on one side of the stage and the other so far over to the other side that the audience is left looking at a hole in the centre, or moving their heads from side to side as if watching a tennis match without a ball!

The use of contrasting levels, and of the spaces that are created between these levels, is often an effective device. Similarly, if the body shapes of the dancers *overlap*, the spaces *in between* can be of as much interest as the overlapping shapes themselves. Using the space between dancers to create dramatic tension or simply to connect one dancer to another is also a possibility worth exploring. This can serve to *isolate*, to put the dancers in *conflict* with each other, or it can bring about feelings of *harmony* or *uniformity* between the dancers.

RELATIONSHIPS BETWEEN THE DANCERS

This follows on quite simply from the use of spaces between the dancers. The dancers' body shapes may be deliberately chosen to copy, complement or contrast with one another.

TASK 16 ⧖

Draw the shape shown in Figure 6.3 on a piece of paper three times. Add a shape to the first drawing which copies it. Add shapes to the second which complement it, and add shapes to the third which contrast with it.

The interest of group shapes, placements and timings are enhanced by using *contact* between the dancers. There are special skills involved here, as well as a need to build trust between the dancers. A whole technique was created around this concept by Steve Paxton in the 1960s as part of the Judson Church postmodern group in New York. Paxton was a gymnast who later studied dance and who combined his experiences to produce a style based on giving and taking weight. Trust between partners, if you decide to fall or lean on them, was the priority. Paxton tried to create a Western type of martial art that did not contain any combat. There was an emphasis on equality of partners, between genders, races, abilities and so on.

It is worth experimenting in duets and larger groups with simple handholds and counterbalances, feeling exactly how much or how little energy is appropriate to maintain a counterbalance and to lose it. Similarly, other contact situations, such as lifting, lowering, supporting, catching and throwing, initiating turns or assisting jumps, can all have exciting results.

The dance company Motionhouse are well-known for contact work in their choreography. In a dance entitled *The House of Bones* (1991, available on video – see the 'References and resources' section at the end of the chapter), they use contact work to great effect to depict how a town laid to siege in mediaeval times became infected by the plague. Instead of the dead and dying being looked after with compassion, their bodies were catapulted over the city walls at the enemy! This is used as a metaphor for the present-day treatment of AIDS victims,

Figure 6.3 *Body shapes*

and as a reminder of the need for compassion. Similar concerns for the humane treatment of our fellow human beings come through in the work of the company VTOL, and in the work of the company DV8 (director Lloyd Newson), whose *Dead Dreams of Monochrome Men* (1988) is set in the desperate world of gay bars. In this latter piece, the desire and loneliness of desperate men in need of company is portrayed. There is frantic, frenetic contact work as desire turns to demand:

> Newson transforms emotion into movement via several big physical set pieces where the dancers fling themselves full tilt at one another like combatants in a war dive-bombing one another's bodies.

(Allen Robertson in Dance Now, *1996)*

Newson explores issues of how people hurt and love each other in a hard-hitting, highly emotionally charged atmosphere. His work here is similar to the work of the German choreographer Pina Bausch:

> Her ... performers seem to use their innermost secrets of their lives as a springboard into these performances. They spew out their guts both physically and emotionally with an honesty that has become a byword for all of the Bausch imitators.... [in *Café Muller*, (1978):] ... A woman repeatedly throws herself into a man's arms, but he does not bother to catch her. ... she simply grows more frantic ... clambering and tossing herself down again as fast as she can...

(Allen Robertson, Donald Hutera, in The Dance Handbook*, 1988)*

Concerns such as these are important in postmodern work, which regards the creation of a truly human world as a priority. Here is an extract from the information which accompanies the video *Different Dancers, Similar Motion* (1989) by Motionhouse.

> This video is designed to encourage you to change the way you think about dance. It shows ... how people can learn to overcome ignorance, anxieties, prejudices and inexperience through constructively led workshops.

(Information from Different Dancers, Similar Motion, Motionhouse, 1989)

The video shows an integrated group, i.e. a group comprising those with and without physical disabilities, working during a fortnight with Motionhouse. Contact improvisation is used a great deal, and there are some enchanting moments as the participants talk about their discoveries both about dance and about themselves.

TASK 17

1 In threes, let two people dance while the other person reads the following instructions slowly enough so that the dancers have time to feel the movements.

'Sit back to back and gently let your backs rub together as if you are mapping out the surface of your partner's back. ... Let this movement enlarge until you begin to roll around each other ... feel the circular movement. ... As you move, find a couple of stillnesses which are resting points. They are comfortable for both of you. Pause in them before continuing the movement. Try to share supporting and being supported equally.'

2 Dancer No. 1: go on all fours, holding a strong flat back. Dancer No. 2: hang over. ... Ensure that your centre of gravity is over the supports'. ... Relax as you hang ... feel balanced. Breathe, melt down to the floor softly and roll off your partner.'

TASK 17 CONT.

3 ⧗ 'Stand close to your partner. ... Slowly melt down to the floor, giving way together in contact all the way. ... Roll apart and return to standing easily.'

4 ⧗ 'Take a walk together, not allowing your partner to fall. ... Support your partner all the way down, going down to the floor yourself if it is necessary. ... Speed this up so that the falls are followed by rapid rebounds, and so that the recoveries are seamless with the falling and walking.
When you are more confident, add jumps.'

5 ◣ See photos (a), (b), (c) and (d) below for the illustrations to this task. Practise making the five shapes shown in the photographs. Connect them, in any order of your choice, with suitable movement which emphasises contact and loss of the same. Try to make the whole phrase as fluid as possible, but with some clear changes of tempo. Make sure that you share roles equally.

Helter Skelter Youth Dance

(a)

(b)

(c)

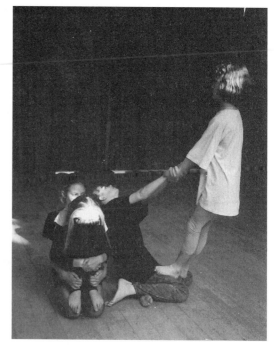

(d)

Other simple dancer-to-dancer relationships may include the use of *unison*, and here, the more dancers who are doing the same movement, the more forceful the impact of that movement. Any of the following are also worthy of exploration:

meet and part	complement
waiting	different facings
match/mirror	passing
side-by-side	back-to-back
alone, together	conversation
lead, follow	one behind the other

Having come thus far in the book, we now have a reasonable overview of many aspects of the constituent features of dances, the form in dances and the dancer in training. After the studio technique class and rehearsal, the inevitable happens: lights, curtains, ACTION! The next chapter will present important matters for dancers and choreographers to consider before, during and after the actual performance.

References and resources

BOOKS

Banes, S., *Terpsichore in Sneakers: Post-Modern Dance*, Boston: Houghton Mifflin Company, 1980

Denby, E., *Dancers, Buildings and People in the Street*, New York: Horizons, 1965

Horst, L. and Carroll, R., *Modern Dance Forms*, New York: Dance Horizons, 1973

Teck, K., *Ear Training: a Dancer's Guide to Music*, USA: Princeton Book Co., 1994

Vaughan, D., *Frederick Ashton and His Ballet*, London: Dance Books, 1988

VIDEOS

Motionhouse, *Different Dancers, Similar Motion*, 1989, and *The House of Bones*, 1991, both available from Oxford

Independent Video, Pegasus Theatre, Magdalen Road, Oxford OX4 1RE, tel.: 01865 250 150

MUSIC

The Chieftains, *Strike the Gay Harp*, 3 Claddagh Records, 4CC10, PCO 1984, recommended for Task 1

Penguin Café Orchestra, *Broadcasting from Home*, EGDC 38, recommended for Task 4

The Go-Gos, *We Got the Beat*, IRS 7243 8 31756 2 8, 1994, recommended for Task 6

Tchaikovsky, *The Nutcracker*, recording by the Royal Opera House Orchestra, Conifer Records, ROH 002 (or similar recording), recommended for Task 7

Parampara, *Moving in Time*, available from Mandy de Winter, 3 Brandywell Road,

Broseley, Shropshire TF12 5ST, tel.: 01952 883 242, recommended for Task 10

Handel, *L'allegro, Il Penseroso ed Il Moderato*, Soli Monteverdi Choir, English Baroque soloists, Erato, 2292-45377-2, 1980 recommended for Task 13

Kronos Quartet, *Purple Haze*, Nonesuch, 75559-79111-2 1986, recommended for Task 14

Sheila Chandra, *Speaking in Tongues II*, RW24 07777 7 867227, recommended for Task 14

chapter seven

DANCE APPRECIATION

The significance of dances

The dance has been choreographed, and the long hours of rehearsal and production planning are over. Now the dance meets its audience, which is ready to enjoy its particular significance, character, content, style – from the surreal to the most minimal, anything and everything may appear. The dancers are nervously anticipating their appearance, and they have a large amount of responsibility for the dance from now on. This, indeed, is the reason they have been training. The choreographer, audience and critics are looking on and evaluating the overall impact of the dance. This chapter will examine aspects of this special moment when the process becomes the product – live and direct!

> It only demands the dance be a moment of passionate, completely disciplined action, that it communicate participation to the nerves, the skin, the structure of the spectator.
>
> *(Martha Graham in* The Vision of Modern Dance, *1980)*

An appreciation of the *significance* of the dance may come from the points of view of the choreographer, the dancer or the spectator. As such, each one of these people is involved in different considerations in the analysis, understanding and appreciation of the performance – they will *all* be evaluating whether or not the dance is successful:

1 *Choreographers* will evaluate as part of an ongoing process of developing a personal style which is both spontaneous and organised.
2 *Dancers* will evaluate according to the specific demands that the performance places on them.
3 *Audiences* will evaluate according to the particular context of the dance.

In order for this evaluation and appreciation to occur, an understanding of the craft and artistry of choreography is needed. The constituent features of the dance as described in Chapters 3, 4 and 5 are what make up the craft. The artistry, however, is a far more mysterious, and yet equally essential, matter. Think back to the beginning of Chapter 3. The choreographic process starts with *ideas* and ends up producing a product: a dance. The artistry is what *links* the two and makes for the success or failure of a performance.

Hence:

● ideas
● the artistic process and style

will be the concerns of this section.

Ideas

Ideas have to do with the type of subject matter chosen by the choreographer, and they form the starting point for the creative choreographic process.

> The art object ... is an original – a first presentation of a possibility truly felt and imagined.
>
> *(Arturo B. Fallico, in* Dance from Magic to Art, *1976)*

The original idea itself may indicate certain approaches in which it may be treated most successfully. This may bring about a certain 'look' or style in the movement.

> ... art is vision or intuition. The artist produces an image. The person who enjoys art turns his eyes in the direction which the artist has pointed out to him, peers through the hole which has been opened for him and reproduces in him self the artist's image.
>
> *(Benedetto Croce in* Dance from Magic to Art, *1976)*

The idea should be made clear to the dancer by the choreographer. The dancer is the instrument of the expression of that idea to the audience. We may note the way that Lea Anderson emphasises the use of 'inner narrative' for her dancers. She is concerned that the dancers be aware of the reason behind each of the tiny gestures which they perform:

> The inner narrative is something that the audience doesn't know and is nothing to do with them. ... I'm very interested in the physical attitude of the performer. For example the traditional way of ... holding your body and relating to the audience. I'm not much impressed with those ways of being ... not how you remember the movement but thinking of the given image. The dancer must go through the same thought process every time.
>
> *(Lea Anderson in interview, in the Flesh and Blood education pack)*

The audience make up their own minds, but the choreographer still has a job to do – as the American post-modern choreographer Anna Halprin points out:

> .. as an artist ... essentially your job is to be a vehicle for other people. ... But when you take responsibility for an audience, you are then accepting the fact that you must go through some sort of distilling process in which the personal experience has become so zeroed and so heightened by a clarity that you know exactly what you're dealing with. ... Then you find the movement ... essence of that idea inherent not only in how your body moves, but in ... an awareness of the total thing.
>
> *(Anna Halprin, in* The Vision of Modern Dance, *1979)*

So now a pattern is appearing. The choreographer has an idea. During rehearsal, the idea and its accompanying images are transformed into physical and mental images for the dancers. The dancers then present these to the audience. Exactly how they do this, and the necessary skills required, will be examined later in the chapter.

In this way, the significance of the dance is conveyed to the audience, and it is possible that the choreographer and dancer give form and life to ideas, feelings and sensations that are close to all of us.

Ideas in the genre of classical ballet are – as already pointed out – likely to be different from those for modern and post-modern dance, the former tending towards the lyrical, balanced view, and the latter towards a disruption and visible tension, as seen in modern life in the twentieth century.

TASK 1

Try to do this exercise as quickly as possible – allow 15 minutes maximum . . . in groups of 3 or 4, brainstorm ideas that would translate into movement. Try to make the list of ideas as long as possible. It could include poetry, relationships, art, sculpture, stories, photographs or current events and issues in the news.

Keep this list handy because this task continues in Task 2 on page 177.

The artistic process and style

The final impression which a dance makes is a result of the choreographer's process of selection and abstraction in reducing an idea to its essence. It is rather like cooking a fine meal: starting with all the separate, recognisable ingredients and selecting the right amounts of everything, timing to perfection, and then presenting them in the right order to make something, with a unique flavour all of its own, that even Delia Smith would be proud of! This process will have involved treating the original subject matter in certain ways, and it will engage your intellect, imagination and intuition. The latter two inner senses result in creative and sensitive choices as to what will be most successful at conveying the intention and physicalities of the dance to the audience. The artistic decisions involved in transforming an idea into a final image are closely linked to a sense of personal taste: selecting and abstracting from your live experiences and allowing the onlooker to see something from a fresh point of view.

In the world of fashion, clothes by the famous fashion designers Katherine Hamnett, Christian Dior and Calvin Klein each have their own distinctive style and taste. When worn, they give the wearer a certain look. Similarly, in the music world, the music of Enigma is unmistakably different from that of Bach or The Beatles. *Style* is the key here. The choice of an idea and its treatment puts personal taste into action in the creative process. Look at the photographs below and you will see the great contrasts in style between the classical ballet of Frederick Ashton and Lea Anderson's post-modern dance.

> Until the artist is satisfied in perception with what he is doing, he continues shaping and reshaping. The making comes to an end when its result is experienced as good.
>
> *(John Dewey (philosopher) in* Having an Experience, *1934)*

Just as in compositional structures there are certain styles of art, and of choreography, which suit certain ideas more than others and which audiences will recognise, so in fashion there are recognisable styles like that from the 1970s or a classic look or a completely over-the-top fantasy. And similarly in music, painting, literature and, of course, dance: you would not mistake a Martha Graham dance for a Merce Cunningham piece. These different styles are the approaches that a choreographer chooses to use to transform an idea into dance. They may arise from the history of visual art and music, or as a result of the social conditions and context of their time. The artist may be responding to or rebelling against the social values of the time, and in so doing brings a certain style to life. This style holds within it the artist's own attitude to society.

To show the differences of style between Frederick Ashton (Les Patineurs, *1937) and Lea Anderson* (Birthday, *1992*)

Some of these named styles from history are as follows:

- *Classicism* is formal and concerned with balance and objectivity. It is seen in Greek and Roman art and in the music of the mid-eighteenth to early nineteenth century.
- *Realism* attempts to copy reality, as seen by the artist.
- *Romanticism* involves a concern with the emotions of love, beauty, harmony and sentiment. 'Dancers aspired to skim and spin like heavenly puffballs,' was how Louis Horst (musical adviser to Martha Graham) described it. The well-known ballets of *Swan Lake*, *Giselle* and *La Sylphide* are typical of this style.
- *Expressionism* chooses from inner feelings and emotions to translate reality into a personal statement – as seen in the psychodrama of the dances of Martha Graham and Mary Wigman laying bare the heart and soul of woman in crises of decision. It is also seen in Van Gogh and Edvard Munch paintings,

and in the work of playwrights Samuel Beckett and Arthur Miller.

- *Impressionism* suggests or exaggerates a certain aspect of reality, as seen in the paintings of Cézanne, Seurat and Monet, or the music of Debussy.
- *Cubism* arranges shape and form in surprising, unexpected ways which may shock or disturb. The work of Picasso and the music of Stravinsky are examples here.
- *Surrealism* interprets reality in a dream-like way. The paintings of Salvador Dali and Magritte are examples here.

In recognising stylistic differences, an interesting point arises. Although the ideas and subject matter may be different for ballet than for modern dance, the main difference lies in the treatment of the *content*. In ballet, there is a tendency towards realism. On the other hand, the modern dance may include romantic fantasy, but transforms it imaginatively into something else. The choreography of Matthew Bourne in *Highland Fling: a romantic wee ballet* (1992) shows this modern treatment clearly. It is based on *La Sylphide*, the classic romantic ballet, but cleverly tells the story of James, an unemployed welder, who is lured from his nuptial bed by a rather grungy-looking fairy temptress. It is a witty cocktail of Glaswegian life in the 1990s, 'rude, funny, stylish … a true instinct for magic' (the Independent).

The style of work will be a personal choice, but it does seem that what all styles have in common during the making of dance is a process of *abstraction.* You have been abstracting in many of the tasks that you have done so far in this book. The choreographer can abstract from any aspect of life – other art forms, emotions, everyday life, stories, anything. Then, out of the remaining essence of the abstraction, a dance is built. The dance is an intense experience for the audience, bringing with it as it does the quintessence of an encounter with life.

> Of this deep responsiveness between body and mind the art of dance is formed. … It is built of symbols abstracted from daily living and intimately associated in the memory of experience with action and emotion. … Any human being who is willing to give it his attention should be enlivened by dance.
>
> *(Louis Horst in* Modern Dance Forms, *1961)*

Your personal movement and choreographic style is something which will develop over time. As you work, analyse and evaluate both your own dances and the work of others. Combine these two aspects into a process of growth and personal development. This process of development is seen in the work of all great artists. Picasso went through various periods, namely Blue, Primitive and Cubist. In the work of Martha Graham, we see certain times when America was the main focus and other times when Greek dramas or the Bible

were important. This personal development has also produced certain named techniques like the contraction/release of Martha Graham and the fall and recovery of Doris Humphrey. Your own personal development may be enriched by a physical experience of such training methods.

Similarly, an experience of dance from other cultures such as South Asian or Afro-Caribbean dances, or folk from the rest of the world – can broaden the scope of your personal style. This multi-cultural influence is seen in the work of many post-modern choreographers. Lea Anderson's work *The Clichés and the Holidays* (1984) is based on Spanish/Latin American dance.

> Their hands, like those of an Indian dancer seemed to have a life of their own … a curious network of looks and gestures. Sometimes these simply reinforce the parody; like the flamenco dancer's exaggeratedly smouldering gaze … catches perfectly the kind of dingy, motheaten atmosphere which hangs around special 'tourist' performances.
>
> *(Judith Mackrell in* Dance Theatre Journal, *vol 4, no. 2, 1986)*

In typical post-modern style, Shobana Jeyasingh mixes the technical skills of Indian *bharata natyam* with contact improvisation and everyday gestures. The melting-pot is further explored by using Indian music as well as Western minimal music and architecture in the videodance *Duets and Automobiles* (1994, for the *Dance for Camera* series, director Terry Braun, BBC2).

The key is to explore and not to be afraid of mixing styles. Working with *other* art forms can also enrich and enhance your work. Your personal style is not a limitation but a beginning. Once you are aware of your preferences, explore how to make the most and the best of them. Finding your weaknesses and trying to make these stronger is another route. Beware of the most dead-end route which is to always rely on the same movements, the same type or way of relating to music, or the same dynamics. No matter how good and brilliant these may be, after a short time they will become predictable for your audience and hold no more surprises.

In music and the visual arts, there is a tradition of studying the 'greats'. This could be so in dance too. At first, identifying with someone else's style will be difficult. However, eventu-ally, you may find that a style other than your own actually has similarities to yours as well as elements which are very different. Therefore, it can reinforce your personal style as well as offer up new ideas to be explored and pursued. It may well, of course, throw up things which really do not fit your own body and mind, and it is useful to know what these are too. Remember: 'If you haven't anything worth throwing away then you probably haven't anything worth keeping.'

TASK 2

1 ◣ From the list which you prepared as a group in Task 1, individually choose one of the ideas and write down as quickly as possible how this idea would translate into the main images, movements and contrasting material that would be appropriate for a dance. Make notes on information which you would *not* use. Choreograph a short solo (1 to 2 minutes) from the images which you have abstracted.

or

2 ◣ ◣ ◣ Choose the work of a choreographer who has a recognisable style, and choreograph a short solo (1 to 2 minutes) from the images which you have abstracted. It would be good to use photographs and videos of your chosen choreographer for reference. Allow 4 to 5 hours for this work, including photo/video research. This task continues at the end of Chapter 7, p. 190.

An idea is transformed and stylised into a co-herent dance form using all the craft and skill which is to hand. The choreographer now hands it over to the dancers, and the dancers now rely on their own skills to recreate it for an audience. Again, think back to the beginning of Chapter 3. Having started with ideas, the choreographic process ends in:

- performance
- evaluation.

These will be our next concerns.

Performance

PREPARING THE DANCER FOR THE PERFORMANCE

At the moment of performance, the dance becomes the responsibility of the dancers. The time for the choreographer's corrections is over, and they must now be content with the dancer's perception of the intentions of the dance, and of how to express these.

The choreographer has now given the essence of the dance to the dancers:

A choreographer, though possessing the same emotions as other creative artists, has no way of expressing himself but through movements which he must implant in the muscles of other dancers.

(David Lichine, quoted in Making a Ballet, *1974)*

Different choreographers do this in different ways. The German post-modern choreographer Pina Bausch describes here how *she* does it:

Well of course, I have asked them hundreds of questions. The dancers have answered them, tried something out. ... Everyone has a think about it and gives an answer. Sometimes we'll be trying to put things into words. ... Gradually we build up short dance sequences and memorise them. I used to get scared and panic and so I would start with movement and avoid the questions. Nowadays I start off with the questions.

(Pina Bausch, in Ballet and Modern Dance, *1992)*

Preparing a dancer for the role is crucial for a successful performance. The ballet choreographer Antony Tudor was reported as being difficult to dance for by one of his dancers, because he demanded that the movement must be technically strong but also that the expression must follow its most natural and obvious route in performance.

The flow of the movement phrase must never be broken, and this is what makes his choreography so difficult technically. He may want ... four pirouettes, but you can't let the preparation ... show.

(Hugh Laing, dancer, in Ballet and Modern Dance, *1992)*

Similarly, a dancer describes below how the choreographer Alvin Ailey helped her to understand a role. She describes how she needs personal images in order to find the right dynamic in her movement.

In *Streams,* I'm a woman who, perhaps, is in the stream of water trying to move with it, or trying to move through it. Or I can take the idea that it's like life and then you try to move as smoothly as you can through everything.

(In The Dance Makers, *1980)*

The quality of the audience's experience can be directly affected by the standard of performance of the dancers. Whatever the genre, a dance can be evaluated by how well the dancers have performed. A part of the art of choreography involves making sure that it shows off the dancers to their best advantage. Finding movement which is not only successful in terms of compositional form but also sits on the dancers like well-fitting clothes and suits their abilities is essential: not too difficult for them, but at the same time challenging and using their specific strong points. Dancers who achieve greatness in performance are those who have, at some point, taken what the choreographer has intended into their own body and mind.

PERFORMANCE SKILLS

As well as the technical necessities of the physical skills of dance training, a dancer in performance also needs other important skills. A dancer must be able to communicate and express the overall intention of the dance. In order to do this, certain skills of interpretation and expression are a necessity. The great romantic ballerina Marie Taglioni was greatly admired for such performance charisma. In this description of her by an actress of the time, we have a feel for that inspirational quality that she had, dancing the lead in *La Sylphide,* (1832), the first romantic ballet.

> What was it then? It was, once again, the ideal Beauty that radiated from depths of the soul into this body, animated it, lifted it with such power that something marvellous took place before our eyes as we saw the invisible made visible.
>
> *(Maxine Shulman in* Ballet and Modern Dance*, 1992)*

As a natural presence on stage, the ballerina Taglioni is well-known, but there must also be *training* beforehand. We know that the physicalities of training are rigorous, and virtuosity alone is not enough. In the end, it is the expressiveness of a performer which must be right for a particular dance. Jean Georges Noverre, the great reformer of ballet in the eighteenth century, remarked that the corps de ballet should harmonise their feelings with their movement. He believed that only then would they be able to express the emotions of the dance and give life to the dance.

> A true dancer has a temperament which directs him to express feelings and ideas through moving the body in space. This instinct must be greatly enhanced by training so that he not only has a strong and coordinated instrument, but an immediate impulse to translate his com-

ments and reactions into rhythms, muscular dynamics and spatial arrangements.

> *(Louis Horst in* Modern Dance Forms*)*

There are some specifics which can be learnt. In the work of many choreographers, the technical aspects are learnt in daily class. Then, subtle and sometimes demanding changes are added for a performance. Sir Frederick Ashton would use this approach to give syncopation to an everyday classroom step. This is the surprise for the audience. The dancer must be capable of tricky technical adjustments and yet keep the flow and expression of the movement.

Other performance skills include:

- projection
- emphasis
- group awareness
- musicality
- involvement of the whole self.

Projection

Projection involves throwing the energy out from the body so as to give a quality of life to the movement. When a dance is performed technically correctly but lacks projection, it is unlikely to reach an audience in a significant way. Projection enables the dancer's movement and energies to reach out beyond the body and 'touch' the audience's feelings. In this way, it makes dancing come alive. There should be an inner awareness in the dancer that is part of each movement and that sparks off various corresponding tensions and muscular reactions in observers.

An efficient and correct use of energy contributes to projection. Isadora Duncan was one of the first to talk about energy flowing from and to the centre of the body and the extremities. She believed that this enabled the feel of the movement to travel across space.

Correct breathing also aids projection. The technique of breathing through the movement should be practised first of all in class.

An appropriate use of facial expressions is also important. A calm, pleasant, open face will help to animate a performance. Cheesy grins, however, are not often appropriate, and likewise, downcast or stressful expressions can kill a dance stone dead for an audience. This was observed as a problem when executing the very difficult *fouettes* of classical ballet. The great choreographer Mikhail Fokine did not favour dancers showing virtuosity for its own sake. He believed that the movement should serve as part of the expression of the dance, and that 'tricks' like the fouette undermined the projection of feeling:

> The fouette ... is the most hateful invention of the ballet. The dancer expresses ecstasy and joy, but her face – what does that express? Quite the opposite. She seeks for balance and her whole face proclaims it. The face betrays her losing her balance. ... unity of pose and movement is a law which, to my regret is not felt by everybody.

> (*Mikhail Fokine in* Mikhail Fokine and his Ballets, *1945*)

Hanya Holm has this to add:

> The face is of course the mirror of all that goes on, but it should not be more prominent than is intended and it should not be a substitute for all that isn't going on in the body. The face should have a relationship to the whole attitude and complement it. ... I very often see absolutely dead eyes inside a multiple moving body.

> (*Hanya Holm, in* The Vision of Modern Dance, *1979*)

Focus is also an important element of projection. Traditionally, this should be thrown out to the back part of the auditorium. This is par-

To show face in use in performance, in DV8

ticularly necessary when the audience is seated above the stage looking down. A dancer who continually looks down is not delivering a real performance, and this has the effect of cutting the audience out of the action. This approach is not, necessarily, accepted in post-modern dance. For example, the choreographer Yvonne Rainer describes the performer as a 'neutral doer'. She believes performance to be something artificial, and an unnecessary display of technical virtuosity. This 'problem' of artificiality is addressed by:

> ... never permitting the performers to confront the audience. Either the gaze was averted or the head was engaged in movement. The desired effect was a worklike rather than exhibitionlike presentation.

> (*Yvonne Rainer, in* Trio A, The Vision of Modern Dance*)

In addition, the dancer should correctly *orientate* the dance to the audience, ensuring that body facings are accurate, and that the audience sees movements and body shapes at their most expressive angle. These facings and angles will have been determined by the choreographer, but the dancer must make sure that their reproduction is accurate. In classical ballet, it is often important to present the *front* of the dancer's body towards the audience. This has its roots in the early ballets for the royal court where every movement had to address the lord or lady present: to have turned your back on them would have been considered very rude and ill-mannered. This tradition survived in the theatre for centuries, and was followed religiously.

Jules Perrot, the romantic ballet dancer and choreographer, was one of the first to choreograph dancers to turn their *backs* on the audience for dramatic effect. Of course, this is now widely used. There is a moment in *Sergeant Early's Dream* (1984) by Christopher Bruce where the dancers are all looking to the back of the stage, turning their backs on the audience. Their focus is out to sea, as painted on the backdrop. This expresses the main theme of the dance which is a longing for, and memories of, their homeland of the past. It is thus a highly appropriate moment for the dancers to turn their backs on the audience.

Similarly, the dancer must realise the need for a high *energy* level throughout the performance – in the quieter moments, indeed, as well as in the faster, stronger sections of the dance.

Being generous with your gestures and movements when dancing will also help an audience to enjoy the performance more. These serve to engage them in the dance and make them feel that they are interested to know more about what they are looking at. This is particularly so in classical ballet, whereas in modern dance, particularly if it is expressive in style, the choreographer's intent may involve a more closed feeling. Either way, the dancer must use the appropriate gestures and movements.

Emphasis

Emphasis involves knowing what aspects of energy, space and time to accent at different moments throughout the dance. The dancer is responsible for giving a clear performance to the audience. This involves colouring the movement with the right kind of expressions, namely those which the choreographer intended. The dancer must be able to direct energy impulses, and to make use of space and time in the way laid down by the choreographer. Energy impulses may be directed between dancers, or to a certain fixed point on stage. They may sometimes have an inward, thoughtful feel, one directed in at the dancers themselves. The shading of the dynamics and qualities by the dancer is vital to the expression of the dance.

> You must master the physical experience so that it becomes a kinesthetic experience. ... You will find out that movement can contain only a certain amount of emotion before emotion outdoes the physical experience. ... Emotion is only a stimulus not an end result. ... It is arrived at but not emphasised.
>
> *(Hanya Holm in* The Vision of Modern Dance, *1979)*

This process of taking in the physical emphasis begins in rehearsal, and it can be a tiring affair. It is important, however, for the dancer to keep energy levels up throughout for two reasons. First, the choreographer often needs to see the dance danced flat out to decide if it really works. Second, the dancers themselves need to repeat the movement over and over again so that they too know intimately what is required. This may involve discovering what kind of quality a particular role or character needs, or it may involve acquiring a feel for where the movement phrases begin and end. There may be a particular highlight in the dance which requires a certain dynamic emphasis. Or the climax of the piece may need a very specific timing or position on stage which is crucial to the expression. Many small subtle details thus need close examination and practice.

Through rehearsal and practice, the dancer will build a secure knowledge of the emphases that occur in a dance. This will provide support and will help the dancer to remain calm during those last few moments before the performance begins when stage fright may be a problem. Being able to focus clearly on the movements and expression, marking these through calmly in your mind, will take your mind away from yourself and your nerves and put it exactly where it should be: on the dance for the audience, not on your ego.

Helter Skelter Youth Group

Group awareness

When dancing in groups, the dancer has to think not only about the content of the dance but also about movement cues which may come from others. *Peripheral vision*, i.e. what you see from the corners of your eyes, is useful here. Some dancers have a 'sixth sense' or a 'third eye' which helps them to feel where others are in relation to themselves even if they cannot actually see the others. Of course, these responses also have to do with good timing in relation to others, and they make for accurate unison, canon or action–reaction relationships.

My company is fortunate; it's not very large, but it is nonetheless filled with people who are willing to take responsibility, not just for themselves, but for every other member of the company, which means that a dancer doing one of our pieces not only knows her own part, but knows everyone else's part who is working at the same time, and knows how that fits into the whole work ... it's something few dancers seem to take seriously. Musicians are much better about it because harmony is easier to hear than it is to see.

(Twyla Tharp in The Dance Makers, *1980)*

When the dancer is learning the choreography, dancing flat out – as already mentioned – will help to build an awareness of the motion, timing, spacing and dynamics of the other dancers. Furthermore, *sensitivity* to the other dancers is vitally important for cues given both for you and for them. The dance requires a group rapport if it is to be presented as a whole, unified item. If one of the group is having an 'off' day, you can guarantee that they will be the one the audience notices most. This will ruin the dance for the audience, and so is not to be tolerated. Each individual dancer is responsible to their own self, to the group, to the choreographer and to the audience.

In rehearsal, dancing with others demands that you maintain a pleasant, professional and responsible attitude to each other. The disciplines of warming-up before rehearsal, punctuality, and approaching problems such as timing and spacing efficiently and sensitively with others are all vital if the work is going to succeed.

TASK 3

Work in groups of at least 5 dancers. Using a short phrase learnt in technique class, dance it:

- in unison, facing the same way as each other;
- in unison, facing different ways from each other;
- in canon, facing different ways;
- dance the phrase, starting at different points within it. So some may start at the end and others in the middle and so on.

If possible, take turns to watch to check the dancer's accuracy and sensitivity to the group timings.

Musicality

Musicality is the sense of rhythm and musical structure in a dancer's movement.

At my feet, my dancing-mad feet, you threw a glance, a laughing, questioning, melting tossing glance.

My heels raised themselves, my toes listened for what you should propose: for the dancer wears his ears in his toes!

(Friedrich Nietzsche (philosopher), Thus Spoke Zarathustra*)*

As a dancer learns a new dance, information is received from the choreographer, and various body images become related to the music and to the content of the dance. Gradually, the kinesthetic memory stores these, and the dance communicates, through performance, the various sensations and feelings that arise from inside the dancer.

The dancer David Blair explains this process during the creation of *La Fille Mal Gardée* (1964) with choreographer Sir Frederick Ashton:

The music suggested a choreographic shape and I timed it to finish on the knee on the last note. But Sir Fred said 'No, bunch yourself up into a tight ball and then EXPLODE.' So he did a bit of rubato, we stole from the phrase before, did the double tour on the quiet music and the exploding thing happened not on the expected double tour music but on coming up out of my bunched position on the ground.'

(David Blair, in Making a Ballet, *1974)*

So the dancer has ears in the feet, and they listen carefully for cues and shadings in the music. This may involve picking out certain instrumentation in the music or particular changes in tempo, metre. The basic ability to count within the music helps dancers to fix certain phrases of movement in their minds within the rhythms of the music. Large ballet and dance companies often have musical directors who may assist dancers to do this.

Of course, in the choreography of Merce Cunningham – as we have seen – the dancers may not hear the music until the first performance. The music can often be very loud, and the dancer's role then is to dance with total accuracy in spite of sound crashing around them. One of the Cunningham Company dancers remarked once in the video *Travelogue* (1987) that the audiences often remarked on the ear-splitting sound, but that he didn't even hear it! This is musicality almost in reverse, and it needs just as much discipline and skill in order to be true to the rhythms in the movement.

TASK 4 ⧗

Using the same phrase as in Task 3, dance it to different pieces of music. Let the music affect your phrasing, emphasis, dynamics. Add to the phrase in improvisation, exploring the different possibilities for each piece of music. (Suggested music: The Chieftains; Parampara; Sounds of the Dolphin; The Orb.)

Involvement of the whole self

You can do the steps with muscle memory, but once you get up on the stage, it's not about steps at all. You really have to reason why you're doing it. You can't just go through the motions; it has to involve your whole self

(Alvin Ailey in The Dance Makers, *1980)*

Moving from the centre of the body is an important physical sensation necessary for the correct execution of movements. However, the involvement of the *mind* is just as crucial: without this, the performance would be uninteresting and dull for the audience. The dancer needs an inner focus which relates to the content of the dance, to the movement and to how the latter engages them in giving an expressive performance. This inner focus is well described by Hanya Holm:

> The same moment you discover that focus you will burst forth in your outward appearance. Your audience will recognise it immediately. The people won't have to look inside of you for emotional overtones. Your chest will be right, your hip will be right, you will have a carriage that is supported and that is right for that which is intended.

(Hanya Holm, in The Vision of Modern Dance, *1979)*

This involvement of the *whole* dancer in performance has to involve a response to the *style* of the dance. Margot Fonteyn and Rudolf

Nureyev were recognised as having this ability to immerse themselves in a role, but of course they looked nothing like a dancer from the post-modern point of view. However, both types of dancer, traditional and post-modern, share the ability to look natural and at ease with the demands of the movement that has been choreographed.

In the sixties, a trained dancer was a person with a puffed-out rib cage who was designed to project across the footlights in proscenium arch stage. He or she couldn't necessarily do a natural kind of movement, even a simple one. So what I looked for was a person with a natural, well-coordinated instinctive ability to move.

(Trisha Brown, in The Vision of Modern Dance, *1979)*

It may be true to say, therefore, that whatever genre a dance may be based in, it is the understanding of the artistry and a feeling for a natural expressive power which makes a sensitive performance. The whole person, body, mind and spirit, must be totally involved in the moment of performance. In the following description, Isadora Duncan reveals what she believes dance could be. You may be struck by the *total involvement* of the dancing child being the thing that captivated and transfixed Duncan's attention. It is a strong memory recalled with great impact for us nearly a century on.

I gazed across the vast expanse of surging water, wave after wave streaming past. . . . And in front of it all, the dainty figure . . . dancing on the edge of the measureless sea. And I felt as though the heart-beat of her little life were sounding in unison with the mighty life of the water . . . she dances because she can feel the rhythm of the dance throughout the whole of nature. To her it is a joy to dance; to me it is a joy to watch her.

(Isadora Duncan in The Dancing Times, *April 1926)*

TASK 5 ▽

This task needs to be carried out either while you are involved with a performance or during a theatre visit to watch dance.

- If *you* are performing, ask another dancer to watch you in the performance and give positive criticism of your projection and performance quality.
- If you are *watching* a performance, be aware of which dancers have the most stage presence, and try to analyse why. The answer should not refer to the fact that one dancer is more beautiful or attractive! Instead they should reflect something of the effectiveness of the dancers' projection skills and general expressiveness. Try to write down your thoughts immediately after the performance, and use terms that are given in the text above.

Evaluation

Evaluation is a process of analysis which judges the success, or lack of it, of a performance of a dance.

> Evaluation is creation ... is itself the value and jewel of all valued things. Only through evaluation is there value: and without evaluation the nut of existence would be hollow.
>
> *(Friedrich Nietzsche (philosopher), in* Thus Spoke Zarathustra*)*

The process of evaluation is crucial for the choreographer for personal artistic growth. You will probably be your own most critical critic. Dancers must be able to evaluate what a dance demands of them in order to do it justice on behalf of the choreographer in its performance. The audience too needs to appreciate the significance of a dance performance. As Nietzsche puts it in the quotation above, the process of evaluation gives *value* to the performance.

Often, dance students may think that analysing is a dry and rather unnecessary process. Indeed, if overdone, it can kill the impact and enjoyment of a performance. However, if it is done with passion and uses imagination, it can enhance the enjoyment. I often try to encourage students to write creatively about what they see – to try to use imaginative language that is as creative and formed as the dance they are watching. Take for example the passage below, and note its rich, descriptive use of words:

> Against a heavenly blue backdrop, the dancers are dressed in bright, often primary colours, twelve soloists co-existing as only in one of Cunningham's comradely democracies. ...
> Its setting of steps to Charles Amirkhanian's brilliant collage of words

or phrases of speech trains us to look more intensely at movement – its components, the steps and phrases.
Alston in 'Rainbow Ripples' draws wit and beauty from the dancer's achievement of balance; we constantly notice a dancer at the peak of a wave before falling – as in the multirefracted figure on the backdrop. Or in reverse: we watch dancers dive deep without dropping. Alston builds this daring into pouring lyric lines which have a silken flow that I, chauvinistically no doubt, like to label as a sign of English classic dancing.

> *(Alastair Macaulay in* Dance Theatre Journal, *1 March 1983)*

This critic writes artistically and leaves us feeling almost as if we have seen the dance ourselves. Finding the words and language that a dance is worthy of requires great powers of analysis and appreciation. It is an art form itself! Often, dancers sneer at writing as a way of approaching dance. But if done properly and well, writing can add value to the work for the audience, choreographer and the dancers alike.

There are three stages in all for the dance critic to follow:

1 description
2 interpretation
3 evaluation.

1 *Description* involves the close observation of all the constituent features and form of the dance, as described in Chapters 3, 4, 5 and 6.
2 *Interpretation* involves an appreciation of the ideas, content, images and style contained within the dance.
3 *Evaluation* – as already mentioned – involves judging the success, or lack of it, of a performance. This takes into consideration how effectively the constituent features have

been used in the actual performance of the dancers to portray the content and the quality of the dance. There must also be some thought as to the *context* of the dance because this will indicate how successful a dance is in achieving its function for a specific audience.

In the description above by the dance critic Alastair Macaulay, we see clearly all three of these stages. He describes the dancers, the movement, the set, the costumes and the accompaniment. He also recreates the images and impressions of the dance. Finally, he puts it into a context for us, and labels it as the success of a certain style. The style of the dance is interesting because it mixes the influence of Merce Cunningham with that of the lyrical mood of English ballet. Macaulay says: 'It is just as much a tonic to the dance-goer's eye.' Key phrases such as this confirm its success for the reader.

Below is an example of a list of headings under which a dance may be analysed and then evaluated:

Title of dance
Choreographer
Date of first performance
Genre/style
Accompaniment
Dancers/company
Any specific demands placed on the dancers in performance
Movement and form
Set
Costume/prop
Lighting
Designer name(s)
Context and significance
Evaluation

An example of a specific dance analysis and evaluation is now given below:

Title of dance: Five Brahms Waltzes in the Manner of Isadora Duncan.

Choreographer: Sir Frederick Ashton.

Date: 1975.

Genre/style: modern ballet.

Accompaniment: originally Brahms's Waltz Opus 35, number 15. In the full-length version of 1976, four more waltzes were added (Nos. 2, 8, 10 and 13) and the first waltz (No. 15) was played as a prelude as in the original Isadora Duncan performance. The piano was played live on stage, again as in the original Isadora Duncan version.

Dancers/company: solo female. Originally, Lynn Seymour for The Royal Ballet, and later Lucy Burge for the Ballet Rambert (1984).

Specific demands placed on the dancers in performance: a very wide range of dynamics was required.

Movement and form: Ashton had strong memories of Duncan in performance – in particular, a lasting impression of the freedom of her movement – and this influenced his choice of movements, which included:

- subtle, light shifts of weight;
- movements relating the body to a universal space and not just to the stage space;
- plastic, fluid, expressive head, body and upper-torso movements;
- movements conveying a range of emotions from lyrical through heroic to reclining.

The choreographic form of each waltz was wide ranging, and so were the dynamics. The phrasing required the dancer to control movements of great intense energy which faded and then accelerated again. In performance, Seymour and Burge made this look easy, but it actually required a high degree of technical control. They were acclaimed for their authentic Duncan 'look'. Seymour was particularly praised for her emotional expression, musicality and fluidity, which followed Ashton's intention to express the spirit and genius of Isadora Duncan.

Set: a bare stage except for a piano.

Costume/prop: a long piece of floaty fabric was used to enhance the spatial patterns of the movements. The costume was a tunic made of flimsy fabric very similar to the original worn by Duncan. This emphasised the flowing, rippling movements.

Designer name: David Deane.

Context and significance/evaluation: it was originally choreographed for the 1975 Hamburg Gala night to celebrate the 50th anniversary of the Ballet

Rambert and entitled *Homage to Isadora*. The later version (1976) was entitled *Five Brahms Waltzes in the Manner of Isadora Duncan*, danced by Lynn Seymour and dedicated to Dame Marie Rambert who, like Ashton, had been inspired by Duncan.

In 1921, Ashton had seen Isadora dance in London. He went back many times, fascinated by her grace, intensity and use of arms. He later stated that he used these influences in his own ballet.

The original Duncan waltzes were choreographed in 1902 and performed with great success in North and South America, Europe and Russia until 1924. Ashton's gala piece was so successful that, unusually for a gala piece, it was placed in the Royal Ballet repertoire in a fuller version. Later still, it was revived for the Rambert repertoire. We may safely assume its value and worth from these facts.

TASK 6 ⧗

The next time you go to see a dance performance, imagine that you are the dance critic for a newspaper. Write not more than 100 to 200 words on your thoughts about the show. Remember that this piece is not about your simple likes and dislikes but should analyse the craft, artistry and degree of success of the performance. Your review should be a constructive criticism, written from an informed point of view.

In work with students, the word 'context' sometimes seems to cause great anxieties. I would like here to give it some extra attention in a separate section, which may demystify it for you.

CONTEXT

A dance is always created at a certain time and in a specific place. When we analyse and evaluate a dance, these two factors must therefore be considered. In particular, we may look at:

- the history and social conditions;
- the function and role of the dance;
- the genre/style of the dance.

History and social condition

When we watch a romantic ballet today, we must consider the time when it was first choreographed in order to truly understand its significance. Thus, we appreciate that the pointe shoe, white net tutu and wings of the costumes of the wilis in *Giselle* were chosen in order to enhance the sense of an ethereal presence, which was such a vital part of the romantic palette. Similarly, in Sir Frederick Ashton's *The Dream* (1964), we note such romantic references as the use of the distinctive position from the *Pas de Quatre* (1845), originally adopted by Fanny Cerrito, Marie Taglioni,

Carlotta Grisi and Lucile Grahn in the ballet by Jules Perrot. In Ashton's ballet, the fairies Cobweb, Moth, Mustardseed and Peaseblossom copy this group shape.

In considering an appreciation of Ashton's choice of a romantic style for the dance, the audience should bear in mind the story itself. It is of course a love story set in a fantasy world of fairies, magic and spirits. So what could be more suitable than a romantic style which makes direct references to the dances of the 1840s and 1850s? If the audience or dance critics have a knowledge of such a context, it will help them to understand, appreciate and enjoy the performance all the more. It is clearly not possible to judge a classical ballet by the same criteria as those one would apply to a modern dance, or even to a modern ballet.

Dance can be totally mystifying for an audience when it is first performed, and it is easy to dismiss what has been presented as obscure and pointless. Martha Graham was one of the first to challenge her audiences in this way. By presenting what she saw as stark movement and hard-edged truths, she put demands on her audiences to *contribute* to the final performance by choosing to interpret the piece in a particular way. Dance was no longer just entertainment, as it had been in the previous years of vaudeville and rather poor ballet: the audience itself now had a greater role to play in the success of the final product. This still goes on today.

Experimental work, by its very nature, pushes back the boundaries of understanding for the audience, and so to evaluate its success, new strategies may have to be adopted by the onlooker. One of these will involve taking a *retrospective* view. For post-modern dancers in North America in the 1960s, the success and significance of their work may only, indeed, be truly understood when looking back in time:

> It may be true that neither critics nor audiences absorbed what happened in the sixties but I don't think I'd be doing what I'm doing now if that happened.

> *(Trisha Brown, in* The Vision of Modern Dance, *1979)*

Therefore, we see that the impact that a dance makes at the time it was created may be very different from how it is viewed later on. Again, the criteria by which we measure its success must consider the whole social and historical conditions of its time. We could never really experience romantic ballet as audiences did in the 1840s because we live in a very different age from theirs. We can appreciate it for what it is and enjoy it, but we cannot relate to it as something new and fashionable in the way that the original audiences would have done. Similarly, their experiences of the value of the French Revolution which turned society upside down are also difficult for us to recreate directly for ourselves. No longer were the social values of classicism acceptable. The aristocracy were no longer to be worshipped as perfect.

Now was the turn of the peasants to be glorified and idealised. This directly affected the choice of ideas and subject matter in the romantic ballet. The types of character, role, setting and story are all a result of the social context of the late nineteenth century when fairies, spirits, exotic foreign places and peasants were all the rage.

On the other hand, to *us*, the late-nineteenth-century discovery of ether light would seem unimpressive given *today's* lasers and other extraordinary technologies.

When modern art burst into existence at the start of the twentieth century, it rejected all the accepted values which had previously dominated art and society. In so doing it reflected a society in turmoil from war as well as the discovery of new psychologies and philosophies. The modern dance as all genres and styles of dance, was born in response to social upheaval and concerns of the time.

As a dance student, you should have a close knowledge of the history of the arts and perhaps use certain periods and styles to influence your own dance. Experimenting with various styles of the past and how they may give you new ideas and approaches in your choreography will add depth and breadth to your work. As one dance writer questioned:

> Why is it ... that a young choreographer is still more likely than a young painter or composer or playwright to regard an intimate knowledge of tradition as something that inhibits originality – rather than something that feeds and nourishes it?

> *(Roger Copeland in* Dance Theatre Journal, *1994)*

An understanding and appreciation of the past and present contexts will assist dance artists and audiences to respond appropriately in their evaluation of a dance. The context may include any or all of the following:

- social structures;
- social changes;
- technological developments;
- philosophies;
- psychologies;
- dominant social values
- other art forms.

The function and role of dance

This book concentrates on Western classical ballet and twentieth century modern and post modern genres, so the dances which we are concerned with have mainly artistic function. It may be worth mentioning briefly that other dances of for example, South Asian or Pan African origin, could well have very different functions for the societies that they come from. The audiences may watch the dances as part of their religious or social lives. This does not mean that they are not artistic as well, but they may contain meanings which carry important messages for the culture in which they were made. They may tell stories of important gods and goddesses, or they may be a part of social rituals which are important celebrations connected with successful growing and harvesting of crops. (Interestingly enough, as Britain in the twentieth century becomes a multi-cultural society, dances of Asia and Africa are performed more and more for their artistic function rather than for the religious or social

meaning. Also there is more mixing of styles and genres. This will be looked at in more detail in Chapter 8.)

Most Western theatre dance has significance as *art*, including most of the dance which we see at the theatre. Its role is to be watched by an audience, and functions as a way of improving the quality and depth of experience for the on-looker. The audience is the final judge of whether a dance has been successful in enriching and energising their lives. Each one of them will have their own thoughts, preferences and interpretations from any single performance.

Style and genre of dance

Social values clearly change over time and so the conditions in which dancers live must affect the style of their work. This was examined closely earlier in this chapter. From the traditional *Swan Lake* to the most avant-garde, all require special considerations of the context in which they were created in if their success is to be meaningfully judged. The style of a dance must be considered when evaluating it and appreciating the whole of its significance for human experience. In simple terms, this is the reason why, when naming any specific dance as well as its title and the name of the choreographer, the date is always mentioned. This can be a very important clue as to the genre, style and context of the dance.

TASK 7

Turn back to Tasks 1 and 2: return to the group to share the final short solos. Offer comment to each other about how successful they are in:

- putting across the original idea; and
- showing the style of the chosen choreographer.

EVALUATION – A SUMMARY

The process of analysis involves a sensitive set of comparisons of how effectively the constituent features are combined with the artistry in creating the success of the dance. Dances which have significance as art and function to make an impact on an audience are judged by certain criteria. Is the content of the dance presented to the audience in a form which they can receive and can add to their life experience? Or is there little to interest or stimulate an audience?

There are spin-offs from the process of analysis and evaluation as used by dance students and critics. It means that there is also a record of dance performances. This adds to the possibilities of developing a future for dance. As such, using dance notation as a tool for dance appreciation can add to recording dance for future reconstruction and performance.

The analysis, evaluation and appreciation of dances for future generations is also made possible by film and video recordings, which are a vital way of preserving the history of dance. The description, interpretation and final reconstructions or judgements of works preserved in writing, on film or in a notation score play a vital part in ensuring *progress* in the art of the dance.

By evaluating dance, we *enhance* its value or worth. Dance is then treasured as a precious jewel in the lives of all who come into contact with it. It has a vital part to play in life, as an aspect of a truly human world.

References and resources

BOOKS

Anderson, J., *Ballet and Modern Dance: a Concise History*, New Jersey: Princeton, 1992

Binney, E., *Glories of the Romantic Ballet*, London: Dance Books, 1985

Bland, A., *Observer of the Dance 1958–1982*, London: Dance Books, 1985

Clarke, M., Crisp, C., *Making a Ballet*, London: Studio Vista, 1974

Dewey, J., *Having an Experience*, New York: Minton, Bach & Co, 1934

Guest, I., *The Dancer's Heritage: A Short History of the Ballet*, Dancing Times, 1988

Jordan, S., *Striding Out*, London: Dance Books, 1972

Jordan, S. and Allen, D., *Parallel Lines*, London: Libbey & Co., 1993

Koner, P., *Elements of Performance* (out of print)

Lowenthal, L., *The Search for Isadora, the Legend and Legacy of Isadora Duncan*, New Jersey: Princeton BRS

Mackrell, J., *Out of Line*, London: Dance Books, 1992

Patsch-Bergsohn, I., *Modern Dance in Germany and the United States: Crosscurrents and Influences*, Harwood Academic Publishers, 1996

Preston-Dunlop, V., *Dance Words*, a review of words used by the dance world

Quirey, B., *May I Have the Pleasure?*, London: Dance Books, 1987

Siegel, M. B., *The Shapes of Change*, Avon Books, 1979

Spencer, P., *Society and the Dance*, Cambridge University Press, 1985

Stearns, M. and Stearns, A., *Jazz Dance: the Story of American Vernacular Dance*, New York: Da Capo, 1993

MUSIC

The following music is recommended for Task 4:

Parampara, *Moving in Time*, available from Mandy de Winter, 3 Brandywell Road, Broseley, Shropshire TF12 5ST, tel.: 01952 883 242

The Chieftains, *Strike the Gay Harp*, 3 Claddagh Records, 4CC10

chapter eight
DANCE TODAY

In the UK and the Western world today, dance activity is rapidly expanding. New technologies and a concern for staying in touch with the past in order to *learn* from it are part of a pattern of growth. This chapter will focus on the following areas:

- computer technology;
- cross-cultural dance in society today.

As a dance student, you may well be considering making dance a career, and it is important to be in touch with the ever-increasing possibilities that are available to you. The traditional options of stage school, West End musicals and performing are nowadays only one part of a much wider range of possibilities in dance careers. Moving into the twenty-first century, we see dance as joining the other art forms as a grown-up sister. In this final chapter, various options and considerations will be presented to you not only to help you pass the course which you are studying on at present, but also to support your decisions concerning where you might be heading afterwards.

Computer technology: new realities

The Information Superhighway is the communication medium of the future. Everywhere, this network spreads information as fast as you can think it up, from and to any part of the planet.

> The movement of information at approximately the speed of light has become by far the largest industry of the world.
>
> *(Marshall McLuhan in* Hot and Cool, *1968)*

Computer technology can serve a variety of exciting purposes. You can choreograph on it, notate on it. With *virtual reality*, the flesh-and-blood human dance may even be a thing of the past! No need to put ourselves through all that agonising training and injury any more. Well, this may be an extreme view, but it is certainly a consideration. Preferences for the human presence may well still be the final choice over virtual reality.

A basic definition of virtual reality is that it is the technology used to provide an intimate interaction between humans and computer imagery.

> *(Susan Kozel in* Dance Theatre Journal, *1994)*

In various experimental works, there seems to be a great potential for dance within this newest of human experiences. The 1994 conference at the ICA in London featured various works which used performers interacting in technological environments. The computer-generated information affects the performance space and the bodies performing in it. In the words of the critic Susan Kozel quoted above, the virtual reality as seen by the audience takes 'inspiration from physical experience to create new reality from art'. So, as the two dancers in *Chemical Wedding by Blast theory* (1992), suspended above the heads of the audience, communicate by means of a video camera, new realities are presented. Or as Orlan, in *The Reincarnation of St. Orlan* (1994), transmits by video the painful transformations of her plastic surgery, the dilemma felt by dancers in training is expressed: dance is painful and yet at the same time uplifting. It attempts to control, an yet also always involves a *loss* of control. There is a moment where the inner self reaches out into the general space. In the words of the artists: 'in cyberspace we are choreographing experience … the interaction between people and computers as a sort of choreography' (*Dance Theatre Journal*, vol 11, no. 2, p. 36, 1994).

What are your basic information-technology skills like? It may be worth your while exploring and investigating a future in the Information Superhighway. The possibilities in *multi-media* work for performance and study are ever-increasing. Software packages – like Life Forms – which model the body and can allow you to compose dance phrases or reconstruct from Labanotation scores make the physical presence of dancers no longer necessary. The software director offers the chance to combine text, graphics, sound, animation and video to create multi-media CD-ROMs (Read Only Memory). Clearly, the learning and performance potential here is enormous. A recent project by dancer and choreographer William Forsythe of the Frankfurt Ballet presents a CD-ROM containing categories of: Laban writing and composition; anatomical exercises; isometrics. Forsythe demonstrates about 100 short lessons, and shows some dancers from the Frankfurt Ballet rehearsing and performing his choreography for *Self Meant to Govern* (1995). The viewer can click back and forth, interacting with the screen, and so change the viewing angle, gain a close-up or distance shot, and of course switch between lessons. The research team which Forsythe worked with is called ZKM. They regard the project to be the creation of 'digital dance school'.

COMPUTER TECHNOLOGY – CONCLUSION

These new computer technologies are only as much value to dance as we care to make them. Information on dance has always been available through writing, film and notation across the ages, and CD-ROM is a development of this. But if we are to take responsibility for putting dance on the global map of the future and making it count in people's lives, then we have to increase research and increase people's involvement. Computer technology is part of the future for dance.

Cross-cultural dance in society today: the 'global village'

The history of ballet goes back over centuries. In other non-Western societies, many forms of traditional dance have similarly existed over centuries. At the beginning of the twentieth century, the revolution and rebellion of modern dance shook the world of dance. As global travel and communication has increased, and as populations have migrated, a melting-pot of dance and music, in fact of all the arts, has been the result.

> Cultural theorists now argue that national identities are not fixed but are in a constant state of flux.

> *(Sarah Rubidge, in* Dance Theatre Journal, *1995)*

There is a new world order, and with it a new arrangement of cultural and political contexts. This exchange and mixing of identities has been happening for a long time in music. We only have to look at the work of composers like David Byrne and Peter Gabriel in the pop world to see the mixing of music from many continents. In the world of modern classical music, composers like Steve Reich draw on structures of Indonesian *gamelan* music to enrich the Western traditions. A new type of contemporary music is the result.

The Arts Council in the UK has been active in encouraging cross-cultural work in dance. Choreographers like Shobana Jeyasingh – as already mentioned – experiment and explore the mixing of Western dance and traditional South Asian *bharata natyam* dance. The recent show by the Kokuma African dance company *Guddi* (1995) appeared to be working from an African base but mixed together the movement vocabularies of Graham technique, ballet (I could have sworn the set was from Act Two of *Giselle*, and there were a few wilis around too) and something resembling a funky Tamla Motown/Elvis Presley showbiz style.

In 1992 the director of The Place Theatre, London introduced a new season called *Vivarta*. This focused on choreographers working in India who were experimenting with their choreography so that it was not wholly in the classical traditions of Indian dance. A similar season featuring Chinese modern dance has since followed in 1995. Entitled *Re:Orient*, it includes works by artists from China, Hong Kong, Taiwan, the UK and the USA. The following review of the *Spring Loaded 1994* season gives a flavour of what has been on offer. It is describing the Nina Rajarani Company in *Kalpa Virksh*:

> In terms of visual effects, the piece offers an interesting fusion of cultures. While the movement is drawn from South Asian dance, all three dancers are white, and the costume, while broadly drawn on classical lines would not look out of place on the club scene ... makes effective and original treatment of British Asian culture.

> *(Uzma-ameed in* Dance Theatre Journal, *1994)*

The fusion of two or more cultures in dance is not an easy task. In these early days, there are bound to be some less successful attempts. Ameed, in the same article, points out that in another piece, *Golden Chains*, the claim to be 'progressive Indian dance' was not really justified. It lacked any depth of treatment in the narrative of the position of Asian women in society today:

> ... the plot lends itself more to a Hindi film style melodrama rather than to the deconstruction of stereotypes and the highlighting of cultural issues.

> *(Uzma-ameed in* Dance Theatre Journal, *1994)*

Similarly, the performance by the Australian Bangarra Dance Theatre in the UK in 1994 threw up problems of fusing traditional and modern movement and ideas. Sarah Rubidge noted that the choreography of director Steven Page was a mismatch of the groundedness of Aboriginal movement with the lightness of a modern dance style. Page himself was aware of the shortcomings of the attempted cross-cultural exchange, and remarked:

> Next piece. No split leaps, no pirouettes, no attitudes!

> *(Steven Page in* Dance Theatre Journal, *1994)*

Rubidge suggests that he may have more success using a more 'released' style of modern/post-modern dance. This would offer a more sympathetic context in which to place the traditional Aboriginal intensely concentrated face and body by using the natural body weight and generating energy from the centre of gravity – by framing the traditional in a postmodern anatomical-release skeletal style.

There is a real clue here as to where these cross-cultural explorations are coming from. In any classical tradition, the baseline values are those from traditional societies. Along with that go all the stereotypical roles and clichés that are the targets of post-modern art and values. It would seem that the basic ideas and material for choreography need as sensitive a treatment as does the mixing of the movement.

The post-modern values in society at large place dancers, and indeed all artists, in a situation where their traditional art forms and values are no longer solely enough to support their work. In the above-mentioned *Re:Orient* season, dance from oriental cultures was seen alongside the work of artists from the same cultural backgrounds but living in the West. The traditional style of Chinese dance was clearly evident – for example, in the use of props like fans, scarves and drums – but was mixed with other more Western influences. In the work of Taiwanese Ming-She Ku, release techniques and contact improvisation, which she had been introduced to during a stay in the USA, were both used. Similarly, the Chinese dancer and choreographer Pit Fong is concerned with exploring the differences between how Chinese people move and how people from Western cultures move. In doing so, she mixes her own natural oriental rhythms with Western contemporary dance structures.

It is important to note that although the cross-cultural exchange process may be accelerated by new technologies and more and faster travel, it is in fact nothing new:

> … no story belongs to any one culture. What is interesting is to see the transformations that take place in various cultures. Take Romeo and Juliet for example. It originates as a kernel of a story in Arabia amongst the Moslems. It travels to Italy, becomes a novel, a searing romance, and then it becomes an English play, a classic.

(Jatinder Verma in Dance Theatre Journal*, 1992)*

Of course it also travelled again, this time across the Atlantic, to become one of the best known musicals of all time, *West Side Story.* Verma further says that he believes that there is no longer any purity in the arts, and that 'Today interconnectedness is a fact of life.'

The 'global village' was a concept thought up originally by Marshall McLuhan in 1968.

> Today the globe has shrunk in the wash with speeded-up information movement from all directions. We have, as it were come to live in a global village … on one hand a community of learning, and at the same time, with regard to the tightness of its inter-relationships, the globe has become a tiny village.

(Marshall McLuhan in Hot and Cool*, 1968)*

In the 1990s it sometimes seems we are only just catching up with McLuhan's ideas. In an article by Roger Copeland (*Dance Theatre Journal,* vol 9, no 4, 1992), surprise was expressed by an African scholar, Robert Farris Thompson, when an African villager told him that the dance he was performing had been learnt from a Michael Jackson performance on MTV. Such fluency and frequency of exchange has been seen as inevitable over the last thirty years.

From this point of view, there needs to be a long hard look at traditions which are openly resistant. The genres of ballet or African people's dance forms are open to question sometimes. Is it sufficient to present replicas of Pan-African dance culture or the classics in such undiluted pure doses?

> … the 'No Trespassing' disclaimer is un-

masked as cowardice or imperialism of the most arrogant.

(Dwight Conquergood, in Performing as a Moral Act, as quoted in Dance Theatre Journal, 1992)

The alternative is to allow cross-fertilisation with ballet, modern and South Asian genres as part of a natural growth pattern. This process reflects the different cultural backgrounds of choreographers, directors and dancers alike. There seems little point in pursuing what may easily be misconstrued as a rather élitist direction if exclusion is the policy. On the other hand, it must be done thoughtfully and deliberately, and not in a manner as described in the following account:

(To) gain artistic acknowledgement of their work ... some companies, in their frantic pursuit of acceptance, abandoned identification with their Black heritage and history, aspiring to be contemporary dancers who just happened to be black.

(David Bryan, in Advancing Black Dancing, Dance Theatre Journal, vol 10, 1993)

There may be a very fine line to draw between these two approaches of exclusion or cross-fertilisation, and each case needs individual consideration.

In the ballet world, mention has already been made in an earlier section about modern versions of the classics. Such choreographers as Mark Morris and Mats Ek have transformed classics like The Nutcracker and Giselle to such an extent that the whole value system of the narrative changes. Ek's Giselle (1982), for example, changes from a tragic romance to a commentary on the foolishness of romantic love, casting Giselle as the village idiot. In Act Two, she is punished by being sent to the lunatic asylum where the wilis become her fellow patients. Their white tutus become white hospital gowns. The values being examined by Ek are testimony to the treatment of women in mental health. The heroine is interred forever, while the real perpetrator, Albrecht, is symbolically purified and ready to start a new life – she the victim, he cleansed. Let it be a warning to us all. Similarly, in his Swan Lake (1966), the evil sorcerer is recast as a woman, and there is an implication that the hero, Siegfried, was the victim of an Oedipus complex (the desire of a child to possess sexually the parent of the opposite sex). Thus, the ballets offer fresh insights for their twentieth-century audiences.

Royal Ballet-trained Jonathon Burrows is another interested in finding new directions for classical ballet. Burrows describes his working in the show Our (1994), combining the use of low and high weight (which he associates with classical ballet) in the body. He states:

In a sense those are the skills of the next generation of dancers ... I have no argument with classical ballet ... it has a three hundred year history. It's more like a martial art in that each subsequent dancing master has taken it and developed it, it's grown very humanly.

(Jonathon Burrows, in Dance Theatre Journal, 1994)

From his point of view, the repetitious nature of training undertaken by a classical dancer results in an ability to move with great freedom and openness. It is this that he sees as the classical style. Burrows sees himself as being on a creative continuum within this style, but without being restricted by the classical compositional structures.

I would rather wrestle with the clichés of ballet than wrestle with the clichés and mannerisms of contemporary dance ... it's horrible when an idea becomes a habit.

(Jonathon Burrows, in Dance Theatre Journal, 1994)

Burrows is concerned with *humanness* in dance, and this is of course a concern which many dance cultures have as a focus in one way or another. In non-Western cultures, the place of dance at the heart of the *community* is of great priority. African dance, like classical ballet, is a strong cultural force, and it exists all over the globe nowadays. Certainly, there are many African people living all over the Western world, and they bring with them their own cultural agendas and packages. The variety of ways that these translate into UK culture, for example, is an interesting situation. In Brighton alone, there are two different African people's dance companies, namely Kakande and Mashango, and they seem to function differently when it comes to the cross-cultural process. Kakande describe themselves as:

> African and European dance and percussion ensemble ... comprising both Europeans and Africans from Guinea and The Gambia ... combine high energy dance and strong West African rhythms with traditional stories to depict the hidden world of African heritage through rhythm, songs, symbols and gestures.

Mashango describe themselves and their show as:

> An all-black African Caribbean dance company ... 'Ekhaya' uses the symbol of a mask that belongs to an African village to show the conflict between rural and urban life in Africa today. For the village the mask represents the power and soul of village life. It is stolen to sell purely for its commercial value. The dancers are all black and a mixture of British and African born. The dances are from Ghana, South Africa, the Caribbean and Brixton.

It seems that the concern for cross-cultural exchange is happening from different flight paths here: one company allowing white European performers to address a purely African repertoire, the other only allowing black performers but integrating Western culture into the content of the show. The melting-pot in operation is thus by no means a predictable process, but what these companies do seem to be concerned with, however, is again dance as an important function of the community in which it is living, rather than just as a visual spectacle which happens in a specially appointed space. One group involves members of the local community as performers irrespective of their colour, while the other uses the community concern as the *idea* or *content* of the choreography itself. This community focus is in itself more of a non-Western idea.

In the Philippines, there is a recent development to use dance as a way of protesting to the political leaders and to build a sense of national identity. Denni Sayers visited the Philippines in 1992 and became deeply involved with the work of dancers there. She describes some choreography she did which was to be part of a May Day rally. The chosen music was a Filipino reggae sound by a local subversive band.

> They were clear about the topics that they wanted to convey. All their improvisations were narrative dance pieces, centred on the struggle of the people. ... The thing that bound them together was their ambition to develop a dance form that could help their fellow Filipinos find their own feet. ... At the May Day rally 2,000 workers turned out to watch. ... The dancers came out on stage to the pulsing reggae beat, bent under the burden of poverty and oppression. As the dance built they began to exert themselves and stand up against the symbols of power. Then they broke into a local dance, which was greeted with triumphant cheers by the Filipinos, recognising something of their own.

(Denni Sayers in Dance Theatre Journal, *1992)*

Contemporary African dancing (a) Kakande (b) Mashango

(a)

(b)

Sayers intended to make a return visit and then follow up by establishing a link with a group of British dancers.

In Australian Aboriginal culture, it has been noted that women are encouraging younger boys to make dances about what it felt like to drink alcohol for the first time. Here we see old values being preserved through consideration and reflection on the new.

CROSS-CULTURAL DANCE – A CONCLUSION

The distinction between 'traditional' and 'modern' cultures is these days a tricky one. Some dance genres may try to cling onto their pure traditions, but the writing is on the wall. Traditions will undergo metamorphosis. Like the egg, larva and caterpillar, in the end they are all parts of the butterfly. Western and non-Western cultures are all undergoing change. You may be a tourist in West Africa watching a traditional dance, and it may be upsetting to notice that the dancers are wearing Ray Bans and Reeboks. Too bad! These performers, like you, live in the global village and are not museum exhibits. Their traditions and our traditions are undergoing an alchemical process in the melting-pot.

It thus becomes apparent that the real East/West contrast isn't 'tradition *or* change' but rather 'continuity *and* change'. *All* traditions evolve, albeit not at the same pace.

(Roger Copeland in Dance Theatre Journal, *1992)*

It is vital, during such a complex exchange process, that the quality of the work be preserved. It is also vital that, whenever possible, the exchange be a *two-way* process which results in something new and not a mere copy or a fashionable pick 'n' mix as in The United Colours of Benetton. Perhaps a final word could go to Denni Sayers, reflecting on her Philippines visit:

We as dancers and choreographers have so much to give, and we can learn from these extraordinary artists about the value of our craft in this constantly developing world.

TASK 1 ▽▽▽

In groups of 4 or 5, choose one of the statements/questions below and construct a 10-minute presentation which can be given to the rest of the group. Wherever possible, use examples of companies and performances that you have seen or know about from research. If possible, use publicity and other visual materials to illustrate your ideas.

1 Consider the role of African traditional dance or contemporary reworkings of African traditional dance in the UK in the 1990s.
2 How far can ballet address the concerns of the 1990s without losing the distinctive characteristics of its genre?
3 Ballet-trained choreographers make barefoot dances, and the influence of African and Indian dance is to be seen in contemporary dance. What is the characteristic of contemporary dance in the 1990s?
4 How might the dance of Indian dance artists develop in the UK in the 1990s?

References and resources

BOOKS AND ARTICLES

Bauman, R. (ed), *Folklore, Cultural Performances and Popular Entertainments*

Burt, R., *The Male Body: Bodies, Spectacles and Sexualities* (out of print)

Foster, S. L. (ed), *Choreographing History*, Indiana Univ. Press, 1995. How the body is presented as political, aesthetic and physical objects

McLuhan, M., *Hot and Cool*. Harmondsworth: Penguin, 1968

From *Dance Theatre Journal*:

Copeland, R., 'The black swan and the dervishes: cross-cultural approaches', vol. 9, no. 4, 1992

Sayers, D., 'Dance in the Philippines', vol. 9, no. 4, 1992

Rubidge, S. and Verma, J., 'Cross-cultural theatre', vol. 10, no. 1, 1992

Semple, M., 'African Dance Adzido', vol. 10, no. 1, 1992

Badejo, P., 'What is black dance in Britain? vol. 10, no. 4, 1993

Rubidge, S., 'Aborigine dreams', vol. 11, no. 2 1994

Kozel, S., 'Virtual reality', vol. 11, no. 2, 199⸲

de Marigny, C., 'Jonathan Burrows', vol. 11 no. 2, 1994

Hameed, U., 'Spring loaded', vol. 11, no. 2 1994

Copeland, R., 'Revival and reconstruction' vol. 11, no. 3, 1994

Kozel, S., 'Spacemaking: experience of a virtual body', vol. 11, no. 3, 1994

Rubidge, S., 'Reconstruction and its problems', vol. 12, no. 1, 1994

Kozel, S., 'Reshaping space: focusing time', vol. 12, no. 2, 1995

Rubidge, S., 'Cultural identity and the new aesthetic', vol. 12, no. 2, 1995

chapter nine

THE WAY AHEAD

A brave new world – with inequalities

You may have had dance lessons at school before you started your A or AS Level or the BTEC studies, and these may have been accompanied by lessons out of school time at a private dancing school. The fact that dance became part of the National Curriculum in 1992 is a fair measure of the progress it has made in the UK education system. In this way we are ahead of most of the rest of the world. This section will examine opportunities for your future dance education and training. It will also address some of the gaps in provision in dance education and throw in a few contentious issues that you should feel free to take away and discuss with dancers, non-dancers, parents, friends – in fact, anyone whose ear you can bend!

So first to the issues:

- dance education and gender;
- the financing of dance education;
- dance and disability.

Dance education and gender

Unfortunately, dance is only optional at secondary level. The National Curriculum Council recommended this because it had been 'persuaded by agony stories from schools about boys having to do dance when they don't want to' (*Times Educational Supplement*, 1992). It seems that dance, to some educationalists, is only important for the younger age group, and then only for the girls! A strange sort of logic in the age of gender awareness, I hear you say. Of course, I would agree with you. One of the most disappointing aspects of my years of involvement with dance and education is the sexist treatment of it as an art form or as a subject on a curriculum. Such prejudices and opinions about the status of boys are quite unacceptable, and all students must be made aware of restricting traditional views of maleness and masculinity. How many boys are in your class? How much longer are females expected to endure living in a world which has its base in a chauvinistic value system? Where are the postmodern values that you have read so much about in this book? What are you doing to reinforce them in your day-to-day encounters? Remember, if you're not part of the solution, you are part of the problem. To give you some ammunition for your assault on the college football team, here are a few fascinating facts:

- The Physical Education Working Group that was appointed to name which activities were to be included in the National Curriculum did a great deal of thorough research, and decided that:

  ... a broad and balanced programme of Physical Education, sensitively delivered, can help to extend boys' restricted perception of masculinity and masculine behaviour.

  (*P.E Working group report National Curriculum Council*)

- 'Real men wear tights!' and 'Male dancers are happy to be hunky!' (in *The Sunday Express*, 2 February 1992).

- The wearing of tights is not compulsory, and reflecting on various forms of street dance and dance from other cultures – such as Banghra – it seems clear that dance *can* carry with it heavy amounts of masculine value and status.

- Pre-industrial revolution, it was the role of *men* to lead the dancing in the community. Similarly, in ancient Greek and classical culture, a soldier was expected to be a good dancer also. Much of this is lost in the UK today. It seems that as people left the land to work in the towns, they left their culture of song, dance and story-telling behind. This happened alongside the growth in ballet of the importance of the ballerina and the lowering of the status of the male dancer. The outcome was the attachment of *effeminate* images to male dancers. This totally unjustified image remains ever strong today.

So, a tricky situation for the dance world to address.

> ... to what extent can man's achievements in dance be celebrated without at the same time reasserting male dominance and thus reinforcing the imbalance of power between men and women in our society?

> *(Ramsay Burt in* The Male Dancer: Bodies, Spectacles, Sexualities, *1995)*

If you do promote dance to male students, are you able to do so without using male-dominated values? If not, dance may become a mere spectacle of athletic prowess within such a value system, one which overlooks the other sensitive lyrical side of dance and human nature in case it implies that the dancer is homosexual. Often, the image of the male dancer is one of muscularity and body beautiful. These images only serve to reinforce the very male-dominated stereotypes which we are

trying to avoid. In modern dance, 'men are men and women are women', like in any good Western film. In this way, the value system is the same as that for classical ballet. We only have to look at the works of Martha Graham and her followers to notice this. In many of her works, for example *Appalachian Spring* (1944) and *Errand into the Maze* (1947), the norm for the male roles is one of strength, with high jumps and the like. It is interesting to note that in the early years of modern dance, the pioneers were women. Since then, as modern dance has become more accepted and mainstream, more and more dance-company directors and choreographers are men. Indeed, the women seem to be their own worst enemies in this matter. They have given away the power bases of whole companies from women as the founders to a complete succession of male directors, almost thoughtlessly.

The problem is not entirely solved in post-modern work either. The androgyny of The Cunningham Company conveniently ignores the gender issue. The high-powered hype and aggression in some contact improvisation reinforces a male-dominated social norm. What is necessary is to be aware of these values and to deconstruct them thoughtfully in order to produce reasoned alternative options. This is your role.

Current work by such choreographers as Lea Anderson, Lloyd Newson (DV8), Matthew Bourne (Adventures in Motion Pictures), the Europeans Pina Bausch and De Keersmaeker and the American Mark Morris offer audiences such options. Just as Anderson is at pains not to show women being 'beaten up', she is also concerned with revealing the feminine side of men as acceptable. This is particularly noticeable in the Featherstonehaughs' *The Bends* (1994) which 'explores the role of men in isolation' (programme note, 1994). The dancers present a number of fast-moving images, from tough commando Action Man-type soldiers

Swan Lake, *Adventures in Motion Pictures, Matthew Bourne*

through to the wearing of feather boas and the carrying-out of domestic chores.

In the recent *Swan Lake* by Matthew Bourne (1995), the swans in Act Two are played by a corps de ballet of men, beautiful classical dancers with soft curving lines as well as tensile strength. This strategy reinforces a more balanced view of maleness, and allows the narrative of the ballet to be told through the eyes of the Prince.

> When the torsos are bare and male, the arms are powerfully muscled and the tutus replaced by ruffled feather breeches, the effect is both peculiar and mysterious. ... These are dangerous feral creatures. ... After the second half I was snuffling into my handkerchief – which is more than I do at the Royal Ballet's or ENB's *Swan Lake* ... Not bad for a small contemporary dance group with a daft name.
>
> *(Jan Parry in* Dance Now, *vol 4, no 4, winter 1995)*

When people ask me what the themes of our work are I always resist, because I feel they are often trying to reduce it. Sexual politics, what's sexual politics? If you are talking about homosexuality what you mean is equality, you know, human equality. But the Royal Ballet is about sexual politics. I mean, when you see *Swan Lake* it's all sexual politics, they just don't call it that. It depends on how you view it. And to me too many critics want to categorise. ... In order to analyse it's often reduced, the issues are reduced, not expounded. And obviously being gay, the issue is oppression ... and conformity

(Lloyd Newson, in Dance Theatre Journal, *1993)*

It is a matter not of forcing boys to do dance classes but of allowing them to relax and feel safe to enjoy movement for its own sake, in all its width and depth. It is an issue which all teachers and students need to grasp and feel able to speak up about. Otherwise, if it is swept under the carpet, how will things ever change? When will a balance ever be struck?

The gender battle in dance is only one example of the unlevel playing field that exists in the education system. The matter of financing dance students is also cause for question and concern.

The financing of dance education

We are too familiar with the Cinderella role of dance in state institutions. Music and art students receive mandatory grants whilst dance students are subject to the discretionary grants lottery.

(Jeanette Siddall, in Dance Theatre Journal, *1992)*

Siddall reports similar injustices in the awarding of Arts Council grants and in the provision of musical and dance tuition opportunities in education. When comparing the provision of dance and music education in many counties of the UK, it is unavoidable to notice that there are usually serious injustices. In one county known to me, there is – and always has been – a music adviser and provision running into millions of pounds for the Youth Orchestra but no dance adviser and no funding at all for youth dance provision at any official level. This is the picture for much dance education provision for the young dancers of the future: patchy, and at best random.

Soon, you may be thinking of embarking on further dance study. The doors of well-admired institutions like the Laban Centre, the London School of Contemporary Dance and the Rambert School, or of many stage schools, will be firmly closed to you unless you can find the money to open them. This may come from your local authority. You know that the school you want to go to is accredited by the Council for Dance Education and Training; *and* you have paid for an audition at the school of your choice and been accepted; *and* the schools seem to think you are good enough. So now you may ask 'What's the problem?'

Well, the problem is that pursuing study at a 'private' dance institution has not been seen until recently by the government as something worthy of a mandatory award. Local government money is, as we know, squeezed to a trickle, and their provision of basic education is much threatened. So where does that leave you? For that matter, where does that leave places like the Laban Centre? For the most part, their options are to fill their courses with students who have the money, and many of these are from overseas (whose governments may pay). The recent introduction of lottery money for dance and drama students has gone some way to improving this situation. You may not have the money, but may be prepared to scrimp, work, save and battle your way through three or four years of gruelling training; training which in itself is going to stretch you to your limits in every aspect of your person. Training which many undergraduate science students would never be able to withstand because of its total demands. Even within the other arts areas such as music, the visual arts and drama, students stand a better chance of receiving the necessary grants.

The final picture shapes up like this:

- the UK's finest dance institutions delivering top-quality education but often not to the UK's most talented;
- dance students who are subject to the rigours of dance training and study and

who also have to work long hours in bars, shops and restaurants just to scrape by. This is not sympathetic to their studies and may be the cause of substantial stress, injury or even the drop-out of the most capable and talented.

So now you are probably in some state of depression. But it's not all despondency and gloom. Over recent years, many universities have started up courses in dance to degree level, and students on many of these courses receive mandatory grants like those given to their colleagues studying languages, drama, science or philosophy. Perhaps you are anticipating that these courses are not able to give you the same intensity and quality of training that you could expect elsewhere. But fear not, for many of these courses are excellent. The only problem may be the written content of the course (present because of its degree status). Over the years, one thing that has been noticeable is the large numbers of dyslexic dance students. After all, their condition may have been one influence in their being attracted to dance in the first place. Indeed, many of them are fine dancers, but to follow a course of study which contains a large amount of written work may be catastrophic for them. This reminds me of an answer in a GCSE Dance examination several summers ago. After several questions on a written paper, the student wrote: 'I can't answer any more questions, but I can dance. You can ask my teacher!' Students who are not comfortable with the written word have to be thoughtful, therefore, about the suitability and unsuitability of certain courses. Although this is a problem specifically for unacademic dancers, it does lead me to a consideration that *all* dance students need to think about.

This consideration is that finding and choosing a course which is right for *you* is the most important thing. You may be interested in theatre, and may therefore be suited to a course which *mixes* dance and theatre. Perhaps a course which takes you into the musical theatre world is more your cup of tea, so that you can use your singing talent. Or perhaps at heart you like to write and analyse dance, in which case a course with a more academic content would be suitable. Or maybe your interest lies in working in the community as a dance animateur, and there are specific courses for this too. Be wary of assuming that the course that your friend may have chosen must be the right one for you also.

The wide range of courses on offer these days is well worth careful research, and it is vital that the one you choose suit you as a dancer, as a choreographer and as a person. *Dance: Education, Training and Careers* by Chris Jones, published by and available from The National Resource Centre for Dance, University of Surrey, is a very good book which lists many courses, but I must add that the growth of these courses is so great that it is difficult for publications to keep up with them. It is worth asking your own dance teacher for some helpful information and advice here. Many universities, colleges and schools have open days, and if you could go along to them, you could make some valuable comparisons before you make any final choice.

Finally, perhaps after your sixth-form or further-education studies you may choose to pursue a career in something completely different, keeping dance as a life-enhancing interest. Remembering the hours of pleasure, challenge and value it brought you, you could still be part of the growing supporters of dance for the future. The dance world needs dancing dentists, accountants, health and social workers, and most of all politicians! As they live their day-to-day lives, they could include as a priority the support and promotion of dance for all of society. In this way, they could help to redress some of the imbalances which have been mentioned in this part of the chapter. Peter Brinson, the famous dance educator, comments that the dance world:

... doesn't pay half enough attention to the powers and the politics which have sustained it, or cast it down, throughout history.

(Peter Brinson, in Dance as Education: Towards a National Dance Culture, *1991)*

It is as much your responsibility to put dance on the political map as it is anyone else's. At present, dance is working towards recognition in terms of funding for education in order to have equal status with the other arts and other subjects generally. We must all help to put this message across to as many people as possible.

Dance and disability

In recent years, the work of such companies as Motionhouse and Candoco has done much to provide opportunities to dance for those with special needs. A contact-improvisation and release workshop being taught to an *integrated group* (that is one consisting of dancers with and without disabilities) is well documented on the video *Different Dancers, Similar Motion,* 1989. It shows work done on a residency over a fortnight in Oxford with integrated groups of adults and youth, and it demonstrates:

- how people can learn to overcome ignorance, anxieties, prejudices and inexperience through constructively led workshops;
- how some forms of movement, such as contact improvisation, are especially suitable for integrated workshops;
- how everyone can value everyone's role in the workshop;
- how people can learn to respect different rhythms, energies and styles of movement in one another.

(From the sleeve notes for the video, Different Dancers, Similar Motion, *1989)*

Such techniques as contact improvisation and release work have allowed far greater access to dance for those with learning difficulties, but there is a strong body of opinion that it should not end there: i.e. that dancers with disabilities

should be encouraged, where appropriate, to attend other technique classes, say for ballet, in order to articulate arm and hand gestures. There may be many technique classes which could be adapted for the benefit of certain individuals, and training programmes could be made more flexible to accommodate such personalisations.

These values are becoming more and more a part of the whole dance picture, including the integration of dancers with disabilities into dance education. At Coventry University Performing Arts, a recent partnership has been struck up with the integrated dance company Candoco to establish the first course which runs through further and higher education. It allows students both with and without disabilities to study together through BTEC National Diploma and on to a BA Hons Degree in Dance. The Laban Centre also reserves places on its Community Course for students with a disability.

Celeste Dandeker was a dancer with London Contemporary Dance Theatre. Her career was ended when she broke her neck on stage. She now dances with Candoco and uses a wheelchair, which may be seen as a drawback, to *advantage*:

> You have to remember that you've got a high-tech piece of equipment under you, if you're in one of our chairs. It's very

Candoco Dance Company

mobile, very light and can move incredibly fast.

(Celeste Dandeker in Dance Theatre Journal, *vol 10, no 1, 1992)*

Candoco's work is based on a belief that confronts the élitism of a dance world which believes that only perfect bodies matter. In a recent article by Adam Benjamin, joint artistic director of Candoco, the point is made that if disabled and non-disabled people are encouraged to study dance together, there is a chance to develop much more the possibilities of employment and research, as well as other opportunities generally, for the disabled dancer. I think the words of Adam Benjamin act as inspiration and guidance for us all moving into the next century of dance develop-

ment. Speaking about the issues that will be brought up during the development, and the raising of the profile, of the disabled in dance and in dance education, he reflects on problems that will have to be solved, and on lessons that should be learnt from dance history:

... the lessons we learn therefore will be more than academic; they will have an impact not only on dance as an art form, but on the way we perceive, treat and respect each other as human beings. Surely this in the end is the test of a vital, effective and truly contemporary art form.

(Adam Benjamin, in Dance Theatre Journal, *1995)*

Conclusion

You may have noticed that this last chapter uses fewer book references and more material from current newspapers, programme notes and dance magazines. This is because it has focused on the present and the future, which are unfolding around you all the time, and have hardly enough time to appear in a book – except for this one. The story of dance is still being written and choreographed, and you as a student of dance are a part of it, walking backwards into the future. Your own contribution to making dance a part of a truly human world is as important, unique and vital as anyone's.

References and resources

BOOKS AND ARTICLES

Banes, S., *Dance Writing in the Age of Postmodernism*

Beal, R. and Berryman Miller, S. (eds), *Dance for Older Adults* USA: NDA/AAHPERD, 1988

Benari, N., *Inner Rhythm* – dance training for the deaf

Brinson, P., *Dance as Education: Towards a National Dance Culture*, London: Falmer Press, 1991

Jones, C., *Dance: Education, Training and Careers*, published by and available from The National Resource Centre for Dance, University of Surrey

From the *Dance Theatre Journal*:

Addair, C., *No Concessions in Condoco*, vol. 10, no. 1, 1992

Benjamin, A., 'Unfound movement', vol. 12, no. 1, 1995

Alexandra Carter's Review of *The Male Dancer*, by Ramsay Burt, vol. 12, no. 2, 1995

Lloyd Newson on MSM, vol. 10, no. 4, 1993

Adair, C., 'No concessions to stereotypes (Candoco Dance Company)', vol. 10, no. 1, 1993

Siddall, J., 'Fair play: the debate about dance and the National Curriculum', vol. 9, no. 4, 1992

GLOSSARY

Abduction   movement away from the midline of the body.

Abstraction   process of reducing something to its most basic form.

Acetabulum   cup-shaped cavity of the pelvic bone, in which the head of the femur bone sits.

Adduction   movement towards the midline of the body.

Accelerando   gradual increase of tempo or speed.

Accent   stress on a beat or movement.

Actions   the six dance skills of travel, turn, jump, stillness, gesture and fall.

Aerobics   exercise which develops cardiovascular (of the heart) endurance.

Agonist   the muscle or muscle group that is contracting.

Alignment   proper posture as near to a straight line as possible from head to toe when standing.

Anacrusis   an up-beat before the main accent at the start of a phrase; equivalent in movement is a preparatory motion.

Antagonistic muscle   the muscle or muscle group in opposition to the agonist (contracting) muscle.

Anterior   sited in the front part.

Articulation   the meeting point of bones forming a joint.

Assemblé   a jump when one leg lifts as one foot brushes off floor, take-off from supporting leg. Land on both feet in fifth position.

Asymmetric   uneven in space, time or dynamics.

Atrophy   tissue wasting away.

Augmentation   increase in the time a movement or sound takes up.

Ballet   a highly stylised technique of dance which originated in Europe in the seventeenth century.

Ballistic stretch   achieved by bouncing (not generally recommended).

Bar   a vertical line that divides one bar of music from another.

Battement   the free leg gestures forwards, back or sideways with a downward accent. Petit battement is small, leg only just off floor. Grand battement is large, leg raises to medium level.

Beat   the underlying regular pulse of movement or music.

Binary   a two part form in composition, AB.

Body image   the picture in one's mind of one's own body.

Brush   a leg lifts with foot brushing along floor with an upward accent.

Bunion   Inflammation of the bursa over the first metatarso-phalangeal joint.

Bursa   small sac of synovial fluid which reduces friction where muscles or tendons glide over the bone.

Bursitis   Inflammation of a bursa.

Cadence   the closing section of a phrase.

Calcaneus   heel bone.

Canon an overlap in the dancers' movements.

Cartilage in joints, hyaline cartilage protects the ends of bones from wear and absorbs shock.

Centre of gravity the densest part of the body, sited just below the navel.

Centring bringing together the physical centre with that of the mind.

Cervical spine curves forward, 7 vertebrae of the neck.

Chiropractic therapy to treat illness/injury by manipulating the spine.

Choreography art of arranging movement into a finished performance.

Climax the main highpoint of a dance.

Chronic a long term, recurring injury that may not respond to treatment.

Coccyx the bottom of the spine, the tailbone.

Collapse a released fall which gives into gravity through the centre and does not usually rebound.

Complementary movements which are similar but not the same.

Composition organising and arranging sounds, words, movement, images into a unified whole.

Concentric muscle contraction which involves fibres shortening.

Consonant harmonious balance, opposite of dissonant.

Contemporary dance see *modern dance*.

Content the central idea of the dance.

Contact improvisation spontaneous movement to support, bounce off and onto etc. a partner or group.

Contraction musuclar shortening that changes the shape of a limb. In Graham technique, contraction of the torso is a main principle.

Contrapuntal forms two or more themes interweave independently.

Contrast movement unlike those in the main theme of a dance.

Contusion a bruise caused by external force in which the skin does not break.

Counts the number of beats within the measure.

Crescendo gradual increase in speed, dynamics or sound.

Criticism a judgement of a dance based on careful consideration of choreographic and technical principles.

Curvature of the spine distortion of proper alignment of spine, usually in a sideways direction.

Curves of the spine natural forward and backward bends which spread and support the weight of the various sections of the body.

Cyclorama a stretched curtain or wall at the back of the stage.

Development altering the action, space, time and quality of motifs so that when they are repeated, they remain interesting.

Diminuendo gradual reduction in force or volume.

Disc cartilage in between the vertebrae.

Dissonance clashing harmonies which feel strange or disturbing. Opposite to consonant.

Dorsiflexion the foot pulls upwards.

Downstage the space towards the front of the stage.

Dynamics   variety of force, accent and quality of movement.

Eccentric contraction   muscle contraction which involves the fibres lengthening.

Effort actions   when weight, time and space are combined, there are 8 possible ways of moving. As identified by Rudolf Laban.

Elevation   jumping or rising.

Endurance   the ability to keep moving over time.

Enchainment   a linked series of movement.

Energy   potential to move.

Eversion   the sole of the foot rotates outwards, away from the midline.

Extension   lengthening of body part/s outwards. Important factor in a dancer's training. Opposite to flexion.

Fall   a controlled movement towards the floor either a total collapse or followed by a recovery.

Femur   the thigh bone.

Flexibility   the range of movement possible in the points. Important to increase this in dance training.

Flexion   movement when a joint bends, opposite to extension.

Floor pattern   an imagined path on the floor let as a dancer travels. Part of spatial patterning/design in dance composition.

Flow   free or bound in movement; flexible or direct through space; successive or simultaneous through the body. (As named by Rudolf Laban.)

Focus   the dancer's sight line used to increase communication with the audience.

Force   intensity of weight, ranging from firm to light.

Form   the structure of a planned dance composition which organises the themes and motifs.

Fresnel   a device used on a light to change the size of area lit.

Fugue   (in music and dance) the theme is varied and played versus itself.

Gels   transparent plastic in different colours, placed in front of lights.

Gesture   movements which do not transfer or bear weight.

Gradual stretch   stretching through held stillness. Opposite of ballistic stretching.

Ground Bass   the basic theme is repeated as background for other themes.

Group awareness   to dance in relation to others by taking cues from each other.

Hallux Rigidis   degenerative disease of the bone of the metatarso-phalangeal joint of the big toe.

Hallux Valgus   big toe deviates laterally.

Hammer toe   big toe deformed so that it points upwards, while second and third phalanges flex downwards.

Hamstring muscles   at the back of the thigh, extend the thigh and flex the knee (biceps femoris, semitendinosus and semimembranosus).

Highlights   the moments of greater visual note in a dance.

Holistic health   approach to health that considers every aspect of the whole person.

Hyperextension   movement of a joint beyond a normal extension.

Improvisation   unplanned exploration in movement.

Inversion   the sole of the foot inwards and lifts up.

Inflammation as a result of injury or infection, tissue will appear hot. There may also be redness, swelling and pain.

Isolation movement restricted to a single joint or muscle group, frequently used in Jazz Dance.

Isometric muscle contraction when muscle length does not change.

Isotonic a muscle contraction when muscle shortens.

Jeté a leap, take-off one foot land on the other.

Joint a place where two bones meet. There are 4 types which allow for varying amounts of movement.

Jumper's Knee pain in the knee caused by excess strain on the patellar ligament.

Kinesiology study of movement.

Kinesthetic sense sensing through nerves to muscles of body positions, movement and tension.

Lateral on the outer side of the body.

Legato musical term to describe a flowing, smooth style.

Ligament band of tough tissue which connects bones and stabilises joints.

Lumbar the small of the back. Five vertebrae curve forwards.

March Fracture stress fracture of the metatarsal bone.

Mark rehearsing movement without going flat-out.

Mental rehearsal going through movement in the mind without actual movement.

Measures groups of beats separated by bars into intervals.

Medial on the inner side of the body.

Meniscus half-moon-shaped cartilage of the knee.

Metabolism All the physical and chemical processes which maintain the human organism.

Meter notes how many beats are in a measure.

Mixed meter rhythm made up of underlying beats in different meters.

Modern dance a dance genre which emphasises the importance of choreographers' choice of theme, intent and style. Originating in the twentieth century.

Modulate musical term to moderate tempo.

Motif the central movement theme of a dance which is repeated, developed and varied.

Muscle groups of fibres which contract and extend to produce a movement.

Nervous system the brain, spinal cord and nerves that send messages to the muscles to produce movement.

New Dance a style of dance in Britain which has evolved as a reaction against more traditional contemporary styles.

Opposition a natural movement of an opposite body part to maintain balance.

Orthopedist doctor specialising in the skeleton.

Osteoporosis bone atrophy.

Pace the overall speed of sections of a dance.

Parallel when standing the thighs, knees and toes facing directly forwards.

Patella kneecap.

Percussive a quality movement which has sharp starts and stops.

Phrase a sentence of movement of varying lengths.

Physiotherapy use of physical elements such as heat, water, massage or machine to treat injury.

Placement balanced alignment of level hips, legs placed in line in the hips, shoulders relaxed, spine extended, abdominal area lifted.

Plane the result of joining two dimensions, flat, not three-dimensional.

Plantar flex ankles extends so that toes point.

Plié a bend of the knees keeping the body aligned. When grand or deep, heels peel off, or demi.

Podiatrist treats foot disorders.

Port de Bras various arm gestures in combinations as they move through the five positions.

Positions the 5 positions of the feet in Ballet, invented in seventeenth century France.

Posterior the back of a limb or torso.

Post modern dance started in New York in the 1960s, to experiment with dance.

Preparation movement which allows the body time to prepare for a specific turn, step, jump or fall.

Projection communication by the dancer to the audience of the content of the dance, by throwing out energy.

Pronation foot rolling inwards on the arch, combines abduction and eversion.

Proprioceptors receptors in the muscles, joints tendons and inner ears which monitor the body position in relation to muscle tension and position.

Proscenium the frame of the stage through which dance is seen.

Quadriceps muscle group at front of thigh (rectus femoris, vastus lateralis/medialis/intermedius). Flexes thigh and extends knee.

Quality determined by the varied use of weight and dynamics e.g. percussive, swings, vibrate.

Release letting go of tension. In Graham technique it usually follows a contraction. In New Dance it is used to relax the body and mind so as to encourage ease of movement and creativity.

Relevé raising onto half-toe.

Reciprocal stretching stretching which uses the stretch reflex. Contracting one muscle releases the opposite one which is then more effectively stretched.

Rhythm a structure of movement patterns in time.

Rondo a dance form of three or more themes which alternate with return to the main theme.

Rotation movement that turns around the long axis of a bone.

Sagittal a plane which gives rise to advancing/retreating movements.

Scoliosis lateral curvature of the spine.

Screwing the knee caused by incorrect technique in plié, when turn-out is obtained by rotating the tibia, instead of from the hip.

Section a large separate part of a dance composition.

Shin splints painful strain of muscles, common in lower leg.

Sickling rolling in or out of foot and ankle while on demi-pointe.

Skeleton the frame of bones that supports the body.

Spondylolysis a displacement of the vertebrae.

Spotting during turning the eyes fix on a spot and the head is quickly brought round at the last possible moment to refocus on the spot again. Avoids dizziness.

Sprain   injury to ligaments.

Sonata structure in music which uses 3 or 4 contrasting rhythms and moods that relate in tone and style.

Staccato   abrupt sharp movement or music.

Strain   tear of muscle/tendon.

Strength   muscle power to be increased through dance training.

Stretch   range of movement to be increased by lengthening muscles through dance training.

Style   an individual manner of choreographing or performing.

Supination   foot rolls to its outer border, combines adduction and inversion.

Suspension   a floating, breathy, light quality of movement.

Sustained   a constant, continuous smooth movement.

Swing   pendulum-like movement with an easy natural feel.

Symmetry   balanced or even in time, space or dynamics.

Syncopation   stress on the beat which is not in the usual place.

Synovial   type of joint which allows for largest range of movement.

Talus   ankle bone.

Technique   skill in dance movement.

Tempo   the speed of the movement or music.

Tendon   tough chords which end muscles and connect them to the bones.

Tendinitis   inflammation of a tendon.

Tension   nervousness which may tighten muscles.

Ternary   a three part form, such as ABA.

Thoracic   chest area of spine: 12 vertebrae curves backwards.

Tour de force   highly skilled spectacular movement.

Transition   links between movement themes, motifs, phrases or sections.

Triplets   a 3-step pattern.

Turn-out   outward rotation of the legs from the hips.

Ultrasound   use of mechanical vibration to treat injury.

Unguis Incarnatus   ingrown toenail.

Unison   dancers moving at the same time.

Unity   a sense of an harmonious whole in the dance form.

Upstage   the space towards the back of the stage.

Variation   a motif or theme is modified without losing its character.

Vertebrae   single bones that make up the spine.

Vibratory   a quality of movement which is jittery, fast stops and starts.

Visualise   holding a picture in the mind.

Warm-up   muscle preparation for exercise to avoid injury.

Wings   sides of the stage.

Xylophone   musical instrument of flat heavy wooden bars struck with a hammer.

Yoga   Hindu system of relaxation and mediation.

Zapateado   dance with rhythmic stamping of the feet.

INDEX

A, AS level dance 202
abdominal muscles 11, 26
abduction 8, 14
abstraction 176
acceleration 156
accent 137, 152, 159, 181
Achilles tendon 19, 24
accompaniment 126–32, 138, 145, 149, 187
accuracy 30, 39, 41–2
actions (dance) 69–79
adduction 8, 14
aerobic exercise 27–9
African dance 43, 54, 129, 190, 196, 198
Ailey, Alvin 178, 184
air pattern 81
Alexander technique 11
alignment 3–5, 9, 11, 20, 40
Alston, Richard 60, 62, 77, 93, 97, 113, 119, 123, 126, 132, 147, 183–4
anaerobic 29
anatomical imagery 38
Anderson, Lea 15, 58, 61, 76, 77, 82, 83, 88–90, 92, 97, 98, 104, 110–11, 113, 138, 162, 173, 174–5, 176, 202
ankle 15, 18–19
antagonistic muscle 24
arabesque 40, 42
Arbeau, Thoinot 50
Armitage, Karole 58, 86
Arts Council 195, 205
Ashton, Frederick 56, 67, 70, 71, 91, 93, 96, 101, 109, 117, 137, 146, 158, 160, 166, 174–5, 179, 187–8
asymmetry 153
Atlas, Charles 58, 59, 62, 63
atrophy 17

balance 30, 39–41, 78, 128, 139–40, 180
Balanchine, George 61, 92, 122, 126, 159, 163
Bakst, Léon 108, 116, 117
ball and socket joint 13
ballet, 8, 10, 16, 41, 90, 91, 93, 173, 180, 181, 194, 196, 197, 207
Ballets Russes 108, 122, 158
Banes, Sally 165
Bausch, Pina 107, 168, 178, 203
Beginner's Paralysis 33
Benesh notation 52

Benesh, Rudolf 51
Benjamin, Adam 208
Benois, Alexander Nicolaievich 108, 117
Bharata natyam 76, 176, 195
binary 143
Birmingham Royal Ballet 22, 29, 46, 51
body image 39
body shape 85
bones 5, 12
bone density 46
Bourne, Matthew 175, 204
brain 30, 31
Braun, Terry 59, 62
Brinson, Peter 207
breath 40–2, 87
breathing 180
Brown, Trisha 60, 165, 185, 189
Bruce, Christopher 61, 71, 77, 82, 120, 121, 128, 146, 181
Bryan, David 197
BTEC 202, 207
Buckroyd, Julia 11
Burrows, Jonathan 197
bursa 15
bursitis 15, 18
Burt, Ramsay 203
Butcher, Rosemary 94, 96, 104, 106, 110, 123, 163

Cage, John 58, 127, 128, 147, 163
call and response 162
calories 43–5
Candoco 61, 63, 207, 208
canon 136
cardiovascular system 27, 29
cartilaginous joints 13
cartilage 13
CD ROM 194
centre of gravity 41
centred 41
centreing 41
character 160
Chopinot, Regine 119
choreologist 49–50, 54
Cholmondeleys, The 77, 96, 119, 176
circle group formations 103
circumduction 14
Clark, Michael 59, 93, 97, 113, 129, 136·
classicism 175
climax 138–9, 145–8, 182

Cohan, Robert 59, 62, 73, 90, 95, 119, 121, 122, 128, 139–40, 144, 147, 161
computer technology 193–4
contact improvisation 168
contraction 23, 27
contrast 136, 141, 145, 165
control 30, 39–40
cool-down 30
coordination 30–2, 34, 37, 41, 42
Copeland, Roger 196, 200
costume 114–19, 187
Council for Dance Education and Training 205
Coventry University Performing Arts 207
crescendo 156
cubism 175
Cunningham, Merce 8, 34, 58, 61, 62, 63, 86, 93, 96, 102, 103, 110, 117, 123, 127, 140, 147, 148, 163, 166, 184, 187, 203

dance
    description of a 156
    function and role of 190
    historical and social conditions/ context 188–90
dance compositional structures
    chance 147
    collage structure 147
    contrapuntal structures 145–6
    episodic structure 146–7
    natural structures 147
    sequential 143–4
Dancelines 59
dancers
    choosing 92–3
    dancers' counts 130, 150
    gender of 96–7
    number of 94–5
    physique 96
    relationship with choreographer 93
    role 96
Dandeker, Celeste 208
Davies, Siobhan 59, 113, 119, 131, 147, 161, 163
deceleration 156
Decouflé, Philippe 119
De Keersmaeker, Anne Teresa 203
Diaghilev, Serge 108, 117, 158
diet 43–7
digestive system 30

dimensions 82
diminuendo 156
directions 81, 113
dorsiflexion 8, 10
Duncan, Isadora 8, 16, 56, 117, 185, 187–8
Dunn, Douglas 58
Dunn, Judith 3
Duprés, Madée 106
DV8 97, 167, 202
dynamics 42, 88, 90–2, 137, 156, 181, 182

eating disorders 46
Ek Mats 61, 197
effort actions 90
elevation 71–3
emphasis 181
endurance
    cardiorespiratory 24, 29
    muscular 26–7, 30
energy 90, 181
English National Ballet 117
episodic structures 146–7
evaluation of a dance 186
eversion 8
Expressionism 175
extension 14

face 180
facings 181
falling 77–8
Featherstonehaughs, The 60, 77, 96, 203
femur 5
fibrous joints 13
film 58
filming 61–5
flexibility 12–13, 17, 20, 29, 31, 34
flexion 14
floor pattern 81
focus 73, 84, 180, 181
Fokine, Mikhail 158, 165, 180
Fonteyn, Margot 93, 103, 184
food abuse 43
foot, 4, 5, 8–11, 15, 17, 25
force 90, 156
form in dance 86, 87, 133–4
Forsythe, William 194
fugue 145
Fulkerson, Mary 77

gastrocnemius 24
GCSE dance 206
gesture 75–7
Giselle 50, 57, 61, 74, 101, 102, 117, 121, 146, 160, 175, 188, 195, 197
Graham, Martha 8, 10, 15, 16, 34, 54, 56, 61, 70, 71, 75, 76, 82, 85, 87, 96, 109, 110, 117, 119, 121, 133, 144, 146, 147, 150, 157, 159,

161, 172, 175, 176, 188–9, 195, 203
grants 205
ground bass 145
groups 164–5
    relationships between dancers 166–70
    shapes/formations 165–6
    spaces between dancers 166

haemoglobin 27
Halprin, Anna 173
Hameed, Uzma 195
hamstrings 17, 18, 25
harmony 157
heart 27–9
    rate 27
    target rate 28
highlights 137–8, 181
hinge joint 13
hip 13, 15, 16, 24, 25, 34
holistic 37
Holm, Hanya 3, 33, 53, 74, 133, 180, 181, 184
Howard, Robin 147
humerus 5
Humphrey, Doris 55, 77, 85, 102, 126, 130, 137, 145, 176
hyperextension 18

imagery 37–9
Impressionism 175
in the round 103
inner self 37
injuries 6, 9, 10, 17, 18–19, 24, 25, 26, 34, 37
injury prone 34
interpretation 186
inversion 8
involvement of whole self 184
isometric 22
isotonic 21

Jeyasingh, Shobana 129, 176, 195
joints 13–16
Jooss, Kurt 53
Jones, Bill T. 74, 96
Jordan, Stephanie 96

Kakande 198, 199
kinesthetic sense 37
kinesthetic imagery 37
knee 17–18, 25
Kokuma 195
Kozel, Susan 193–4

Laban, Rudolf 51, 53, 90
Labanotation 53–7, 71, 77, 81, 95, 135, 154–5, 194
Laban Centre 205, 207

Lambert, Gary 127, 138
Lanchbery, John 146, 160
Lawson, Joan 22
levels 77, 82, 166
levers 23
lifting 36
ligaments 12, 13, 16, 17
lighting 111–13
    colour 112
    different sorts of lights 112
    direction 113
    effects 113
    intensity 113
Lockyer, Bob 59, 61, 62, 63, 64
logical sequence 140
London Contemporary Dance School 55–6, 205
London Contemporary Dance Theatre 147

McLuhan, Marshall 193, 196
Macaulay, Alistair 158, 162, 186, 187
Mackrell, Judith 176
Macmillan, Kenneth 61, 160
Marks, Victoria 58, 61, 63
Mashango 198, 199
masks 120
Massine, Leonide 58
melody 157, 159
menstruation 46
mental rehearsal 39
metre 153, 156
mobility 20
modern dance, 7, 10, 15, 16, 41, 173, 181, 197
Morris, Maggie 138
Morris, Mark 50, 97, 197, 203
motifs 134–6, 137, 145
    development of 134–5, 136, 139, 143, 145
    variation of 135, 139, 144, 145
Motionhouse 167, 168, 207
multi-media 194
Mumford, Peter 59, 60
muscles 22–6, 45
    contraction of 23
    groups 4
music 128–32, 135, 145, 149–64, 177
    choosing 128–9
    live 129
    notation of 151
    structures 143–5
    style 129
    using 129–32
    visualisation 150–60
musicality 183
mutual coexistence 162

narrative 137, 146, 147, 160–1

National Curriculum 202
National Resource Centre for Dance 206
neck 7
nervous system 30–3
neurons 31
Newson, Lloyd 97, 167, 203–4
Nikinsky, Vaslav 69, 162
Nikolais, Alwin 113, 117, 150
North, Robert 59, 73, 104, 160, 161
notation dance 50
Noverre, Jean Georges 76, 107, 115, 116, 179
Nutcracker The 50, 97, 137, 197
Nureyev, Rudolf 103, 184

osteoarthritis 16
osteoporosis 46–7

Pace 137, 138
Parker, Monica 54
Parry, Jan 204
patella 17
Paxton, Steve, 123, 167
pelvis, 6, 7, 13, 15, 16, 25
Perrot, Jules 181, 188
personal space 79
Petipa, Marius 158
phrases 87–90, 139, 157, 178, 181
Phoenix Dance Company 138
Physical Education Working Group 202
placements of dancers 101
planes 82
plantar flexion 6, 8, 10
Pilates technique 11
plié 17, 18, 40
pointe work 10
polyphony 145, 157
post modern dance, 36, 43, 93, 110, 113, 146, 173, 196, 197
posture 4, 5, 35
postural problems 7, 9, 10, 11, 16, 17, 18–19, 25, 26, 37
pre-performance nerves 34
preventative training 21, 29
progressive overload 22, 30
projection in performance 179
pronation 8
proportion 139, 140
props 121–4, 187
proscenium stage 100, 165
protective reflexes 19, 20, 30
psychology 33

quadriceps muscle group 17, 18, 22, 125

Rainer, Yvonne 39, 119, 180
Rambert School 205
Realism 175

receptors 11, 31
reciprocal 18, 30
recovery 29
reflexes 29, 30, 31, 32, 34
    muscular 32, 33
    righting 32
relationship of dance to music
    call and response 162
    direct correlation 158–9
    disassociation 163
    mutual co-existence 162–3
    showing/emphasising character and narrative 160–1
    visualisation 159–60
relaxation 35, 37, 42
relevé 40
respiratory system 28
rhythm 149, 150–1, 159, 161, 162, 163
    accumulative 150
    even 150
    resultant rhythm 153
    subtractive 150
    uneven 150
ribs 5, 28
Robertson, Allen 167, 168
Romanticism 175
romantic style 108, 116, 150, 188
rondo 144
ronds de jambe 16
rotating 14
rotation 75
round 145
Rubidge, Sarah 56, 194, 195

sacroilliac 7
Sayters, Denni 198, 199
section 87, 139, 140
semi-circular canals 11
sensitivity 183
set 107
shoulder 15, 35–7
Siddall, Jeanette 205
sickling 18
silence 126–7
site-specific 104–6
skeleton 5–6
skill 33, 39
skills 134
Sleeping Beauty 50, 137, 158
smoking 28
soleus muscle 24
somatypes 33–4, 96
sound 127–8
South Asian 15, 20, 43, 54, 176, 190, 195, 197
space 79–86
spine 6–8
Spink, Ian 124, 129, 137, 145
speed 86
stages 104

stamina 26–30, 34,
stillness 77–90, 137
strength 21–2, 30, 34, 36
strengthening 36
stress 34–5
stretching 12, 13, 19, 20, 21, 35
Strider 147
style 129, 172, 177, 187, 190
stylistic blocks 34
supination 8
Surrealism 175
Swan Lake 197, 204
swing 40
syncopation 159, 162
synovial joints 13
synovial membrane 13
synovial fluid 13

Taglioni, Marie 18, 116, 179, 188
technique 3, 30, 87, 207
tempo 149, 156
tendons 13, 22, 24
ternary 143
tension 34–5, 40
Tetley, Glen 79–80, 95, 96, 120, 123, 149, 160
Tharp, Twyla 59, 92, 100, 121, 138, 183
The Place 195
time 86–90
time signature 153
torso 23, 36
transition 140, 143, 144
travelling 69–71
treatment of injuries/problems 7, 9, 10, 16, 18, 19, 24
Tudor, Antony 178
Tufnell, Miranda 6. 37
turning 73–4
turn-out 16

unison 170
unity 135, 141, 143

vegetarian 45
Verma, Jatinder 196
vertebrae 5, 6
video 49–50, 55
virtual reality 193
visual cues 11
visual imagery 38
voice 127

warm-up 20, 29, 183
weight control 45, 146
weight training 22, 29–30
wheelchair 208
Wigman, Mary 53, 150
Williams, Margaret 61, 63, 98

Zane, Arnie 74